CW00500224

L.F.C.

PEP LIJNDERS

INTENSITY

INSIDE LIVERPOOL FC

OUR IDENTITY

PEP LIJNDERS is one of Jürgen Klopp's right-hand men. He began his coaching career in 2002 with PSV Eindhoven and later went on to enjoy success at FC Porto. In 2014, he moved to Liverpool, beginning at the Academy as U16 coach before moving up to the first-team set-up, working first with Brendan Rodgers and then Klopp. After a stint as manager in his native Netherlands, he returned to the LFC coaching staff as assistant manager in 2018. Lijnders has been key to everything the Reds have achieved since: a sixth European Cup, UEFA Super Cup, FIFA Club World Cup, a first Premier League title, Carabao Cup and FA Cup.

L.F.C.

PEP LIJNDERS

INTENSITY

INSIDE LIVERPOOL FC

OUR IDENTITY

With James Carroll

Reach Sport

www.reachsport.com

For Danielle, the love of my life.

For Romijn and Benjamin, the ones that make the earth turn in the most beautiful direction I could ever imagine.

Us together, always!

Written with James Carroll.

Published in Great Britain and Ireland in 2022 by Reach Sport.

www.reachsport.com
@Reach_Sport

Reach Sport is a part of Reach PLC.

Hardback ISBN: 9781914197482
Trade paperback ISBN: 9781914197550
Ebook ISBN: 9781914197574

Photographic acknowledgements:
Liverpool Football Club, Alamy, Getty Images, Pep Lijnders.

Editing and production: David Cottrell, Roy Gilfoyle, William Hughes.
Design: Rick Cooke.

Printed and bound by CPI Group (UK) Ltd,
Croydon, CR0 4YY.

CONTENTS

FOREWORD
BY JÜRGEN KLOPP

I HADN'T KNOWN THIS YOUNG, ENTHUSIASTIC, bright, ideas-filled Dutch football coach that long when I realised he was constantly making notes. Always writing things down, be it on a device or with pen and paper. Staff meetings, team meetings, snatch conversations here and there or immediately after training sessions and games – he was detailing information. Constantly. Eventually I asked him, "Why do you do that?"

"Because all of this information and these experiences are valuable...they're like a gold mine. Why wouldn't I?"

That guy was Pepijn Lijnders and although I didn't realise it then, he would go on to become one of the most important figures in my professional life. When I arrived at Liverpool Football Club in 2015 I was specifically asked by our owner Mike Gordon to keep Pep as part of my staff. It was a request rather than a demand. Now I can't imagine how different and less fulfilling things would have been if I'd have said no.

We've enjoyed successes and failures together, incredible highs and some heartbreaking lows. He left, for a brief period, for NEC Nijmegen and came back. And since then, his contribution to this organisation cannot be overstated. I'm blessed with two sensational assistant-managers in Pep and Peter Krawietz, supported by Vitor Matos, and many other wonderful, talented staff throughout our football set-up.

Pep is unique, though. I've never met anyone like him before and I'm not sure I'll be fortunate enough to do so again in the future. He is studious and coaching-obsessed; he believes in the training process with a passion I've never seen before. It was his obsession with chronicling everything we do that led to this project happening. This diary, this book, our story of 2021/22.

Typically, he was conscientious about it. He was tentative when asking whether or not he should do it. We had just arrived in Evian from Austria for the final part of our training camp in July 2021 when he raised it. At that stage no-one knew the adventure we were about to embark on over the next nine months, but Pep could sense something special was brewing. His only motivation for this project was to give our supporters a closer insight into our world. The decisions, how we reach them and the reasoning behind them.

One of his key characteristics is that he wants to share his joy and passion for football with everyone. He doesn't make distinctions. He's never a snob or judgemental, like some within the professional game can be. He doesn't think some are more worthy of a football opinion than others, or that certain insight is beyond anyone who's not an employee of a club, has the relevant coaching badges or been a professional player.

I've no idea if there is anything such as football socialism, but if there is then Pep is at the forefront of that ideology. He believes that by sharing ideas and experiences with each other we enrich the game we love and make the experience of watching and supporting even more fulfilling. I'm sure a project such as this will raise eyebrows in some quarters, but to be honest I couldn't care less. We do things our own way at Liverpool Football Club. People who read this will feel an even greater connection to our team and our environment.

It's not about giving away secrets or lifting a veil. What we do isn't that serious and we shouldn't kid ourselves that it's some sort of special, mystical world. It's football, the greatest sport in the world, enjoyed by most people on this planet of ours. It's about community and engagement. It's about something that brings people together in a way very few things can. It's about making strangers into friends. Individuals into a collective.

I'm so proud of Pep. He's family to me. I love the guy so much. I hope you enjoy reading this as much as we did living it.

You'll Never Walk Alone
Jürgen

PROLOGUE

IT ALL STARTED IN PRE-SEASON. IT ALL STARTED during the 28 days we spent as a group across two bases in Austria as well as the final leg in Evian, France. Of course, I am talking about what unfolded on the pitch for Liverpool Football Club during the 2021/22 campaign, but also this book you're about to read. Could I have imagined how this season would ultimately turn out? Of course not. Especially because of the well-documented difficulties we'd faced and felt during 2020/21.

Heading into the first phase of our training camp in Saalfelden, Austria, I felt there was a do-or-die season in front of us – and therefore it was the most pressure I'd ever felt during a pre-season. The incredible efforts of our players in the final stages of the previous campaign gave us a base – and Champions League football. From there, it was about getting our whole building back together and moving forward as a collective, powerful unit once again.

That month away from home was tough, both physically and mentally, but it provided the foundations for us to go on and achieve what we did. Everything was mapped out, visualised and worked towards during that time. It's where the new ideas were introduced and the old ones finessed and fine-tuned. The team needed inspiration and positivity. That's why I accepted the offer to write a regular diary for the club's official website. With this make-or-break season in front of us, I felt I could use it to give an extra message to our team, to our staff and, of course, to our fans. When we returned to Liverpool, we were proud to be able to say we'd delivered an incredible pre-season – and the wheels were in motion for this book.

It was in Evian when James Carroll suggested a book. I think it was something he said slightly in jest via WhatsApp, but I told him immediately, "Okay, let's do it – why should we wait?" I told James that if we agreed to do this, we'd do it with all we have – with all I have – with no holding back and with no secrets. 'What if the season doesn't go to plan?' was something we discussed, but we agreed we would still write it. Why? Because it is in these moments a season is defined.

What I knew then – and know now – is our journey is something special and deserves to be spoken about. Whatever the outcome of 2021/22, I was committed to detailing it all; the why and how things happened on and off the pitch. I am in a very privileged position of being one of a small number of people able to answer those questions with truth and with insight. Not what others think happened, but what actually happened at the AXA Training Centre during those nine months. All the decisions. All the struggles. All the glory. That's what I have tried to document and convey in these pages.

'How much do we want to give away and make public?' Everything. 'Everything?' Above everything; we are just going to be honest. The more the opposition knows about us, the better because the more they worry. Anyway, how do you stop unpredictability? How do you stop flexibility? How do you stop intensity? Also, if there will be something made absolutely clear in this book it is that we are constantly evolving. The Liverpool of today isn't the Liverpool of tomorrow or yesterday. Never overthink words.

And in the end, it all comes down to the players anyway. The incredible group we have at Liverpool FC. They make the difference; they bring our game to levels of analysis the opposition never can reach with video footage. How? Because in split-seconds they make decisions based on their intuition. You can't prepare for a Thiago Alcantara pass, a Bobby Firmino flick, or Trent seeing something the whole stadium missed and putting the ball exactly there.

Over the course of the nine months – the 63 games, or 'finals' – we wrote together each week as the season unfolded. During downtime in the hotel or when we were travelling, I'd write my notes. Two or three times a week, we'd sit together or I'd send them to James, often late at night. Many of our conversations took place in the early hours of the morning, especially when the team had played an evening fixture. We shared ideas, we bounced off each other, as we put this together. The writing helped to clear my mind; it was a remedy to prevent my thoughts going everywhere. It helped me to have a more organised mind and a better understanding of what was really going on.

This book is not just for Liverpool supporters. It is for everyone who loves the beautiful game of football. There are so many books about tiki-taka, the Spanish way, as well as the German coaching school, but this is a combination of being born and raised in Johan Cruyff's Holland, learning and maturing in Portugal and working with the best manager in the world of football in Jürgen Klopp. Twenty years of experiences went into this particular season and my decisions and input.

I have always had a passion for the training process and

coaching ever since my own dreams of making it as a professional footballer were ended by a knee injury. I began to study the coaches who I loved and admired: Sacchi, Cruyff, Coerver and John Wooden. All for different but obvious reasons. Together they are probably the complete package, I guess. Even now, I feel I study each day, the things I believe will directly help the team and players I am working with. It is a process that doesn't end for me.

I'm fortunate to have worked for some of Europe's top clubs: PSV Eindhoven, FC Porto and now, of course, the mighty Liverpool FC. I'm also blessed to have worked with some of the continent's top talents, including our very own Trent Alexander-Arnold. He is the epitome of a successful training and coaching process with a young talent. I could not be any prouder of the man and the player he has become – from my captain at Under-16 level to one of the world's best players, with every possible major club medal won by the age of 23.

Even at the age of 15, he was this natural technical talent. He had all the characteristics I loved: a mentality to win, passionate to improve – but his emotions sometimes took control instead of him taking control over the emotions. He trained with so much power and competition. He grew step-by-step into the wonderful guy he is now, surrounded by a lovely family, he created this superb personality. He has this aggression in a positive way. If someone represents this quote of Bill Shankly, it's him: 'Playing at the highest level isn't pressure, it's a reward'. I still see the same fire in his eyes in each training session, but I don't see this young guy anymore; I see a leader, I see someone who controls his emotions, a future captain. A leader by example.

The best clubs have one thing in common, a 'one-club'

mentality. The culture spreads through all departments. It's great that our talents, the real ones, can make these steps together with our team – and they continued to do so during this season.

So, I hope this book will show what went through my mind as the weeks passed, how we approached the team and the club game-by-game, week-by-week, month-by-month. Life is about opportunities and timing; we all learn this the good way or the hard way. This book was an opportunity and this season created the right timing. We made it happen together.

I'd also like to hopefully inspire some of you with our thoughts and ideas. As I mentioned, this was written in 'real time' and nothing you're about to read was later amended or changed with hindsight. What you read is what it was at that time, the right and the wrong and the ups and the downs. Jürgen had said to me many times that I should write a book. I couldn't be a prouder man to have done it 'live' during one of the finest seasons in the history of this incredible football club.

During our time together, we've won the Champions League, we've won the Premier League, we became club world champions and we won the domestic cups, but it's what you do after you win that counts. There are so many decisions we make on a daily basis as a staff and a team – small ones and really big ones.

We live in a world that moves forward so quickly that there is almost no time to look back because the next game is around the corner. And in our world the only thing that counts is winning the next game, nothing else. The problem is because there is always the next game that consumes your focus, you forget really quickly all the decisions made, the small plan created and the evolving relationships between staff and players.

Thank you, James. I couldn't be prouder of what you've done

to help me with this book. Because of you, we can take people on this journey with us. Because finally, it's written down – and by a guy who was involved in or initiated many of those decisions. What you're about to read is the truth, my truth.

I hope you enjoy it.

Pep Lijnders

"WE WILL WRITE YOUR BOOK TOGETHER ONE DAY." Pep is correct, I did send those words to him during a WhatsApp conversation half in jest and, in all honesty, with zero expectation. It was the evening of our arrival into Evian for the final leg of our 28 days away from home for the pre-season training camp of 2021. Sitting in the bar area of the Hilton late on that Sunday evening, with the rain lashing down outside, we were discussing the feedback and reaction to his diary column we'd worked on together for the club's official website during the month away from home. Pep's response was a jolt. It shifted any thoughts of tiredness after – by that point – three full weeks on the road, working daily on the content output on the club's platforms. "Why should we wait? Let's do it now!"

And so, that's where and when this concept was formed and from that very moment on, we set about documenting the next nine months in as much detail as possible. As truthfully as possible. We made a commitment that, however the season panned out, we'd go all-in on this project and make it happen regardless. At no point was Pep hesitant or having second thoughts – he wanted to do this as he had belief and conviction this season would be a good one for Liverpool Football Club.

Of course, we had no idea how it would work out. We could never have envisaged it would be the way it was, with two trophies won and outstanding Premier League and Champions League campaigns. The tone of our conversations were a good indicator, from 'This will be good' to 'This is looking like a good season to do this' to 'We've picked a good season to do this' to ultimately 'What a season to do a book!' From a difficult campaign played behind-closed-doors to this. Utterly remarkable.

For me, it was an immeasurable privilege to have had such an up-close, candid insight along the way. I never took for granted being in a position to have detailed knowledge of how things were playing out behind the scenes over those nine months. I never will. I know how fortunate I am to have been on this journey.

Nothing you will read has been changed or watered down. Nothing has been redacted. These are Pep's words and thoughts as they were as the campaign unfolded. And we did it all in real time, as it all happened. Pep's commitment or enthusiasm never wavered – I never had to chase. The arrival of his notes and thoughts were like clockwork, two or three times a week – even with his schedule, even in the most hectic of periods during the season. Or we'd meet in his office at the AXA Training Centre or in The Titanic hotel on matchdays. Having had the opportunity to work directly with Pep for several years in my role at Liverpool, this was never in doubt. He is one of the most dedicated, committed people I've ever had the pleasure of meeting. If he is in, he is in 100 per cent.

Finally, when Pep and I had that honest conversation early in the process about what we'd do if the season wasn't a positive or successful one, his answer erased any lingering doubts I still had: "We will still do it because this is us. And remember, we are Liverpool."

That was enough for me.

James Carroll

DRAMATIS PERSONAE

Jürgen Klopp – manager
Pep Lijnders – assistant-manager
Peter Krawietz – assistant-manager
Vitor Matos – elite development coach
Andreas Kornmayer – head of fitness and conditioning
Ray Haughan – general manager of first-team operations
John Achterberg – first-team goalkeeping coach
Jack Robinson – first-team assistant goalkeeping coach
Claudio Taffarel – goalkeeping coach
Alex Inglethorpe – academy manager
Nick Marshall – assistant academy director
Matt Newbury – head of senior academy recruitment
Barry Lewtas – Under-23s coach
Andreas Schlumberger – head of recovery and performance
Jim Moxon – club doctor
Conall Murtagh – first-team fitness coach
Lee Nobes – head of physiotherapy
Chris Morgan – first-team physiotherapist
Lena Aschenbrenner – prevention and performance physiotherapist
Paul Small – masseur
Michelle Hudson – masseur
Mona Nemmer – head of nutrition
Mark Leyland – performance analyst (left the club in December 2021)
Daniel Spearritt – performance analyst
Greg Mathieson – head of opposition analysis
James French – opposition's analyst

DRAMATIS PERSONAE

Lee Radcliffe – kit-management coordinator
Brendan McIlduff – kit coordinator
Thomas Gronnemark – consultant throw-in coach
Mike Gordon – director
Billy Hogan – chief executive officer
Michael Edwards – sporting director
Julian Ward – assistant sporting director
Danny Stanway – club secretary
Jonathan Bamber – senior vice president, general counsel
Danielle McNally – PA to the manager
Jane Ashton – head of player-care
Warren Scott – senior manager, grounds management
Marc Kosicke – agent for Jürgen Klopp and Pep Lijnders
Dr. Niklas Häusler – neuro11
Patrick Häntschke – neuro11

WEEK 1

"TRAINING IS OUR TRANSFER"

I'M SURE IN THE OUTSIDE WORLD, SOME MAY HAVE wondered why – after four weeks on the road at pre-season training camps in Austria and France – we decided to play two Anfield friendlies on consecutive days immediately after arriving home, with Athletic Club [Bilbao] and Osasuna visiting us.

Well, to be honest, playing two days in a row at Anfield is something we always wanted to do: a mini-tournament to finish off pre-season, similar to Bayern Munich's Audi Cup format. It takes a lot of planning but we had belief it would pay off for us.

We'd arrived back in Liverpool from Evian on the Saturday evening, into heavy rainfall at John Lennon Airport. But our spirits were good; all the backroom team agreed our month away had been hugely successful and we'd see the benefit when the season got underway.

There was an exceptional atmosphere among the squad while we were away, players and staff together, and we were keen to make sure it remained now we were back home. So we spoke with Mona Nemmer about having BBQs on the terrace once in a while, and Ray Haughan about having some table-tennis tables put up in the hallway of the AXA Training Centre.

On the morning of the Bilbao game I sat in Jürgen's office to prepare the line-ups for the two games and the changes we'd make during them, as well as discussing the final week's training plans ahead of the first game of the Premier League season at Norwich City.

The team who were playing in the first game, against Bilbao, were already at the hotel, so we trained with the lads who'd be involved against Osasuna before driving over to join up with the first matchday squad.

Before that, I caught up with one of our analysts, Mark Leyland, to get some more details on Osasuna's set-pieces. It might be a friendly in name but that's not how we approach it – and preparation is key.

When I stepped onto the training pitch I took a moment to absorb the fact we were back at our 'home'. Our base. The pitches at the AXA Training Centre look so quick when you're watching from the coaches' room; the Deso [hybrid turf system] makes them super-fast, which is something we like as it helps develop our passing game. You only genuinely realise how good our own pitches are when you go to a training camp and work on 'normal' pitches, so all credit to our ground staff for the work they are doing here and at Anfield.

That being said, the moment we stepped outside we knew we were back in Kirkby for another reason… the wind. Even the expensive windshields we had installed cannot stop it this morning.

A lot of people ask me about the move from Melwood to Kirkby. It was emotional, of course, as Melwood held so much history, so many memories. It was all we knew. But the ATC is different and we need to create new memories here. Create new icons, new family, new history.

It's true that it all came together at Melwood during our time working with each other. It was an impressive facility on the strength of its history alone. It was here new teams were born, new strategies devised and talents were transformed into icons, and we were able to leave having won the Premier League and the Champions League, adding our own mark to

Liverpool's incredible history. In that regard the timing was perfect.

Back ahead of the Anfield friendlies I discovered that Nat Phillips had a hamstring issue that ruled him out, so we made the decision that Rhys Williams would play 20 minutes against Bilbao and 30 the following day versus Osasuna. Joe and Virgil were still not quite ready for the full 90 and Rhys had made incredible steps with us.

He had a chat with Jürgen during the summer and asked what the plan was for him. Jürgen told him that, long-term, he could be one of Liverpool's senior centre-halves. Short-term, we are not sure yet, but he would be with us until the end of pre-season at least.

Rhys and Nat saved our season in 2020/21. There is an iconic photo of them after the Crystal Palace game, both battered and bruised, applauding the Kop after we'd finished third. It's a photo that would not have looked out of place in the 1980s. Nat puts his head where others don't put their boot. What they did in getting us into the top four shouldn't be forgotten, not least during our unbeaten run in the final 10 matches.

But it was clear we'd need five centre-halves for the new season, particularly with Virgil and Joe coming back from long-term injuries. We also didn't want to have to use Fabinho in the last line again if we could avoid it. It was one thing losing our centre-backs, but we also lost our 'Lighthouse' in midfield as well. So if Nat was to move on in this window, then our feeling was we should keep Rhys as he attacks and communicates so well.

Nat's not the only one who will be absent. Shaq stepped out of training with a hamstring issue, so it created a place for Kaide Gordon – the young talent of our pre-season. I was really looking forward to seeing him start at Anfield as he made such a good impression on us all over the summer; his attitude and desire to win the ball, the dribbling skills, the will to score and run in behind. He will be a top player for us in the coming years. Just 16 years old but great work from our scouting department.

For this season we would have a new team hotel: The Titanic, based in Liverpool's historic docklands. It feels like something of a restart for us, but I will miss Hope Street. It holds such strong, vivid memories. When I first signed for Liverpool I stayed there for three days. The smell of the wooden floor and panelling, the phone call to my best friend to explain my move to England instead of Ajax, the negotiations with the club, speaking with Alex Inglethorpe and Michael Beale about our footballing visions in a restaurant nearby. These are memories that will never leave my mind.

I remember an afternoon when I was sitting outside a café in the Georgian Quarter of the city. The sun was shining, I was sipping an espresso… It felt like I was still in Porto, although that feeling went away quickly when I first encountered the weather in Kirkby!

It's still the best decision of my life to join Liverpool Football Club. There are not many clubs in the world with more culture or history than FC Porto, but Liverpool is absolutely one of them.

When I got into my hotel room at The Titanic, I flicked on the TV to watch Harry Wilson's debut for Fulham, who kicked off their season against Middlesbrough. Harry, for sure, has the best delivery of a ball in the Championship. I really like him as a player: vertical, direct, a finisher. He is one of us.

Middlesbrough were man-marking all over the pitch, which is the exact opposite of our style, but I have great respect for their manager Neil Warnock. He has been in the game for so long and has so many incredible stories. I always say, you can play the game in so many ways and Neil has a clear idea, that's for sure.

Just before Jürgen's team meeting was due to get underway, Vitor sent me a text saying it looked like Lautaro Martinez could be on his way to Tottenham from Inter Milan. I presumed that would mean Harry Kane would join Manchester City. Regardless, we had to be so strong as a collective this year. That was what would give us our chance. We needed to create an ambience within the squad to drive the best out of us all. "Training is our transfer," is what one member of staff always says to me. He couldn't be more right.

Before the meeting, Jürgen asked me about our high press and whether we'd keep the same plan. The answer was 'yes' but we needed to explain the difference in our strategy when the opponent had one or two players in the six position. It's something we identified we could improve upon after our games with Bologna in Evian [in early August]: the moment our attack finishes, to watch the ball and immediately go back to our high-pressing structures. It was one of our bravest approaches, but it took a while to find the exact dynamic that worked against all opponents. Now we felt we'd found it. You have to cherish the moments things fall into place. We'd had this after the Bayern Munich away game during the Champions League run in 2019 with our own goal-kick structure. We'd never changed it since and it became one of our best weapons in attacking a game.

Mo and Virgil walked into the meeting room together. It's funny, they always sit in exactly the same positions during these. Virgil smelled great, so I told him! The amount of times one of them gets a compliment and sniggers with the other is hard to count. The same goes for Robbo and Trent. I like this confidence and little game between them.

For example, Virgil and Sadio have this competition in the pre-match warm-up about who can jump the highest and I always have to judge… I always give the win to Sadio!

On a more serious note Virgil asked about the plan for him as we're leaving the meeting room. I said, "Maybe 60." He said, "Minimum 70." I'm on his side, but during half-time we'll have the same discussion with Jürgen and make the decision. It's true, sometimes it is the best players you have to slow down.

We told the squad during the Bilbao meeting that the only difference should be there are not three points to be won. We wanted to give everything – why would you get everything while you are not giving everything? It was a great chance to make the next step. As we say, the difference is always made in that last four or five per cent. We hated calling it a friendly, we called it a pre-season test – and this would be the hardest one. Firstly, because we'd go to the full 90 minutes, and secondly, because there would be many moments this season where we would come back on a Wednesday night and have to play on a Saturday.

Maybe we didn't feel like it, but we had to create the right atmosphere together. That's what happened this weekend; that's why I planned it like this. A pre-season needs difficulties. Jürgen spoke about the 'new' ideas like playing the first pass forward and also about the improvement points to be made on the last game: quicker re-organising after a chance or when they have a goal-kick.

His final message was a simple but an important one: let's enjoy the fans and give them something to enjoy.

We headed over to Anfield and, walking in, I saw one of my quotes in big lettering on the wall: 'Our identity is intensity'. The fact the players see that when they walk out of the dressing room makes me very proud. 'Gather as team-mates and leave as a family' is written on the wall of the players' restaurant. Wow, if there is one saying that identifies Liverpool FC it's this one. The restaurant is full of pictures of the team. It's a nice place. Before the pandemic we always ate together here after a game. These kind of initiatives became so important in our journey to winning the Premier League. Before these times we got food from Nando's delivered...nothing else to say. With Mona, we have evolved massively in this area.

In our coaches' room at Anfield we have three pictures. One is the coaches lifting the Champions League trophy in the dressing room after the game in Madrid… I can still smell the beer when I look at it. The second is us – the entire squad – raising the trophy in Madrid, with Hendo holding it so powerfully. And the third is all the players and staff together after the Barcelona game singing You'll Never Walk Alone with our fans on the Kop. I'm standing between James Milner, Virgil and the gaffer in the photo. It was an incredible moment that shows when a lot of people dream and work for the same thing, the football world can sometimes conspire in your favour.

It was great that we had the chance to do these final pre-season tests in our own stadium a week before the league starts, just to feel the routines one time before everything was for real. But there was an issue: the countdown clock wasn't working properly. Who else other than James Milner told me about it.

Outside, the game was delayed by 30 minutes to ensure all fans could get into the stadium safely. This had an impact on a lot of things but most of all Bilbao's journey home. They were concerned about the timings and Vitor and Adrian had to assist in helping translate between their directors and our staff to assure them all was fine and we had arranged a police escort to take them to the airport immediately after the game.

When Ray came to tell me about the delay I'd said, "We play for them, the fans, so of course we will wait until they're all in," not knowing about the knock-on effect it would have on Bilbao. But thankfully we got it sorted and were very thankful to them for their patience and understanding.

As we stood together during the warm-up, the fans were already singing inside Anfield and Jürgen turned to me and said, "This is proof the people make a stadium," before saying to Vitor, "We should cherish these moments."

In the additional time we had for the warm-up, we decided to do a 10-versus-goalkeeper exercise we usually repeat a lot during the week, where players have to pass the ball and create as many speed-ups during the three balls they get.

Once the game was up and running it was so intense, especially the first half-hour. Jürgen later said it was like watching a car race.

In my opinion, the most important sign for a good game is concentration – and that will create the right intensity. And we were all in it, everyone together pressing with one brain. You saw an 'all-in' Liverpool FC performance which, after all the sessions and travel, was the most pleasing aspect. Inside our pressing zone we were compact and aggressive – we pushed the red button several times.

Cross-field passes from Robbo to Trent and vice versa; quick restarts from Alisson starting the machine again. Also, Mo and Sadio's combination spirit would get us 15 to 20 more goals this season, I believe. During one of our sessions in the summer, I shouted so hard after they combined: "This is what we need from you two!" It's something we focused on as Sadio and Mo in one-v-one offensive situations is something from another planet. We can unbalance so many defences with this and when they combine before or after these moments, we can become unstoppable again.

With the amount of chances we created against Bilbao, we could see the 'first pass forward' concept was really working. The compactness between Sadio, Mo and Jota, stopping the easy passes to the inside. The team created an atmosphere to hunt in packs. So many short, quick passes speeding up the tempo of our positional game. We scored another goal with our full-pitch press – something we spoke about in the team meeting – but Robbo getting injured just before half-time was a shot to the stomach.

During the break we spoke about how to protect against [Bilbao striker] Inaki Williams and their second striker, and still push up with the other players to get closer to each other offensively. They had come out too easily too many times because we didn't push up enough. All their counters came from us not pushing high enough with Naby, Harvey and the full-backs in and around the area. We could and should improve our counter-press. There is nothing worse for the opposition than when you play super counter-pressing, and many times it's only about five metres forward.

The game finished 1-1 but we were happy with the workout. Afterwards, Jürgen gave compliments for the amount of good spells but highlighted the issue of not scoring enough goals during these periods. Also, becoming passive in possession in the second half made us run more. The ball will never get tired so in these moments we should switch the game more often. When you become passive you get punished, on every level, because everyone can cause everyone problems in the game of football. We needed to play the extra pass in these moments; keep the ball for longer periods with short, quick, low passes to have moved Bilbao much more. With this there would become more spaces through the inside. You make the opposition passive and then you can use the spaces they leave.

Harvey Elliott's performance was a highlight, though. There is no such thing as like for like in football, but he has some of the ingredients of Andres Iniesta and thinks like a creative midfielder.

Afterwards, Jürgen and I headed to the bus to get something to eat as we were still using that as our 'restaurant' after games, something that came in with the COVID-19 protocols. When we boarded, Billy Koumetio was sitting in my seat and Marcelo Pitaluga in Jürgen's. It was cause for much hilarity among their more senior team-mates… but we forgave them.

Late on Sunday evening I received a call from Jürgen telling me that Lyon had made an offer for Shaq. He was heading into the final year of his contract and was keen to get a move. Their initial offer was too low, we felt. My opinion, I told the boss, was that it could be the right time for all concerned: next year he could leave on a free and Shaq had made it clear he'd like a new challenge.

We also talked a little bit more about the team and the game. We were really enthusiastic about so many things and the three midfielders against Osasuna needed to step up their game after the performance against Athletic. And, better still, we had Hendo and Thiago on the bench.

To prepare them, Vitor took Thiago and Hendo on the morning of the Osasuna game for an extra session. They worked on a specific exercise we call the 'spine' where the central players have to combine and counter-press through mannequins. A good team isn't born – it's created through many, many exercises focusing on the same aspects time and time again; searching constantly for an intensity so we can go and the opposition can't. That's what we wanted: to be able to cause each team problems this season by creating as many speed-up situations as possible. A collective display of intensity, provoke them offensively and cut their connections defensively. A red block chasing the ball in packs. The quality of Hendo and Thiago in this 'extra training' reflected the talent of our squad.

One of the big secrets of our success is the way Jürgen speaks with the players. There is a saying that the way you speak to your players becomes their inner voice – and that's what happens with our squad each day. So much positivity, so much will-power, so much game-intelligence. He has this drive of wanting to surprise the opposition non-stop. The moment Jürgen speaks with the boys before training the tone gets set. It's then for me, the other coaches and the players, to use this tone to improve our way. Controlling games by being dominant and being unpredictable.

On my way into the AXA Training Centre early on Monday morning, I read a rumour that Southampton were interested in taking Ox on loan, but after the way he'd played in pre-season there was no chance of that. He played with so much fire and was outstanding.

When I got there, the first person I saw was Caroline. It was so nice to see her again. COVID had meant she'd been away for a long time, so it was good to catch up. It's people like Caroline and Carol, of course, who help make this the place it is.

Next I went to speak to Mark and Greg about Norwich. The main two strengths they have is how they overload the centre and the quality to find the central players between the lines, and the aggression in and around the box. This was great information to start preparing the week's training sessions.

The only doubt we had is they played with a back line of five against Newcastle two days earlier; Greg suggested it could maybe be to match Newcastle, but I was curious and thought they'd probably start with five against us. Why would you change the last game of pre-season when, in the last two years, you've never previously changed to a back-five? We are used to this, though: a team changing their structure and idea against us, mostly to stop our strong parts. This is why we needed to focus on ourselves and stay or become even more unpredictable, which is why we worked so hard on it over the summer.

After this, we went to get the information from the medical department on a number of different issues that needed consideration. Andreas Schlumberger had joined us at the start of the year, someone Jürgen knew well from his time in Germany.

One of the main hopes of Schlumbi is that a player doesn't lose coordination throughout their rehabilitation. Virgil is a great mover but the way he coordinated the rehab was outstanding. Not too much strength work, constant focus on his movements. Communication is key in these processes; trust is key and we signed a world-class rehab coach. He is a great addition to Jürgen's staff. So many small but good decisions are what makes a rehab so smooth. Virgil also did some work with a private physio during the first months of his rehab. The fact he was ready for the first game of the season was down to his drive and passion but also to the precise planning of Schlumbi and the staff within our medical department.

As we drove over to the hotel, Jürgen got the news that it looked like Robbo would be out for three weeks with a small tear in his ankle joint. It was probable that he'd be ready again after the international break. It meant 'Cross-tas' time was here! He had a good pre-season and it felt like the time for him to make the next step. Pre-season is so important for new players. I'd joked about his crossing skills with him on Sunday in training and he said, "Just tell me where the package should be delivered and I will put it there." His appearance against Osasuna would be important for him to step up to 70 minutes.

As we arrived at The Titanic we were still trying to organise a game for the day after Norwich. Only then would our pre-season finally be over. Ray asked me if Wrexham could work but I felt we needed stronger opposition, so he set to work on trying to invite Hearts after both Rangers and Celtic said no. I told him it was important to get everyone as fit as possible for the season. We needed this game to give Hendo and Thiago full game time.

The message in the team meeting was simply to inspire the stadium. We'd seen the day before that Anfield was at its best. From first till last second, we needed to show desire, organisation and be vocal. Throw everything into this game, being aggressive in the best football way. Our counter-press had to be wild, we needed to chase them from all directions. The special instruction for Curtis was to use his skills between the lines to create speed-ups and use our new skill as we did yesterday: first pass forward. Osasuna would approach with long balls – they were second in long passes in the Spanish league the previous season – so it was important we applied our 'have to be first' principle when the ball was in the air.

Again, we had a nearly-full Anfield to perform in front of. The difference in driving to the stadium, even for a friendly – or test – compared to the season before was remarkable. And the players responded to it with a pleasing display to win 3-1.

The sign of a good pre-season is when two different XIs play football like this. This was our best counter-pressing game of this pre-season. There were some great individual performances as well, particularly from Taki, Ox, Fabinho and Roberto. The moment Bobby got involved and freed himself to connect we became so unpredictable, we had options everywhere. I couldn't see our team without Bobby at this moment. He defends like no-one else.

Also, what a performance from Ben Woodburn. The energy he brought to the team was exactly what we stood for. Football-smart, good mover and he unbalanced the opposition constantly with the ball but also with his movements off the ball. I was so happy for him.

Ben was my no10 in the U16 total football team. Trent as the six and Ben 10, wow. The spine of that team was incredible with Trent, Herbie Kane, Harvey Whyte, Ben Woodburn and Rhian Brewster. "Dominate midfield and you will dominate the game," is what we used to say.

After the Osasuna game, there was a quick message of appreciation from Jürgen to the team: "The only bad thing about tonight is that it counts as a pre-season game." Kaide, Harvey and Owen made another step in their development, all playing a minimum of 45 minutes at Anfield. And it was also another step for our commitment in bringing through our own young players. All of them are in different moments of their development, but all are building the foundations of a professional career. That's the most important thing. What this experience has taught us is when the process is fluid and when you have a strong collective idea, it's much easier for young players like Harvey, Owen and Kaide to come through, to be available to have a good and consistent performance. And that's what happened with Owen. He has attributes like Ben Chilwell, so much technique. We were really happy for them; what a dream that was.

As I was driving home that night, I remembered how what we

did in the last ten games of last season was something so special. We started dominating midfield again with Fabinho back in the six, the most important position. Thiago, Gini and Bobby filled up the rest of the spine. Many things came together at the right time. The consistency was there again. All our success in these last three years had come from how we dealt with adversity – just take the Barcelona semi-final as the prime example. In these moments was where we kept our plan, our way. It gave us consistency over long periods.

I believed that after this pre-season we were strong enough to cope with everything that was coming.

WEEK 2

FIRST PASS FORWARD

AFTER RETURNING FROM EVIAN ON SATURDAY night and then games against Athletic Club and Osasuna on Sunday and Monday, the following Tuesday was a day off for the players before we really started to ramp up the Norwich preparations.

I used it to prepare the training week and also to think about all the options we have for our first line-up of the season as I knew Jürgen would ask for my opinion when we were back in Kirkby. Since the summer I'd had it in my head we should use a more rotational approach without losing stability. Utilising all the strengths of our squad, creating with this an ability to attack each competition because of the quality of the team. Our squad is fairly small, so not using everyone would not be smart. Also, it would help to maintain freshness and avoid injuries throughout the season.

I thought the plan was good but it was only on paper. In football you have to play the moment, so we could play with this idea week-by-week. There was also time to train in these first weeks and that made it easier to change things a little bit more.

We felt we should try to keep Sadio, Roberto, Diogo and Mo fresh for the whole season.

There is nothing as strong as talent that gets opportunities in combination with experience. For example, Harvey and Milner together, because from both perspectives they will not let each other down. That's my experience: the younger one feels stronger and guided by the older players and the older ones feels more responsibility to organise, which raises the standards. I love to guide these processes. 'Talents need models, not criticism' is one of my favourite sayings. The young ones always surprise you and they took our game plan over the last year further than we could have ever imagined. For example, Trent gave the right full-back position a new meaning but with Hendo as his mentor.

As someone once said, 'Logic gets you from A to B, but imagination will get you everywhere'. And that's the strength of young talent – they are so brave. One generation will influence the other and then it's becoming a culture. This is where we're at: the ultimate goal no-one really can see or plan. As Jürgen has said in his press conference, we are constantly busy with the long-term. You can't compare us with other clubs, we do it our way.

This also helps the new players a lot as they come into a culture of preparation. When a player like Ibou comes in, it's always about how the player adapts to the team – its mentality

– and how the team understands the player. But you could see that Ibou has everything to represent our ideas, so the adaptation process went very naturally.

Everything about this team is glued by togetherness and character. We know if we give everything, every day, then we can beat probably every team – starting with Norwich on the Saturday. That's why we believe so much in training. We (probably) only have two rules: one, that it's always 100 per cent attitude; and two, everyone is responsible for everything. That's setting standards. That's total football. Flexibility, freedom inside the system.

It's about a strong collective idea which makes the individuals flourish. The team transforms the players, not the players transform the team. This is how we approach our training sessions. And with that, for us, the main ingredient is the defensive aggression off the ball, because the better you are in the 30 per cent you don't have the ball, the more freedom and conviction it will give you to play attacking football. We believe it's that 30 per cent that makes us different to many other teams, with our intensity and togetherness in these moments. In that 30 per cent, we all do it together – the front players who prepare pressing situations and a last line which supports by finding challenges high up the pitch.

If we do this well we could play with eight attackers and two centre-halves… well, that's our dream! That's why Ibou came in, because he could be one of the two centre-backs, he had speed and could catch the quickest counter-attacks. We were getting there.

On Wednesday morning we had our referee, PFA and Premier League meeting. They provided us with updates about changes to the laws. The offside-rule tweak is top – it gives the offensive advantage a new life – but the rest becomes even more subjective, especially when Martin Atkinson said we will go back to "the old times." Beforehand, Jürgen and myself decided not to comment. It's something we decided also in the last ten games of last season.

We had so many situations we discussed last year, from early kick-off times to too few recovery days in between games, to tactical fouls, having five subs… it just went on and on. A lot of lost energy because nothing changed or got better. We try to not get involved anymore with the fourth official, not with the referee, not with the other bench. Just remain calm and control our emotions, focusing on ourselves. It was a common decision so even John Achterberg was calm from that moment on!

Afterwards, I sat with Jürgen to go through our training plans and he mentioned that we should think about rotation. It's great when two minds are so alike; it makes everything much easier. I need this set-up, this relationship with the people around me. We know where we want to go. He asked if I think Virgil is ready to start at Norwich. I told him I don't have any doubts whatsoever.

The training on Wednesday focused on a nine-versus-seven towards goal, where I always brought a second ball into play to train the first-pass-forward concept. It was the session after a day off so we needed to use the time to increase the concentration levels again. Immediately introducing a common plan, it's never an 'easy' session and I'm pretty sure the boys were not expecting a tactical exercise when they arrived. We did it on purpose to make sure after that day we were ready.

The seven when stealing the ball tried to score immediately within three gates, who represent our three strikers. This moment of transition created the focus on our counter-pressing impulse.

With the nine we focused on 'moving' the seven, trying to create space between the lines for Sadio or Mo to turn and speed up. I told them that with Mo and Sadio with space facing the goal, we kill everyone – it's for the other eight to create as many situations as possible like this. "Use the width to attack through the inside!" Jürgen and myself shouted, over and over again.

We spoke about the behaviour of the Norwich centre-halves, dropping with each move we make, so it's important to create space between the lines. After this feedback, the exercise became like the game. Mo, Sadio, and Jota started moving much more freely, something that was an evident change last season in the last ten games, not as 'fixed'. We also did rondos and passing to improve the speed of decision-making, during which Thiago was incredible. "He must have been born in a rondo!" I joked with Jürgen.

We train our passing in a non-conventional way. There is always freedom on where to pass and to move, and we add counter-pressing and pressing dynamics. We completed the session by finishing crosses off. 'Finishing to finish', the best way to end the day on a high. When we can't attack through the inside, we should be able to create with give-and-goes, or overlaps to create dangerous crossing situations. Kostas–Taki–Kostas–Bobby was a good example of this in the game versus Osasuna. First outplay, then cross. It doesn't matter who we play against, where we play, we will press them high and aggressively and we will attack and attack them again. Our style is to attack, with and without the ball. Norwich should be ready for an intense game. We realise that the game is played with one ball, our ball, and we chase it all over the pitch and we use it to play the first pass forward. More Cruyff is impossible.

A clear reference is when we prepare pressing situations by

playing versus the ball. So when the ball moves, we move as a collective. We close the easy passes to the inside with our front three. We have the principle that Mo, Sadio and Roberto are responsible for defending five or even six players of the opposition. When we see, feel or anticipate the trigger, we start our pressing machine. We identified a centre-half of Norwich as the player to press in our drill – the pass towards him sets the trigger for the closest player to apply aggressive pressure. Many teams have this, but what makes us different are two things. One is the last two metres of the press is when we want to win the ball, so we go with all we have, knowing that when you get outplayed the next one is ready. The second thing is our capacity and our will to chase the opposition from behind. For example, Roberto is never really outplayed.

On Wednesday night I watched the UEFA Super Cup final between Villarreal and Chelsea and I remember Adrian's performance two years earlier in the same fixture for us. Some of the best stories are written from out of nowhere.

Heading in on Thursday, I had a padel tennis match lined up against Jürgen after he'd set it up the night before via text. I won 7-5, 6-4, but Jürgen seemed happy about it. It's the age, I guess, when you become just as happy about the performance without winning. To be honest, it was a very equal game, but I was thinking we should keep a competition table.

Training was very competitive that day. The players didn't have time to think as we went through all different types of games in the space of an hour: keeping the ball in possession as a wake-up call; counter-attacks stimulating the last pass and finals to show some magic. I explained during the possession drill that when we can play one-touch football in these spaces, we can play well everywhere. Also, because Norwich defended within such small spaces, we needed to be ready to play combinations in them. Jota, Bobby, Ibou, Taki and Fab won the tournament… after Jota and Bobby drove every other team nuts by creating so much. Afterwards, Pete stayed with the set-piece takers to work on their accuracy. I'd asked Warren, our groundsman, to build a basketball-type ring to be used exactly for this. It was still a prototype at this stage but worked outstandingly for what we needed.

It was just 48 hours before kick-off at Norwich, two days until the season started. "If we play like we trained today, we will be flying," is what Milner said after training. The problem with sessions like this? It makes it much harder to choose a first 11. We were seeing the benefits of a full six-week pre-season – if people want to improve the game and its quality, they should think about allowing for this more often.

That night Jürgen forwarded me a text with the result of the votes for the players' committee. There were three spots left behind our captain Hendo, vice-captain Milner and leader Virgil. I was delighted to discover that Trent was in! Our future captain was a step closer – he should now stay close to Milner to learn as much as possible during this year because it's the next step in his development. Robbo and Ali were the other two to make the players' committee.

Trent had asked to meet me in pre-season for a chat and we sat together for an hour discussing his game. One of the main things he wanted to discuss as well was making sure me and Jürgen knew he wanted to be in now, and not be missed out because he was young or maybe a bit less vocal before games than others. I replied to the boss, "Trent is in, TOP, he represents so much of our club."

On Friday, Virgil signed a new deal. Our rock. The impact of Virgil is huge. We can play a higher line with him in the team. We can also play more aggressively because of how he deals with space and longer balls in to our backline. But don't forget that Virgil is able to be this good because of the player next to him, whether that's Joel, Joe or Ibou now. For me, you can only evaluate or judge a centre-half as a pair. I see it as one position, not two. They lead, they organise protection, and the base for good pressing is the positioning of the last line – they are responsible for this.

I remember sitting in Jürgen's kitchen just before we had a personal conversation with Virgil [when Van Dijk was set to sign for the club]. I've never seen Jürgen so determined: "We have to get him, Pep – it's him and nobody else." We only had a Plan A. Jürgen didn't want to think about a Plan B. We were convinced that with him we could take the next steps as a team, but for a long time it didn't work in trying to get him. Virgil is a great professional and a great person to work with. He deserves all the credit because he works really hard and makes the people around him better. A big player who makes the team great. Virgil and our last line are continuously moving forward, literally and figuratively. I'm often yelling, "Virg! Push up!" on the touchline and he once jokingly said to me after a game: "If I keep listening to you, I'll be defending in the opponent's box!"

Before training Jürgen called me into his office to go through the line-up for Norwich. We felt that if we did the right things, with time we could drag them out of position and make them lose sight of our players between the lines. We'd need players with life to use this and also the initiative from our centre-backs to play these passes. We decided we wanted to respect the pre-season we had, use the ones who were with us from the start and in the best form. Therefore, we chose Ox over Harvey as he was in such a good moment.

We then got a shout from Ray to come into his office where he explained the problems around the international period. Brazil and Egypt were playing in 'red-listed' countries, which would mean the players would need to quarantine when they came back. FIFA had previously allowed us to not release players when games were in red-list countries, but now we could no longer hold them back without their approval. It was unclear what would happen but it didn't look great. However, there were more Premier League teams with the same issues so we told Danny Stanway, our club secretary, to get everyone together.

The main message of our last training session and video meeting was that Norwich should realise it's the Premier League now, it's against Liverpool FC. But Jürgen made it very clear that pre-season was to prepare us for all games, not just Norwich. We showed clips with their stadium full; enjoy the ground but don't wind them up; deal with the atmosphere and use it in the right way. The sign of us playing a good game against them is if we found free players between the lines. That's why we needed to be flexible in our offensive moments, something we repeated in training that afternoon. Jürgen then made sure everyone knew you never play just against one player – always one can defend two, be in between, know about the one at your back. This was important because they put so many players between the lines. When Ox or Naby were jumping on one of the centre-halves, we needed two to protect him closing the gaps. We attack with triangles, but we defend with triangles as well. One of our first principles.

During the session, one of the teams – made-up of those not in the line-up – had Fabinho, Hendo, Thiago, Bobby and Harvey in. Jürgen walked past and whispered in my ear, "I'm so happy we're not playing against them tomorrow!" But that's something you want and it's nice because the other team has to be spot on. On the other hand it's not nice because some tactics don't work as well.

That night we flew down to Norwich. Everything was smooth. I asked Danny Stanway to check the squad to make sure there were no hidden obstacles or surprises. With players having come back from loan, you never know. After a situation with Pedro Chirivella a couple of years earlier, I always double and then triple-check. At night I got the all-clear from Danny.

On the morning of the game I took an hour-long walk over the golf course on the hotel grounds. The sun was shining and I was thinking: it's D-Day… better still, it's Ali's day. He had a very short pre-season and has to be ready.

In the pre-match meeting we discussed how last year we were forced to see the last ten games as finals; there is no other game we play. Today needed to be the same. We should be an intense, high-energy unit, everyone performing with fire. Over recent years we'd set a new intensity in the Premier League, but the journey starts again.

Norwich had been relegated from the top-flight in the pandemic, but having 97 points last year – their highest-ever – and with fans in the stadium, they would be full of confidence. It was for us to put a stick immediately between the spokes of that wheel of confidence. We should also not be surprised that when we crossed badly, for example, they would celebrate these moments. This was the kind of environment we should anticipate. "Ox, whatever you were thinking before the Osasuna game, please think the same this time," we tell him. There are two team rules for today: one, everyone is responsible for defending; and two, be brave on the ball.

Jürgen spoke again to the team at the stadium once the warm-up was done, making sure the boys realised when we were together, close to each other, we were always so strong. Compact and aggressive in our pressing zone. Milner was very vocal... This is the reason you start today, I was thinking. Exactly this, because defending without communication doesn't exist. He is a captain.

We got the breakthrough through Diogo in the first half, but at half-time we showed images of our high press and how we could use Trent and Kostas more often offensively to start the attacks. We also discussed the communication of Virgil and Joel to Milner to control Todd Cantwell better between the lines. He was key and free in each of their attacks in the first half.

When Jürgen had finished, I told Joel and Virgil they should protect each other well diagonally because of the movements of Teemu Pukki. Conclusion of half-time meeting: be better at taking away their offensive routines, cut their connections and exploit the free spaces more on the outside with Kostas and Trent.

Roberto and Mo scored in the second half to make sure we won our first 'final' of the season 3-0 against a technical and brave opponent. The journey had started and I was loving the spirit in the team, though directly after the game we pulled everyone together to discuss our last 15 minutes where we didn't control the game how we wanted and needed Ali to make some spectacular saves. That should really not be necessary.

But our plan had worked well with bringing Roberto and Fab on to improve during the second half. We became more fluid in our combinations and scored two top goals. Trent was outstanding too; all the attention after the game went to Mo and Virgil, but he played as a leader, as a captain.

Game one and three points on the board, but our pre-season was not officially done. On the Sunday we'd agreed for Aston Villa to play us in a behind-closed-doors friendly at Anfield, in which Hendo and Thiago would start. A final pre-season test.

We landed back in Liverpool on the Saturday night and I looked across the aisle of the plane to see Jürgen with a big smile on his face. We were up and running.

'TO INNOVATE YOU NEED GUTS. TO ADAPT YOU NEED AN OPEN MIND'

WEEK 3

"DO IT AGAIN, NABY LAD!"

I BEGAN THE WEEK BY LOOKING THROUGH THE notes I'd made throughout pre-season as I prepared our week's training, which started on Tuesday. I felt we needed to repeat, repeat, repeat so we were ready to go, go, go again. Do it again and again and again and then hopefully Burnley would not have an answer to our organisation and mentality. It was with this in my mind that I prepared sessions where the boys had to be ready to work really hard trying to win the ball back as early and as high as possible, without losing control for the second ball. We also wanted to focus again on 'having options everywhere'.

Pete and Mark had created a brilliant, animated video for one of our earlier pre-match meetings that showed the amount of lines and options we wanted. Our game is a collective one, based on connections... Could you imagine if there was a machine able to evaluate these?

More and more in football, people tend to individualise, but that's exactly the opposite of what we want. What we do, we do together – and at 100 per cent. That's why I choose exercises where players are constantly forced to cooperate, to re-organise, to find a common plan. I believe that like this, we become successful, or are at least closer to achieving success, because at this level you never win when you play poorly. I constantly praise the boys every time I see something I like, to try and motivate them; encouraging attack and stressing the importance of the defensive aspects.

This week presented another full week of training, which we always look forward to. With no midweek games in the first couple of weeks of the campaign, it felt like our pre-season had been extended because we had time to train which we never normally have. So we started the week immediately with a 10 v 0 exercise to simulate making quick, short, new triangles, attracting the opponent on the outside and attacking through the centre with many options and lines, winning the ball back quickly and playing the first pass forward to create.

The main idea was to make our build-up more flexible, with a dropping full-back or dropping no8, and our no6 staying more positionally together with our two centre-backs to form a stable triangle. From there, we changed the outside triangle with Naby or Kostas closer to the centre-halves. This was the first image our players had when they were starting the week, the idea being that there was a greater chance of it sticking in their minds. Give the most important message at the start of training when everyone is able to process all of the words and instructions.

The following day, exercises were carried out faster, giving the boys many different 'Burnley problems' to solve where they had to work hard and together to find answers against this style. With this constant hard work, plus an erase-the-ego mentality, we are creating the competitive collective environment we want. You can't 'sign' an environment [like a player] – it is achieved by a good, stable process.

At the end of the session we did some extra finishing drills with pure striker movements. Mo, Sadio, Jota, Roberto, Ox and Kaide had to move aggressively behind the last line and finish ball after ball. The star of the session was Naby Keita, though. I thought to myself: whatever you ate for breakfast this morning, you should keep eating it! Wow, he basically nutmegged everyone in the squad during our five-a-side identity games.

He should definitely eat the same thing on matchday. When he did yet another nutmeg I shouted, "Do it again, Naby lad!" and five seconds later, he does indeed do it again. Twice. "It's four days too early, Naby... calm down!"

Monday was a day off for the players but our analyst Mark texted me to say that we needed to keep our no6 more central, as we'd discussed before. I agreed with him but it's always good when someone who knows our game so well gives clear, concise feedback. The season had started and now it was about evolving with small tweaks to our game plan.

He had two clips to show the difference when Fabinho is off and on the pitch. Fab has this natural characteristic to be the one who protects us constantly, he's controlling a very important space for counter-attacks. He does that as nobody else can, that's why I called him 'the Lighthouse' – he guides us, he controls this structure. You need organisation, tactical discipline and the right distances, and there are key positions who control these. It's the base which allows you to become more unpredictable. So, in the 10 v 0 we'd focus on creating dynamics with our no8 or our full-back dropping next to our centre-halves instead of Fab.

The goals we'd score from pressing and counter-pressing situations this season could be the difference in our points total at the end. We had to keep 'building the body', adapting to our intensity, training our connections by changing the eyes and the mind of the players; focusing on the process of pressing high in the highest intensity. We should not lose any sleep about the opposition, in my opinion. That doesn't mean that we don't do our homework and create a game plan BUT – in capital letters – always keeping the same mental landscape for the players. For example, I believe each system has solutions for a single problem of a different opponent structure. Burnley would target our last line with many high balls, so we needed to have a clear plan for this, but all the rest should stay the same.

We are lucky Jürgen is with us. To innovate you need guts, to adapt you need an open mind. He has all of that and more. He gives me so much freedom and with this a lot of responsibility. It's all about preparing the team step-by-step towards playing more – and better – counter-pressing football. Burnley was a new chance to play at the end of this week.

There is a well-known saying, 'You are a product of your own environment', and this is so true, but some people have the gift to create an environment just by themselves, giving colour to a whole organisation. When Jürgen speaks to the players, he speaks from the heart and it goes directly into the hearts of the players. The meetings he holds before a session make my life leading training so much easier. Players are curious about what's coming and he has this remarkable capacity to touch people with the words he selects. That's not easy, especially with this level of player. I find it intriguing, how it's possible, the convincing way he has and the ability to touch people. You deal with a lot of egos in football, but at our club it looks like there are none – and the moment the best players put the team before themselves is the moment you can become a success story.

The level of respect the players have for the boss is huge. In fact, even opposition players look up to him. There is a poem that explains it best: 'No written word, no spoken plea, can teach our team what they should be, nor all the books on the shelves, it's what the coach is himself'. The character of the coach becomes the character of the team. You can see it throughout the club. That's the power of Jürgen's personality. He is someone you can't stop learning from because he surprises you so many times. He can create a feeling of belief and determination for a whole group of players in just two sentences.

Off the training pitch, Leighton Clarkson joined Blackburn Rovers on loan this week. I'd spoken with Julian Ward when we were in Austria a few weeks before so we could start organising his loan deal so everything would run smoothly for him. We decided at the end of last season that Leighton and Jake Cain could make a step on their development paths by going into the loan process. It was clear with Fabinho coming back that the time to move on was there. Ben Davies left as well for Sheffield United.

I asked our analyst James French to look at set-pieces and put a document together focusing specifically on corner-kicks. We'd changed our idea of focusing on set routines to a more open approach, with the idea to be really organised for the second phase, and we stayed with this idea during the final ten games of the season when we became much better and more dangerous on the edge of the box – which was exactly what would happen with Mo's goal at Norwich. We felt Bilbao had been our best set-piece game of the pre-season; we attacked centrally and had Virgil, Sadio or Joel making first contact constantly. This is what was in my head, but I'd felt the need to analyse our corners in that game together with Pete and James. Making the idea consistent, attack the centre with three targets and go for the second phase. The outswinger and attacking centrally was really working for us. Virgil and Joel – our two towers – were reading the delivery much better.

After the meeting with James, I went through the training plans with Jürgen and we discussed the idea that Thiago and Hendo should do a 'real' pre-season. Andreas Kornmayer had already said the same thing earlier that morning, so we decided they would play the 'identity game' at the end of the session, when normally on second-day recovery they would only do passing, 10 v 0 and rondos. Then, the following day, when we had our 'competitive volume' day, they would do some extra 'on and off' runs.

Before the session began I walked into the first-team operations office to see James Milner sat there checking through a list at the table. Ray explained to me that the players were giving small gifts to all backroom staff who were with us the whole four weeks of the training camp, as a token of gratitude and appreciation for their help, work and sacrifice. I said to them, I thought I could not have any more respect for James Milner but it went up again. Big respect for our players, this is what makes us different and the staff would give this little bit more in the coming weeks.

Tuesday's training was top, much better than the previous week. Jürgen gave clear instructions on what we would work on and how we would create little advantages in our build-up by changing the formation. From there, I put the team through its paces. The only problem of the session was that Roberto went in after the first half of the identity games with a feeling of discomfort in the outside of his left hamstring. Milner said he'd never seen a player with a hamstring issue running inside, only Bobby Firmino was special, even with an injury. He'd had two recovery days after playing 30 minutes at Norwich, but the problem was he missed 'pre-activation' because of cardiac-screening. These things can't happen again. We were hopeful it was not that bad and Bobby told me it was okay… but he said that as well when we played Barça away. I still see him sitting with a towel over his head after the game. Hopefully this time he would be alright.

This actually reminds me of a story which shows the examples of Jürgen's power after that game at Camp Nou. I'd got a text message from Vitor, who was still at Porto, which said: "If there is one team in world football who can change this around vs Barça, it's you." I got together with Milner and Jürgen and we started showing belief immediately in their dressing room. People ask me, did I believe it was possible? Yes. You know why? There was nothing else to do. We played incredibly away at Camp Nou and had more possession – no other team did that there. Gini as a false nine, come on! If we wouldn't have believed, we would not have had a chance at all.

Jürgen called me into his office after the session. He'd just finished speaking with Ben Woodburn and we wanted to let him go out on loan. I have to admit, I became a little bit emotional because I believe in him so much and he had enjoyed a good pre-season with us. He can play multiple positions, nobody can steal the ball from him even under the highest pressure, he understands the game, can play with a task and will press with high energy.

In the past, a loan process sometimes was a bit like flipping a coin: sometimes it worked, sometimes it didn't. It depended on too many processes which we didn't have control over at the loan club. But now, as a club, I believe we're one of the best around at managing this. In this case, I knew what he could do inside our way of football and the goals and assists in him. Many of our players had a difficult path into our team with not many believing in them early on in their careers elsewhere. For me that's one of our secrets: know how it feels to be undervalued – it's such a motivator. We should give trust to the ones we believe in. We need talent in our team. I prefer talents without many games over players with many games but with not a lot of talent.

In the evening I had a reminder of why we work so hard. I was preparing the session for Thursday when I caught a replica I have of the Champions League trophy gleaming in front of me as the setting sunlight caught it through the window. Start preparing with that cup in mind, the end in mind, but do it game by game. The next day we needed another high-quality session, staying true to our beliefs, pressing high with the highest intensity.

The following morning I wrote down the session again; all details were in now, just before breakfast. A night's sleep always clears the mind and gives solutions. We would use mixed 11 v 11 teams as it was important to keep everyone hungry. Last year we maybe played too much 'starters v non-starters' earlier in the week. We just had to decide which units or triangles we wanted together in both teams. Jürgen chose the last line together, with Ibou coming in, and we also went with a right-sided triangle of Trent, Harvey and Mo.

It was a competitive session. We did the pressing-counterpressing game in the middle zone with long balls played in on my whistle. Each team had to make six passes to create a real counter-press or 'second-ball fight' impulse. Then, after six passes, they were free to attack the goal and leave the zone. By putting the extra long passes in, it became very Burnley-specific, constantly fired into our last line. Our defence needed to be brave and hold it as high as possible to have the advantage of the offside. Jürgen makes it very clear that we can decide how small the pitch is while trying to win second balls. Six passes is one point and a goal counts for three points to create a level of competition. We finished the session with finals to create this extra motivation for the players to give absolutely everything.

To make the teams I just shouted 'groups of five' and the four teams were made automatically. Winner stays on, 40-second games. Trent's team didn't reach the final; everyone knew after the last game because he was arguing with Vitor about the goals scored. Vitor had the toughest job, keeping scores during finishing or finals. I shouted: "It becomes more obvious you are not reaching many finals anymore, Trent…" But a silent Scouser is a dangerous one!

The yellow team was full of experience led by Virgil, but the last team of five was a young one with Curtis, Neco, Harvey, Rhys and Ben, who in the end won the most games. I shouted after the last whistle: "This is the sign of a super strong squad, when your talents beat all the others!" Harvey had even bounced Sadio away from the ball on one occasion and the boys made so many jokes after. This was a day where we felt again that our identity is intensity.

Before Thursday morning's session a member of staff came over to me during the warm-up and joked that he expected to see Robbo parasailing down the side of the building to show he was ready for Burnley, but we were hopeful he would train on the Friday.

During our MD-2 [matchday minus two days] session we focused on finishing situations. There were so many incredible goals – from the edge of the box, the second line, in front of the goalkeeper and headers from late and early crosses. Proper finishing variation, from all different angles and positions inside and outside the box. I'd prepared exercises where Jota had to create space for Mo and Sadio. We felt a crucial point would be the runs into the box against Burnley, unselfish runs to create space. Jürgen explained to the team that it would not be easy, but we couldn't find out in the 75th minute that this was most crucial. After the session Trent went and practised some free-kicks. When Virgil asked Sadio why he wasn't going, he answered with a big smile, "I'll give Trent until January and if he's not scoring them, I will take responsibility!"

Unfortunately, on the same day we lost both our no6s during the session, Fab hamstring and Milner calf. So before training Jürgen and I agreed we should go with Hendo in the 6. I met with Greg and Mark to go through our last two games against Burnley and I wrote down the most important points for when Jürgen, Pete and myself were to meet on Friday to prepare the final presentation.

In the afternoon I'd organised a staff football game to bring the people together in the AXA. After leaving Melwood, I felt we needed these kinds of initiatives. I called it 'the return of the Mummy' because Ray Haughan was playing again! Jürgen said Ray had probably felt his meniscus twice before the game even started. The boss's team won and he immediately put a picture of the winning team on the big screens throughout the building. "You don't mind do you, Pep and Vitor?" he said to us, cheekily. They'd played with one more player for half of the time, but fair play to him, he had some real striker movements still… I won't mention he described them afterwards as "proper Gerd Müller situations."

I scored three goals, one dribbling inside and firing into the far corner, leaving Jack Robinson standing, which was pleasing because he'd played so well in goal. I also tried a bicycle-kick that went just over, although Jürgen made a point of saying afterwards they were still searching for the ball. Vitor showed some Portuguese class on the ball while Kyle Wallbanks, our scout, moved like Ozil, thought he was Ozil, but was dangerous because he tackled with a knife between his teeth. When the game finished we were lying down and Jürgen started urging us to do some warming-up exercises to put more pain in our stomachs.

It was just a great afternoon workout, bringing the departments together. You think you are fit because in the week you do a lot of running, but after five minutes of football you realise it's a completely different animal. That's good for sports science departments to realise; you need to train all three energy systems at the same time to improve game-intensity. Straight-line running has nothing to do with improving football intensity… in fact, I always say straight-line running is the thief of intensity!

On Friday we felt we had to give the team a good 'message' about what they could expect in Saturday's game so there was no surprise when it started. That's why the session was based around forcing our lines to stay high and defending the channel balls. It feels more comfortable for our centre-halves to drop, but sometimes what feels comfortable for an individual isn't good for the team – and this would be exactly the case against Burnley. The space couldn't become big between our lines when our forwards pressed, then they'd have an advantage for the second ball. I always say we want our team to be inside three grass stripes, 18 metres from front to back. That's being together, that's the base of being intense, because what Burnley do when they have space they do really well. More and more, I'm convinced the most important aspect of our game is stopping counter-attacks, so how do we organise ourselves while attacking to be ready for this?

We spent the last part of our training putting Virgil and Joel together v 'Chris Wood' (knowing he wanted to spin into the channel), Hendo v 'Ashley Barnes' and our full-backs high on the edge of the area, knowing this is where they started the counter. We trained this pushing-up of our full-backs on Thursday in the finishing drills, where Kostas and Trent needed to take this position 20 times. Jürgen said strongly in the pre-session meeting to the lads, "I want 11 players here to defend, and I want 11 players here to attack," pointing to our half and the opposition half of the pitch, sketching a great total football picture.

Afterwards we had to have a 'red alert' meeting with Julian, Billy Hogan, Danny, Jürgen and myself. The Brazilians and Mo would play in red-list countries during the upcoming internationals and have an 11-day window instead of nine. This meant they'd play their last game on the Thursday, have to fly back, and we played on Sunday v Leeds. It's just unacceptable, but as well as this they would need to quarantine for ten days on their return. The Premier League wanted an exemption from Number 10, but we would keep them here if that didn't happen. There were 52 clubs all over Europe involved with the same issues. Billy is intelligent, organised and shows understanding towards the beliefs of Jürgen, who was fuming. Eight days from now they would be going, so he wanted a statement from the club ASAP. The best thing, purely from a Liverpool team perspective, would be no exemption provided and the players stay here, to be honest, but we knew and appreciated how important it was for our boys to represent their countries.

Fabinho was actually outside doing some runs to check if he had any pain as we were holding this meeting. He said he felt all good, so the plan would be to integrate him with the team preparing for the Chelsea game.

Later, when we headed over to The Titanic, Vitor threw a grenade. He said Jack was better in goal than John in the staff game. I'd asked five different security guards to ask John when he arrived how the game had gone, as well. The best banter in life is always in the dressing room, even in the coaches' one.

"You should be ashamed of yourselves," John quipped as he walked past us on the bus.

After dinner Jürgen showed me an image of Adam Lallana counter-pressing with a slide-tackle and Sadio finishing it brilliantly. "That's counter-press!" Jürgen said, loudly. It was from Burnley at Anfield in 2019... what a year! After watching the other three goals we decided to put it in the players' group with the message: 'Every way into the goal is the right way!'

We watched PSG play later that evening and discussed the talents of Kylian Mbappe. Vitor asked directly who we'd choose between him and Haaland... "Better for Jürgen to answer this one," I said before Billy walked up the stairs and saved him from having to answer by speaking with the boss about a different topic.

I took a call quite late that night from the owners of a Championship club. It was a great honour to be linked again to the plans there and I knew the ambition and passion of the owners very well. But my focus and commitment was with Liverpool Football Club. It was a relationship based on trust and quality. We were in the middle of our project at LFC and ready to attack this league again. The owners of the interested club told me they wanted a change in management and I was their no1 candidate, but it was not the right timing. You commit or you don't, and when you do, you must be loyal to the project, to the club, to your colleagues.

Later I took another call, this time at three in the morning, when two members of staff contacted me to say Ox was leaving the hotel as his baby was coming earlier than expected. I was just really happy for him. We made sure that it was his day. He could decide when and if he joined the team for the game.

On Saturday morning Ray came to us with Alex on the phone

and he told us it was a little boy named Axel – a typical boyband name already! Jürgen started his pre-match meeting by telling the players the good news and saying, "A baby changes everything in life, the same as supporters change everything for players in a stadium. There was never a great atmosphere during a shit game. We need to give people joy and in return, they will give more back. It means the stadium will feel that it is the same for us as for them. The never-give-up mentality is not only for the big games – it's for these games where things will not work perfectly. And don't forget it was Burnley who ended our unbeaten home run of 68 games last season."

After the week's work, the players' response was a good one and we won 2-0 against a battling Burnley. This was one of the better games we'd played against this kind of team with two great goals.

Jota had told me at half-time that against Norwich he'd been running towards the second post and the crosses had been between the centre-backs, so he thought this time he needed to go in front. He is someone who really analyses the game.

Some of the Burnley players are built like stone and when they switched the side and put the cross in, they were so strong. We said to the boys at half-time, don't play the clock – we can't slow down against them because they will smell it and punish us. We discussed on the bench to keep our subs for later because we were increasing pressure on them and starting to play better and better. It paid off with the second goal: a few great combinations using the width and attacking through the centre, with Sadio finishing the volley.

I would say giving Virgil time on the ball isn't the best idea. He played one of his classic cross-field passes to Harvey, who had taken a position out wide with Mo and Trent inside. He controlled the ball twice with his chest before linking up brilliantly with Trent, who played it first time to Sadio for the finish. Harvey showed his level of technique, Virgil showed the big man was well on his way back.

Nothing feels as good as winning an early kick-off on the Saturday and watching and analysing all the others calmly when they play afterwards.

Another one down.

WEEK 4

A SEASON IN THREE GAMES

AFTER A DAY OFF FOR THE BOYS ON MONDAY, OUR week began with a visit from Arsene Wenger to present Jürgen, Trent, Virgil, Ali and Thiago with FIFA awards on Tuesday. He also watched our session and you could see him change the moment his feet touched the grass. The pitch is his office. He told us he was impressed by the intensity of the training, to which I said to him, "This is after a day off – you have to see them tomorrow!" He also said, "The amount of specific information about your next game is incredible." That was exactly my idea while preparing the session: many clear messages in drills. The preparation for Chelsea had started and some of our pressing dynamics we had to change.

Jürgen explained to Arsene that in our first three games we would already have gone through the whole Premier League: Norwich, technical, brave, good football but with some weaknesses; Burnley, second-ball, physical game; and next Chelsea, with world-class players in combination with a possession style. That's the reason we needed to be clear at the start of the week because 'new problems mean new solutions'. Credit to Thomas Tuchel, we would need to defend better than we ever did before. They were strong, but we believed they were not stronger than we were and our week began with our intensity on show. Our passing and combinations were sharp.

Wenger commented on how great it is to have Anfield full again – he's always been very vocal in his praise for our support. I explained how much we missed the supporters for our emotional type of game. Jürgen said we had both of our legs cut off last year, one leg being our centre-halves and the other being our fans. So true. We then discussed our good start with two wins from two. Wenger said to us: "When you are winning you ask yourself why I'm getting paid so much money, but when you lose you think I deserve every penny and more." The life of a coach is like this. It doesn't get better when you win, but it gets a lot worse when you lose.

As we chatted, Harvey, Trent and Mo were practising free-kicks in the background. Arsene said that in the past, walls came half-a-metre forward, but now it's fair because of the spray and this means you can train much better. Jürgen explained that's exactly the reason we brought neuro11 [neuro-scientific data-based training for elite athletes] into our sessions in Evian. As he said this, the three lads were finishing almost every free-kick perfectly.

We had finished our session with the 'gates game' to simulate quick, sharp switches of play, to create free space and find the free gate'. Play with pressure, keep the ball in possession and attack the gates aggressively – something we would need to do against Chelsea in each spell of possession we had. If I had

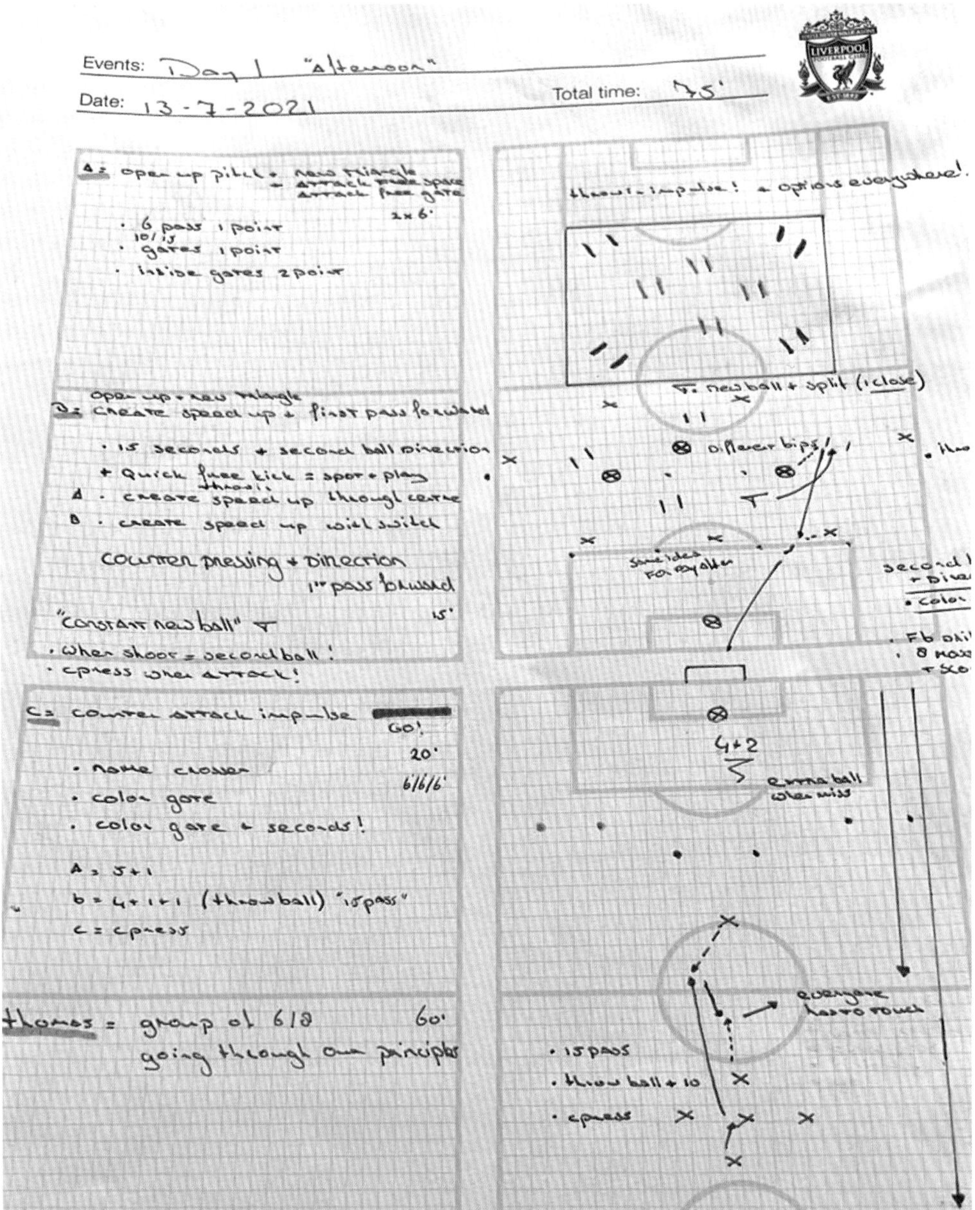

Events: Day 1 "Afternoon"

Date: 13-7-2021

Total time: 75'

A: open up pitch + new triangle + attack free space, attack free gate

2 x 6'

- 6 pass 1 point
- gates 1 point
- inside gates 2 point

open up + new triangle

B: create speed up + first pass forward

- 15 seconds + second ball direction
- quick free kick = spot + play

A - create speed up through centre

B - create speed up with switch

counter pressing + direction

1st pass forward

"constant new ball"

15'

- when shoot = second ball!
- cpress when attack!

C: counter attack impulse

60'

20'

- nome closer
- color gate
- color gate + seconds!

6/6/6'

A = 5+1

b = 4+1+1 (throw ball) "15 pass"

c = cpress

thomas = group of 6/8 going through our principles

60'

throw-in - impulse! + options everywhere!

new ball + split (close)

different bips

4+2

extra ball when miss

everyone has to touch

- 15 pass
- throw ball + 10
- cpress

The journey starts here: Some notes and a picture from the very first training day in Saalfelden, Austria, in July 2021. Little did we know then how the adventure would unfold

Pep talk: Those first training sessions of the summer were key to preparing the players for the challenges ahead

Off to a flier: The three points are secure in our first Premier League game of the season against Norwich City as Mo celebrates our third goal. (Above) Arsène Wenger pays a visit to Kirkby

Mo-mentum: (Top) an expectant Anfield prepares for the visit of Chelsea at the end of August. (Above) Mo continues his strong start to the season with another goal – against AC Milan at Anfield

the chance I would repeat this exercise every day because it shows the necessity to speed up the play as much as possible to surprise. On top of this, we'd need to work harder than every other team they'd played so far. These exercises simulated this so well and our best level was needed. A red block moving back and forward, because when we win our pressing situations it's a one-v-zero emotional advantage with our crowd.

I had watched Arsenal against them closely at the weekend and realised the positioning of the last line would be crucial to apply high pressing. A 'big belief' game, I told our centre-halves and full-backs in the first session of the week. I said this is the main task: against a line of five you need to be brave, jump and become one-v-one in the back line. With a deep line we would not be able to press James or Alonso, and when they can switch they become unstoppable. Arsenal got picked apart like this, to be honest.

All players and all lines should dominate all defensive aspects, then you are never surprised. Read where the next pass will go – together we will force the mistakes, knowing that it's never a mistake to defend forward. We told Robbo and Trent to be immediately in a pressing mood. Full-back to wing-back, and make being braver impossible. We let them do what they like but not what they really like. Jürgen told them, "The only moment to run slow in this game is when we have scored." These two players, Robbo and Trent, should be the ones who set the stadium on fire on Saturday.

In the afternoon I watched the whole training session back in Mark's office to see if everything came out how we'd planned and to prepare for the next day's training. From the 'wake-up call' rondos to our defensive shape vs their offensive routines. You can be good for 98 per cent but missing two per cent and then your press will be shit. It's about finding and winning challenges. We need success – and always when we have success in our first phase of pressing, we play a good game and are fresher with the ball.

That's why we changed our set-up with Sadio and Mo closing the inside passes instead of the outside passes. We focused on finding our front three using the spaces they give us. It can be difficult for teams when you combine winger to winger, for example, and can open up big gaps in the last line. We knew the way we set up could create issues for them. Attacks should make us stronger, unlike last year when we suffered from counter-attacks. Their set-up could hurt us as well, so we should be able to close the pathways to their counter better now. We should try everything to keep the team compact, with and without the ball. It would be about moments, going up, gaining confidence emotionally and using these moments. Mark discussed how Rudiger would come out and when he did we needed to use the space he left. Mo should be smelling these spaces.

Tuesday also brought the news that Robbo had signed a new deal with the club. Another captain who'd committed his future to Liverpool FC. As I was making my notes, I caught a glimpse of Robbo's book in front of me. Now You're Gonna Believe Us: Our Year, My Story. Exactly what [co-author] James and I had in mind for this project.

Ahead of Wednesday's session I spent some time thinking about how, before you go into a game, it's important to know the advantages you have. One is, clearly, Anfield. Secondly, it was our structure plus a common plan against Chelsea, but I felt what separated us from many others was our character. I had the feeling that this would be a special Anfield game when we are in a special mood, so we needed to create another little advantage with our defensive plan: always being 'on the jump'. We needed to dominate our pressing zone again, then we are always on top. Running becomes biting – this is what makes us a defensive machine. What people forget is that pressing is the most offensive idea in football because you immediately create attacking situations. The better you are without the ball, the more you will have it.

So, it made a real difference practising these defensive aspects already on Wednesday, three days before the game, creating so many problems for our players to solve in the session. We knew we couldn't be perfect against Chelsea because they were too good for this and you couldn't control everything against them.

Jürgen, Pete, Vitor and myself watched moments of our press against RB Leipzig from the previous season, then watched Chelsea back and discussed how we wanted it to be at the weekend. The session ended at a high level with our identity game, three teams competing over the whole pitch. A crazy intense exercise. The boys were really training well, fighting for their position. You saw it in the performances of our midfielders. There were not many times we played more sharp, quick passes than today. We trained so sharp, quick, and still there wasn't one foul committed to hurt another player. I love that. LFC players are not just judged on their skills, they are judged on their values as well.

Vitor also started with the talent group on Wednesday. The idea is early acquisition and adaptability of the young players to the first-team game idea. We try to create individual and collective development in relation to the idea and values of the club. We've seen when talents come together, the possibilities in training increase indefinitely and that's exactly what happened. Kaide Gordon, Tyler Morton and Owen Beck were not knocking on the door – they were pushing the door open. In modern football you don't see a group of players who stay together for a longer time and are from the same culture much anymore. But in the past every club had a core group of players from the same culture. This is what we try to create with all the contract extensions.

Historically, the core players decided the way of playing and then the coach came in. Whenever they were touched by a top coach, they won everything. This happened in every country. For example, Sacchi at Milan, Cruyff with Barça and Van Gaal with Ajax. What you can create with your own academy is this: what you had in the past. We started the talent group so we'd have a 15-year-old training with a 19-year-old with the only goal being that they get to know each other. They know the rules of AXA, they know the staff, the kitchen, all those things, but the most important thing is they know each other and connect with each other. Because in the end – and this is our main goal – we hope they will play together in the first team and when they do, that this is not the first time they have played together. This is only possible if you create a situation where the best 15-year-old is training with the best 19-year-old. So, we brought Kaide and Owen up and they can watch Mo Salah up close: the way he prepares himself in the physio room, the way he prepares himself before the training session, how he puts his shin pads on, how he treats his boots, everything. All these small things, these unwritten things, for young players to learn from their models is so important.

That's before you even speak about the pitch: how Sadio controls the ball and turns away, how Virgil is the playmaker from out the back, the motor. They see how Sadio is creating space for himself before he receives the ball – that is one of his biggest strengths – so he can play one v ones in the areas we want him to. It's a one-club mentality, with our vision, with our future, with our ideals, our way of playing that makes us specific, that makes us recognisable. And also how we try to represent the fans. We want to represent their passion, that's why we choose this style, because it all has to link together: the manager, the coaches, the players, the staff, the Academy boys and the fans. That all has to come together and then over time you can compete.

The talent group is something that we created because at a club as big as Liverpool FC, it is impossible for the manager to watch every youth game. I thought if the manager can't go there and can't see them… okay, we can bring the best of the Academy to him. So, one time a week, the first-team dressing room is home for these young players. In doing this, we create a relationship between Jürgen and these players.

With Kaide coming up, we wanted to show patience with him. That's really, really important in my opinion, because in the end these decisions make or break a young player's career. Not only his, but the others who come behind him as well. We want to create something unique. Jürgen always says if it was simple everyone would do it, so it's not that easy. Character is number one and talent is number two. By character I mean the passion, the ambition. I've said before that the love of the game is the most important quality that drives a player.

On Wednesday afternoon I got a text message from someone at the club that said all 20 Premier League clubs agreed we need to stand together to say we won't release players to red-list or quarantine countries and we would appeal to FIFA to reconsider their position. The Premier League would put out a statement making our position clear. They told us they felt it was unlikely FIFA would penalise the clubs, but we'd see over the course of the next few days as it unfolded. The international games were getting closer and the key element was clarity for everyone.

The news was dominated by another topic: the future of Cristiano Ronaldo, who was being tipped to join Manchester City. But even if he did, we had this willpower to prove what we were doing was right. In the summer before the season we became Premier League champions, we'd had the same discussions around that time. Keeping a group together plus talent and training is, for me, the three main ingredients in a successful formula. Training, improving players, improving the team. One thing is for sure: when we sign, we should sign for the first 11 and nothing less.

Mark selected three or four good defensive clips of Tuesday's session. We went through it and I asked him to animate the clips with the most important coaching points. There was still more fine-tuning to do. Especially in midfield. On Wednesday afternoon we had our second staff game which ended in a 9-5 victory for mine and Jürgen's team. I'll be honest, I went to our security room afterwards to see if it got filmed by the CCTV because I'd scored two worldies against John Achterberg: a volley from outside the box and a lob from 35 metres. Unfortunately they didn't have it… so disappointing.

Thursday brought the Champions League group-stage draw, and having got AC Milan, Atletico Madrid and Porto, we were excited by ours. You need to earn the right to progress in a group stage like this. I told Joe Gomez, "We will become a better team with these games." It's the Champions League, the name says it all – and the better the games, the better you have to play. The better you play, the more you improve.

Milan were last out of the pots for us and a couple of staff members at Kirkby were hoping to avoid them given we already had Atletico and Porto, but I was saying, "Bring it on." A historic club to visit for our fans – provided they were allowed to travel – and real history between clubs, despite the fact we only played them in finals. European football at its best. I was at the San Siro with PSV when we got knocked out by them in the Champions League semi-final in 2005. Yes, that year. The Istanbul year. There's a lot of history there and Sacchi is one of my favourite coaches.

I will be honest, I was really happy we didn't draw an eastern European team… away in the snow in December in a must-win would be tough. But we never did it the easy way. When we won the Champions League, we beat Bayern, Barça, PSG, Napoli and had a very difficult away game in Belgrade. I can still hear them singing during the complete duration of our warm-up: 'Fuck off, Liverpool!' In terms of Porto, well I have real history there after seven years as part of one of the world's most well-known training methodologies. And Atletico? Well, we didn't deserve to be knocked out against them last year, with 34 shots and 72 per cent possession.

The draw and the excitement around it momentarily made you forget we played Chelsea in two days, but once it was finished, the focus was back. In the evening I watched Sol Campbell on Sky discussing a game of the Arsenal 'Invincibles' team against Chelsea. "Some games define a season," he said and it's so true, but this is a championship that will be defined in the later stages because it's the Premier League. Campbell was asked how it was to play for that team and he said in response that it was great to play with each player who does everything on and off the pitch to win and has the exact same thinking. When he said this, there was just one thing in my mind: we should cherish these times with the team and players we have because this is exactly our mentality.

Gary Neville then spoke to Jamie Carragher on the next show and told him that emotionally it was so difficult to play at Anfield as an opponent and his Manchester United teams believed winning there would give you a chance of winning the league. He also mentioned how you could hear into the other dressing room before the new Main Stand was built, which I'd forgotten about but then immediately recalled Van Gaal going crazy with Wayne Rooney to the rest of the Manchester United team trying to encourage them at half-time in the last 16 game of the Europa League in 2016.

Friday morning, I arrived at the office when Dr Jim Moxon came in. I could immediately tell something wasn't right. A member of external staff who had been working closely with our Brazilian players had tested positive for COVID and he'd treated the lads on Monday, Tuesday and Wednesday. We decided with Jürgen that we should all take lateral flow tests and then focus on all our normal routines without too much change. We had only just been speaking about how good our week had been so far when the Doc came in, and how we'd had no distractions apart from Mo's situation with Egypt and the potential quarantine requirements.

Training was good, the level was high and we were looking in good shape for the challenge of Chelsea. As we finished up the tactical session, the news came through – Ronaldo to United. It makes us want to prove a point. Pete came by later and said, "Neymar to City," which made everyone laugh.

Before we headed over to The Titanic, we got together in Jürgen's office in front of the tactics board to go through our options for our high press. The magnets go quicker than our players are able to, but we decided there and then we go all in, in the bravest way we can. We thought we could surprise Tuchel. What would he do? We thought we knew. We countered the counter figuratively already before the game. When Pete came in with the analysis footage, we went through the details and decided to change our throw-in defensive organisation. We'd been poor for a long time in that aspect and we'd go to a more zonal approach instead of man-marking. Burnley creating three massive chances hurt all of us.

Later at the hotel in the team meeting, Jürgen said one of football's best rules is 'find the free player' and when there is no-one free, 'create a free player'. This is what we'd be able to do against them as long as we tried to create three advantages for this. First advantage is to have Fabinho behind the strikers so that makes them move more. Secondly, we drop with Robbo or Hendo to pull an opponent out. Thirdly, we play with Sadio, Roberto and Mo really together – a maximum of 10-15 metres apart – in the centre to give us a chance to pick the free space with one of them and always be able to counter-press. This would create gaps in their backline which the other two forwards should try to use, with Trent and Robbo always ready for the overlap.

After the meeting, the staff got together to watch Dortmund beat Hoffenheim 3-2 in the Bundesliga. Haaland was the match-winner. Again. He has so much energy.

On Saturday morning at breakfast Barry Hunter joined us – a great person and a top, top scout. We spoke about Kaide Gordon and about Bobby Clark, who was to join our Academy from Newcastle. Both are signings for the future but with immediate impact. It was great to see him, as we don't see him much because of his role. Vitor started speaking about Lee

Clark, Bobby's father. I said to Jürgen, "This guy has 32 hours in a day..." 'Vitorpedia' we call him.

Manchester City-Arsenal was the early kick-off and I got treatment on my shoulder from Chris Morgan as I watched. He'd helped me so much since pre-season; I couldn't deal with another year of the pain I'd had last year. Chris used to be at Arsenal before coming back to us and I told him I hoped Mikel Arteta does well. Chris is a top physio and a top guy and a really important part of our team.

Arteta had asked me to be his assistant-manager when he was preparing for his new step into management. We were together years earlier on the Pro Licence course. His request came out of nothing. Imagine the assistant of Pep and the assistant of Jürgen together at Arsenal. What a crazy thought. Mikel had said he felt "There was just a difference playing Liverpool before and after you came in." This was the biggest compliment I ever got from somebody, I think, but I politely said no to him. A few months later we won the title for the first time in 30 years.

Just before that game started, a commercial featuring Trent came on the TV for Under Armour. The boys made a lot of jokes. "We never saw you running that quick and with your arms like that!"

Jürgen then held his final meeting and told the boys that all we do and all we did is made for games like this. The recipe for this game: bravery. There will be many little fights, like a challenge, like a throw-in press, and these we need to celebrate. The most important sign for a good game is when our counter-pressing is working. We have to be there, this will create a monster struggle. There were two moments in this game, we were pressing or we were preparing a pressing situation. Pressing doesn't work all the time, but imagine if we didn't press them. We need this common idea. "You hear that I'm speaking really quick, but only because we have to play quick," the boss says.

The game – final no3 – ultimately ended 1-1 against the European champions, with a small taste of defeat for us. They didn't have an answer to our pressing in the first half but found one in the second half by defending deep. They were down to ten men after the sending off of Reece James – but you play the moment, and they did. Fair play to them for that. This happens after winning the Champions League, a lot of moments fall your way.

Mo equalised with a penalty after Chelsea had scored – against the run of play, I felt – through Kai Havertz's header, but we couldn't get the second goal in the second half, even with the extra man, because they defended so well and so deep. Ultimately I blamed this one on myself, to be honest. We should have had a better answer, a braver approach in the last 15-20 minutes of the game. Sometimes our full-backs can tire towards the end of the game because of our style and play in the position outside where we need to outplay more to create dangerous crosses. In these positions we need to have more attacking solutions during the last 20 minutes, with different types of speed-ups. It's too much of a task against a deep-defending team after 60 or 70 minutes going up and down constantly.

In the summer I'd prepared a set-up based on going 3-diamond-3 with two new, fresh players on the outside. For example, Ox and Curtis come on to play on the outside; Fabinho as a false centre-half playing in front of Trent, Virgil and Robbo. The problem was this time we played against Lukaku and we had already made a sub with Jota for Roberto in the first half due to a hamstring injury. Still, it would have been possible if we would have practised it beforehand. Maybe it would have been the same outcome in the end, but it wouldn't go through my mind for the next week with me thinking, 'What if?'

But we were superior – and the most important thing is that our players and their players felt that. For that, it feels like a win. The Premier League is the Premier League; it's a marathon where consistency is the winning word. And... our defensive throw-ins were outstanding, we won all of them.

As we made our way home I organised with Vitor that we'd need the second team to be prepared to play like Leeds in training. He tells me he will look after it – the problems we had away at Leeds last season should be solved early in the coming week.

I couldn't wait to get started but it was now the international break, so I needed to wait. I promised myself that hitting the wall in the last 20 minutes like we did a bit against Chelsea would not happen again. The most important thing in football is to be one step in front, the rest to follow you and not the other way around. We did exactly this in the first half, which is the positive we can take.

‘WE ARE THE PASSENGERS WHO REPRESENT THE CULTURE OF THIS BEAUTIFUL CLUB, ITS PAST AND ITS GLORY’

WEEK 5

MAKE FATE YOUR BEST FRIEND

THE WEEK BEGAN WITH TRANSFER DEADLINE DAY and a whole host of clubs searching for solutions. The pressure was on already, England at its best. In our meeting in February with the ownership, we again explained the importance of signing players early so they could join our pre-season, with all the advantages and benefits of that.

Ibou was the perfect example of knowing what you want and how you want it. That's doing business. It's obviously less spectacular but when you want team play and to create team spirit, this is important. With this you create confidence and trust. These are the real money-makers and this only happens with time. That's why we coach so much with praise; the goal is to change individual confidence into team confidence. Jorge Valdano [former Argentina international and Real Madrid coach] said it well: "The ball only smiles when the player smiles." And the player only smiles when he knows he can make mistakes.

Jürgen forwarded me a news page claiming Michael Edwards will not continue at LFC after the end of the season. It's always sad when people leave who had an influence on our trophies, but life moves on. "The club will always be here, even when we are gone," was a favourite saying of our former kit man, Graham Carter. We are the passengers who represent the culture of this beautiful club. We represent its past and its glory. Mike Gordon had anticipated this move with the promotion of the talented Julian Ward to assistant sporting director almost a year ago, so hopefully the process continues and maybe even improves. You need strong leaders who know what they want and at the same time have great sympathy and great people skills. Julian is all of this and more. We're very fortunate to be able to navigate the departure of Michael with someone as talented as Jools, but what a job Michael had done for us. Unbelievable.

In terms of our deadline day it was Julian who explained to us there was nothing concrete on the table for Nat, so we made a last-minute turnaround with Rhys going to Swansea on loan and Phillips staying. We always said one of them had to stay to avoid having a situation like last year. Nat is an intelligent and very professional guy, so it was great we could keep helping him on his pathway. And one thing was for sure: we'd need him this season.

Hendo also signed his new deal on deadline day. Our 'mini-manager', as his dad explained so well in the video The Journey Continues. The definition for Henderson in the dictionary would be 'determination'. He has the capacity to lead a team, to drive a team to heights no-one would expect. A sergeant, our sergeant. These are the difference-makers. I remember a meeting with him away at Barcelona after our lunch on matchday; he was so disappointed about not starting. I spoke for an hour with him about our ideas, the coming weeks, his importance leading the team out at Anfield because the team needed his presence as a captain. A character like this as well as all the soldiers.

The rest is history. He led us out at Anfield with a level of energy you just couldn't predict. It's as Jürgen once said; it's a dream for us that fans recognise us, our way, and that these fans feel and live our identity. When we reach these levels at Anfield everything is possible, like that night. Hendo was everywhere in this game, always in the right moments. Barça wanted to dictate the tempo of the game and when they do, you play against the best in the world. Our idea was that they couldn't control the tempo and Hendo was crucial in this – that's how we stopped the pathway to Suarez and Messi.

We let them do the things they didn't like to do, but always within our idea that we defend to create chances. Eleven players were chasing, not allowing one of them to dictate the tempo, not even Ter Stegen because when they came under pressure they wanted to use him to do exactly that. Every long ball they played was a small victory for us, because they are not as effective at this part. We told them: don't play one-v-one against Lionel Messi but when he starts dribbling we defend against him with all the players who are close.

The tactical discipline of our three midfielders, led by Hendo, was outstanding. We were a red block moving forward and backwards. That season each single player had important, decisive moments, and that says a lot about the mentality of the team. Just take this Barça game: Divock chasing Ter Stegen with each opportunity; Milner filling in for Robbo in the second half; the amount of times Trent or Robbo in the first half pushed up into attacking zones. I said before, I love to see full-backs in the box. Robbo and Trent became so important on the outsides and arriving in scoring positions; even their cross-field passes to each other at the right time are so unpredictable. But when you play against Barça you can't avoid everything, so Ali had a few incredible moments, too. He has this talent to surprise you with one big save.

That's enough about Barça and the past, but sometimes it's good to look back to understand better what made the difference. Exceptional success requires an exceptional environment. Let's go again.

We noticed there was a lot of chatter about our perceived 'lack of business' in the transfer window. But we like how we do things, we like to create a different path towards success. We are figuratively coming from a hard-working family and we believe that with hard work we can prove the doubters wrong again. We must believe in this. Work harder than everyone else – letting our captains' group believe this is key. It isn't easy, but with Hendo, Milner, Virgil, Ali, Robbo and Trent helping to steer the wheel it becomes possible. There is always a way for the ones who really want it. We need to give them this responsibility, give them complete trust in leading the team. And then, when our team sees a possibility, fasten your seatbelts. But it all starts with everyone working hard, erasing all egos. Whatever you have achieved before, as always in life, without doing the hard work you'll get nowhere near again. For example, these boys have the ability to make a simple rondo competitive, and all the successful teams I've coached have had this in common.

Competitiveness and everyone committed to the team. A team full of strong characters with a great ambition for improvement – with this you make fate your best friend. What I've learned competing in the Premier League is the password for all games is 'Be yourself'. And reach 'consistency'. Three games, seven points, six scored with great variation, one set-piece goal against. It was a good enough, consistent start.

Jürgen called me the day after the transfer window shut as I was driving to Amsterdam. We were on our way back to England after spending a few days with my family in Holland. We have time off during international periods, the boys train with individual running schedules from their home or holiday destination. The running schedule is like the placebo effect, to please their minds – they 'stay' fit. As a manager you have so many decisions to make each day. Some have such a big impact that nobody realises and this is one of them. It helps players and staff stay full of energy in the last months of the season, the decisive months. As I've said before, you don't prepare for finals the week leading up to them, you prepare for them each single day in the 51 weeks leading up to them.

When getting closer to Amsterdam Schiphol airport, I texted Mark Leyland from the car, asking him to animate our defensive throw-ins and our midfield and high press. We were incredible in the first half against Chelsea. Incredible. Also, I asked him to send clear instructions to our second-team coaching staff; my idea is for them to play against us the following Tuesday afternoon with the Leeds United style, man v man over the whole pitch. I couldn't wait to meet Marcelo Bielsa again. I had this picture of him, me and Jürgen taking the knee at Anfield. It was an important picture for me because I respect him so much. I have this same idea that the team transforms the individual and not the other way around. This drive to drill team play.

In the meantime I was just praying all our players came back healthy from international duty. That would definitely be a small victory with them having three games in such a short period.

WEEK 6

WHAT DO WE REALLY WANT?

AFTER A WEEK 'OFF', FINALLY WE WERE ALL BACK AT AXA to begin working towards Leeds United. Jürgen and I sat together straightaway in his office and we went through the week. I told him that I'd organised to bring 12 young players up for the coming days, firstly to keep an overview on our main talents;

second, to stimulate the core players of the second team with our main principles; and lastly, these young boys give everything – it's where they want to be, so with this we have high-quality in training considering the number of enthusiastic players.

I also explained to him my idea for when reaching the last 20 minutes and needing to score, based on Chelsea and pre-season, before we then discussed how to prepare the team in the best way possible for a proper fight at Elland Road. We knew it would be a hostile environment with end-to-end football. Wow, I like the hostile-environment ones the most… it could be that this stems from my history at Porto. When we win, it feels like us stealing three points against the whole world in that moment.

Before a game I always search for more detail about the opposition coach, trying to understand his beliefs and relationship with the club better. At 5.30am in the morning, my youngest son Benjamin had woken me up and was watching Aquaman next to me when I found: 'Leeds supporters never damage the team'. Immediately I thought: this always comes with coaches who are obsessive with attack. Marcelo Bielsa's idea is teaching defence is easier than attack. Their defensive idea is to run all the time. To run is a decision for the will, he explains, but you need an indispensable amount of talent. He tells his team that his football is about four things: movement, rotation, concentration and improvisation. With this method, he believes he has more chance to win. You never win playing badly, you never win if you don't attack. And with this he captured the process of a manager in the world of football: 'We have to win'. He couldn't be more right. I like how he integrated into the Leeds culture. "Any coach would like to work at this club, given how it has been designed." That's how you want to look at the club you work for. This coach changed the fundamental way we see football, the way we understand training. That's why so many coaches in world football have this huge respect for him.

During the international break I'd gone back to my Porto time to find some specific tactical rondos to prepare for this Leeds game. 'A true test of a man's character is what he does when nobody is watching' is a quote I learned a long time ago. I said to Jürgen I never thought these exercises would come in handy again, but they were just perfect for this week. When in life an opportunity comes around the corner, it's too late to start preparing because as coaches you have to act and decide before you are right.

Last year we didn't create enough chances playing at Elland Road and what we created was with long balls in behind. This should be an option but not our only solution. We needed to improve and this started with how well we would bring the ball out from the back. For this we needed to be clear and work with our centre-halves as they would be crucial in bringing the ball out as the free player against a man-marking team. When we do this well, they lose organisation and that's what will make us attack the game – they needed to lose organisation. The second important aspect, after analysis, is we needed more success in our first phase of pressing because we didn't have this last time we played them. The positioning of their full-backs and wingers created this. It cost us a lot of unnecessary energy. So, we'd decided this training week would mainly be designed around these two topics. We would create these problems for them and encourage our team to solve it. What matters always is the process. Thiago, Fabinho and Harvey had to work out the answers.

I said to Jürgen that if we continued and evolved our 'new' way like we pressed against Chelsea then we'd become the best pressing team in Europe again. Our team could do this because they'd mastered all the skills and knowledge of preparing pressing situations. We believed in this, we believed in our group of players. That's most important – telling them they had the ability to change. There is no progress without change, but you can only do new things if you did the old things very well, in my opinion. This should be our target: stay the team no-one wants to play against. Letting our players believe this change was our most important task. As Jürgen always said, we could beat the best teams in world football, we didn't necessarily need to become the best team ourselves. This created the desire to press and this would be decisive if we wanted to achieve and to surprise the opposition again – not only with the intensity of our press but also with our new dynamics, competing for possession.

Keeping this self-belief for the team didn't ensure success but 'self-disbelief' would only work against you, so we needed immediate success. But that's why training exists: to create clarity and repetition to gain confidence, to gain anticipation. You can't compare the player with confidence to the same player without. Isn't this the target for each coach in each sport in each age? Create confidence with your speeches, your sessions and your team protection. That's why I'm so strong on training with everything they have – like that, you never lose in my opinion, you are a champion no matter what. This is the mindset needed. That's why I spend so much time preparing the sessions and the moment the session finishes, I'm thinking about the next session until it starts. I mean thinking-thinking.

For me, it's not about being the smartest, it's about staying with problems for as long as needed. The sessions had to inspire the boys to give absolutely everything. They needed to be in the session with the whole of their bodies, brains, lungs, legs and hearts. And when none of our players or staff cared who got the credit, it's amazing how much I believed we could reach in this intense season. We try to be the leaders who give credit and accept the blame. Like this, we believe we can take pressure away from the people around us. This is, in my opinion, the characteristic of a true leader. This is Jürgen. We try to enjoy this journey of winning and losing but with a continuous focus on our process. Seeing Leeds as the next final. We never give blame to the boys or accept credit.

The first exercise we did with our midfielders this week was a three-v-two rondo where players had to play one touch or were obliged to outplay the one-v-one before passing the ball. It created a great dynamic of hiding the ball and surviving in each difficult situation, promoting connection and interaction between them, risk and offensive aggression to outplay one-v-one situations, rhythm changes, taking players on attitude. These types of rondos we played a lot at Porto to create offensive aggression, a 'create to score' mentality, individual development. It's brilliant to use the rondo in a more attacking way. The limit of creating these types of exercises lies in your own creativity. Thiago, Harvey and Fab outplaying and combining together non-stop, this would be key against Bielsa. Directly afterwards, we gave the three players two balls to keep in possession between them, meaning that there were many one-v-one situations to be won and they had to think quickly. The centre-halves were playing a four-v-three rondo where they had to create a free defender to step calmly into the free space to commit. Then we combined all these rondos together in a ball-possession game.

What I've learned over these last 20 years of coaching is to plant the seeds early and, after that, each exercise becomes like water. Like this, players start anticipating much better situations and each other.

Ox walked in one morning looking so sharp. He didn't look tired at all. Strange... You had to see me after three weeks when Romijn was born, I looked like a coaching zombie. "It's great," he said, "he sleeps so well." Ox was scary in his training. We trained him again as the false 9. I still believed this position could be the trampoline for him to fly again. Milan could be perfect, I thought, as Bobby wasn't available and we'd play every three days. Ox needed freedom, he was good when touching the ball a lot, being involved in positions and space to attack and shoot. This was his best attribute.

I spoke with the young boys before our session and used a quote of [American basketball coach] John Wooden to make sure it was clear what we wanted. "There are many top, top athletes with tremendous God-given talent, but they don't focus on the development of those gifts. Who are these? You have never heard of them – and you never will. It's true in sports and it's true everywhere in life. Hard work is the difference – very hard work." I think it was clear what they could expect from us in those coming days.

After the late afternoon session I walked out of AXA and spotted Harvey's dad in the car waiting for him. He explained to me how hard Harvey had worked during the off-season. We started talking about when we first met Harvey. Jürgen said back then, "You are a player for the middle." Jürgen came out and joined us standing at the car. His dad said they were so grateful for our guidance and trust. Jürgen laughed and said that's likewise. "It's a win-win situation," he added. Harvey went on loan as a boy and came back as a man. It was a great example of how a process can work when a whole structure supports and believes in a talent.

The session ended with a tournament. "Only Ali is able to keep a clean sheet in a five-v-five tournament!" John Achterberg said after the training. "It's crazy," added Mateusz [Musialowski], "he is just everywhere in the goal!" "A top goalkeeper and a top striker win you championships is an English saying," declared Jack. Meanwhile, "Kaide is from a different grape," said Vitor. Our Portuguese philosopher, wine is always in their minds as well...

On Tuesday I continued my research into Bielsa. You have a lot of coaches who set up their teams with a structure and mentality to 'play not to lose', but he is definitely not one of them. There is a saying that you have two different types of coaches: not the 'good' and 'bad' one; no, it's the one with confidence and conviction and the one without. Now everyone thinks it's easy to set up your team attacking-wise, and maybe on Football Manager it is. But when 50,000 people are in the stadium, tens of millions at home, journalists with their laptops at their fingertips, all of these are watching every move you make closely, it's really about if you have real confidence and conviction. That's why I love the quotes from Jose Mourinho after our game away at Barça: "Liverpool were brave in their approach, I don't think in the last 20 years many teams in the Camp Nou beat Barça in terms of possession. Liverpool deserves much more than the 3-0 defeat, much more." My respect is huge for each coach, on each level, with the attitude to attack the game. Because I know how it feels to walk out of the tunnel and the floodlights are shining, the cameras follow you with each step and the noise is louder than a volcano erupting. In football you need to be very strong to deal with the outside. If there is one quality of Jürgen's that makes him different from all the others, it's this one.

You could feel that we were excited for this moment of the season. Fabinho said it well: "The mentality of the group is really good, everyone is ready for this, everyone is in good shape. So we're very excited for this moment to play three times a week." I said to the boys before training on Tuesday: "What if? What if it can turn out even better than we can imagine right now? That's how we should approach it, not as a squad but as a team."

In the afternoon James texted me asking if club media could film the padel match between me and Jürgen and Adrian and Thiago. I answer with, "For me you can live-stream it, but Jürgen always says he feels like he looks like he's been hit by a truck after 30 minutes so I'm not sure if he wants to do it..!" What a padel match it was, by the way. We lost but the rallies were incredible and Jürgen was very good. Spanish technique against German and Dutch passion. Jürgen said, "This is the first time I've seen Pep sweating!" We played well, got close, but it was not enough. Our identity was mediocrity on this occasion…

Then, as expected, on Wednesday – on our day off – FIFA and the Brazilian FA threw in a bomb by contacting the English media to say they would not allow our players to play against Leeds after they'd missed the internationals due to the COVID-19 quarantine restrictions. I wasn't afraid of sanctions because FIFA couldn't take points away – only the FA and Premier League could, and they supported our decision, so they have to keep their promise. What would happen if Chelsea didn't play Thiago, United didn't play Fred, City didn't play Jesus and Ederson – all of these on the Saturday? We had a big decision to make if we played Ali and Fab the following day.

On Thursday afternoon at AXA I stopped for a chat with

Danielle, Jürgen's PA. "Players with fight never lose a game, they just run out of time," I said to her, quoting John Wooden, as we discussed the team's success over the last few years. That's what happened with our team after losing the Champions League final. Any other team in world football would have a terrible next season, but we won the Champions League and lost just ONE Premier League game. Not just a league game – a Premier League game. Complete and utter domination. But we didn't look back because we weren't going in that direction. She was standing in the door of Jürgen's office and I wanted him to hear it… particularly because we lost against his team in the staff game earlier that day. "That's why you get paid so much money – if you can even get John Achterberg back to his levels when he was 25 in a staff game, you deserve each penny," I said to him. We had 70 per cent possession and 30 shots but it was clear after 45 minutes that John would become MOTM. Jürgen laughed and said, "I just told him the world wants to see the real John Achterberg… and if you don't do exactly that, you'll get the sack!" I said to Danielle that Jürgen's team played long-ball and he replied, "Yes, that's true, but with Bobby Firmino up top!" That's because the manager had played as a lone striker. "A loss is only a loss if you don't learn from it," Vitor commented. Andreas asked how many games he'd won so far. "I'm still learning," Vitor replied, quietly. "There's no education like adversity," I told him. You could see the environment improving between the staff members.

It was that afternoon that the Chelsea report from 'Throw-in Thomas [Gronnemark]' came in. "One of our best defending throw-in games in the four seasons I have been coaching," he said. That's what I'm talking about! Chelsea had 15 throw-ins and only kept the ball four times. We were back in business.

For Leeds' throw-ins, it would be important to be immediately in our shape, everyone facing the ball, meaning everyone is ready to press. When we have to decide, we always first close the centre. Wherever they moved or rotated they should run into one of our players because we'd closed the spaces and not opened them up. Make the pitch small with the opposite winger or full-back being in between ready to intercept their big or mini switch.

On Thursday afternoon I received a text. It was Jürgen, asking me to come into his office. That's unusual, I thought. This could mean one of two things...

I walked in and took a seat. "Pep," he began, with me still none the wiser. "What you're doing is absolutely incredible and I want to give you a reward from myself." Wait. What? "It will arrive shortly, so don't be surprised." Wow. I stood up and gave him a big hug. What a character. It was a private gift between us, but it meant so much to me. Passion is momentary but our relationship is enduring. I finish by saying, "That's the real reason you're the man you are – your character."

On Friday I said to Jürgen after training that we were watching something really special growing in Harvey Elliott. "He makes so many good decisions for such a young player," he says back to me, "It's crazy. He never, ever makes foolish runs or decisions. He's already a real, real football player." Vitor said to Conall, "If you ever write a book, make sure you write that you were witness to the development of an unbelievable player." Mo and Harvey had been connecting well. Mo built his reputation as a goal-machine, but most impressive is his creative development over the years, in my opinion.

The day before Leeds, I took Mo out of the gym just before our video analysis meeting and explained to him with pen and paper the importance of pressing Leeds to the sideline instead of closing the outside pass. Their whole idea was to play around our press with their full-backs deep. The more success we had in the first phase of pressing against them, the more energy we would have to attack. He liked it and indeed it was simpler for him like this.

That night, at the hotel, we sat together as we always do. We watched Sporting v Porto, a real classic in Portugal, and it was an emotional encounter, especially now Sporting were champions. In 45 minutes there were more yellow cards than actual minutes played, or at least it felt like that. I'd forgotten about these games. Jürgen said he didn't understand why society accepted this kind of 'winning at all costs' mentality. We then watched Emma Raducanu win the US Open. She was so impressive, 18 years old and so much power and elegance at the same time. Virginia Wade and Tim Henman were in the stands; it was a special moment for the whole of England.

I asked for a beer late at night and got a reaction from all the others as if a Tibetan monk had asked for one. "Pep is throwing his hair loose!" Jürgen joked. The problem is, for the last few days it just hadn't got out of my head that when Bernardo played for City they would not lose many games this season. He'd scored the winner at Leicester earlier.

Game day started with a staff member messaging me about how well Ben Woodburn was playing in the Edinburgh derby. That's my boy. Meanwhile, in our WhatsApp group called 'We Are Liverpool', Roberto texted just before we went into our last meeting: "Good luck lads! Big three points today. Vamos! May the Lord bless and protect you all." Maybe he felt something was coming...

Jürgen delivered his final message before the match: "This is the first game after the transfer market closed, the first after the international break, so it's time to speak about it. Everyone is speaking about our transfer business, but I couldn't care less about what other teams did. We signed Ibou – he will help us a lot – and we got Harvey back. For the outside world, we will finish fourth because of the business of the other teams, but if football was that easy, I would not like it. It's not like basketball, bringing the five best players together and you win. When we were winning so much, there were two reasons for it: first, it was the consistency we played with; and second, it was our mindset and that is what we can create again. A mindset to challenge, a mindset to become the team no-one wants to play against. The other teams don't have this yet. We have a world-class squad, now it's about turning potential into quality.

"How? We need to answer this question: what do we really want? If we want everything, we need to give everything. Ninety-five per cent or 100 per cent wanting something is completely different. What would be the worst thing? If after this season we don't reach our targets, but we look back and think it would have been possible if we wanted it more. My age can tell you – I will avoid this [telling you how old I am] – because I've been through this. We are completely overlooked by the public. Look around you, guys – do you want anyone else sitting in this room? One other player? Exactly. The best and most consistent team will win. That can be us.

"What do we want to show after last year, when we struggled? We won the Champions League because we wanted to show we could do it after losing the final. We won the Premier League because we wanted to show we could do it after missing out by one point. What do we want to show after last year? We are never satisfied! We don't want to tell old stories – we want to create new stories. I want to read stories about you guys. All big stories needed a start. We had one, a good one. Seven points in the first three games. Don't look back at what we could have. We are Liverpool, a great team, and we will show the world this."

Jürgen impresses every single time, it creates a commitment towards our project. If any player needed a little bit more motivation to reach the 100 per cent it would be through this speech.

'Final no4' ended 3-0 to us against an aggressive, man-marking Leeds but was soured with the bad taste of losing Harvey to injury. Bielsa said afterwards, "We were overcome in nearly all aspects in the game. We did not impose ourselves and the result was fair. The way they planned to play, it allowed their forwards to shine." It was the best game that we've played against Leeds. The way that we were able to use and create the free player in the centre and the way that we used the second-line players to attack gave us the advantage we needed. With that, we were much more consistent in defending as well. They needed to run more to defend more and then we used that to be able to be fresher to press higher and really control the side of the ball.

We have to mention Joel's role in the first goal. He stepped in with the ball, going on a real adventure forward. We call this the classic Joel dribble – and it was a new weapon for us. Having this ability to break lines the way he does, especially against man-marking sides. In this moment, he found Mo and then Trent and then a trademark finish from Mo.

However, we lost Harvey through a hard and unfair tackle – from paradise to hell in an hour. When it happened, Naby was standing in tears on the sideline after seeing his ankle, and Jürgen was on the pitch. I had words with Bielsa, he had both arms on my shoulders saying, "No proposito" [not on purpose]. I shouted back in half English-Portuguese, "But it's a badly-executed tackle from behind, it doesn't matter if it's 'proposito' or not." We repeated these sentences a few times. Mo was so upset after the game, throwing his socks in the changing room. He had just scored his 100th Premier League goal, but all our thoughts were with our boy.

I have to highlight the role of our medical staff, Jim Moxon and Chris Morgan, who reacted so quickly under so much pressure to help Harvey. In moments like this, the medical team show what a real difference they make for the individual. It's crucial.

On the drive back to the AXA Training Centre, Gary McAllister called to say how fantastic he thought we'd played. He became a good friend – we worked so well together and he is someone I feel I can count on. A fantastic person with such a huge football brain and this was a nice touch. But already, my mind was on AC Milan...

‘A PERFECT ORGANISATION DOESN’T EXIST, BUT THE BEST POSSIBLE ORGANISATION DOES’

WEEK 7

FREEDOM INSIDE THE SYSTEM

THE WEEK BEGAN WITH THE COACHING TEAM SITTING together in the office to go through our options for the games and it was clear it was time for changes. We needed to attack Milan and we had only two sessions and some video to prepare ourselves to do it. "Italians can't win the game against you, but you can lose the game against the Italians," Cruyff once famously said about their style of football. We'd need to be spot on in our analysis because they finished second in Italy for a reason, with a young team full of ideas.

I also went over some of the post-match reaction and interviews after Leeds and something caught my eye. Football is life as well. You work with powerful personalities, but we all have our good and bad moments and some of us have to play in dark times. Fabinho's comments after the Leeds game showed this so well: "I just wanted to score for my mother and for my father as well. After I scored I wanted to look up and dedicate this goal to the sky to God. I want to thank God because when Alisson scored [last season] he said it was a gift from God and I believe the same as well." Football is life.

The previous night after getting home from Leeds, I'd had a couple of interesting texts. Virgil had messaged me directly: "I want and can play Milan as well, playing so long against 10 men didn't exhaust me." I replied, "You will play against Milan, for sure." So on Monday morning he came to me to ask again and I said, "Yes, Virgil, you will play against Milan," to which he smiled. Then, "Away at the San Siro in December." I don't think he found it funny.

My co-author, James, had also messaged me about Mo's 100th goal in the Premier League, but how because of what had happened with Harvey we hadn't done something to celebrate the achievement with him, so when we regrouped Jürgen and I decided to use a shirt and print the number 100 on it, get the whole team to sign it, and then we gave it as a present before training. Mo's smile when we handed it over was just brilliant. I asked Trent what the message was that he wrote on the shirt. "'Congrats'... but I should have written, 'You're welcome'."

You could see that everyone had a focus, though. The Champions League was starting again and there was a buzz around AXA for it. As a Dutch guy, I speak with huge responsibility about Milan. When you speak about Milan as a Dutch guy, you speak about Gullit, Van Basten and Rijkaard, the three who went beyond the limits of logic. You speak about 'Total Football' and that's in Italy. Indirectly, you speak about a coach who changed Italian football. When we'd arrived in Madrid in February 2020 for our away game against Atletico Madrid, Jürgen showed me his phone as we were getting off the plane. "Look, Pep, look who we got compliments from... Arrigo!" The boss had a big smile on his face. Sacchi wanted Jürgen to go to Italy to talk to him about football for a newspaper article. "I told him, Arrigo, tell me where, anywhere in the world, and I'll make sure I'm there." That shows how much he respects him.

This Liverpool team has been inspired by the Milan of Arrigo Sacchi. Jürgen said before that the foundations of his philosophy were based on the principles of the Milan coach. There are so many elements that touched us both. First, the emphasis on the offside trap. Second, the zonal defending. And third, how he kept his teams tight with and without the ball. But above all, he is an example with his principles of training. The way he created focus was unbelievable: clarity – repetition – correction. That's what appeals to me most. I still watch his training video over and over, probably about 300 times, because that's how he created organisation within his teams, with tactical discipline and the right distances between his players on the pitch, with work on the training ground. Those are the basic principles for creating a team as constant as we have.

A perfect organisation doesn't exist, but the best possible organisation does. That's why his vision is so authentic and still very powerful in 2021. I even watch his video sometimes when I'm on the treadmill on game day – it's just perfect to gain focus. Sacchi was a forerunner in collective defending and zonal pressing. Step-by-step, he developed a coordinated pressing style, together with organised attacking play, without losing sight of the individual qualities inside his team. That's not easy to do, but that applies to good coaching in general – it's not that simple. That's what I believe in: freedom inside the system. Him signing Rijkaard for his Milan team was on the same level of impact as when we brought Virgil, the big puzzle piece, and both ended up with the European Cup in their hands.

Sacchi gave the Italian style a new dimension with high pressing and attacking play, where entertainment was the guiding principle. That was exceptional – it's a Dutch basic. He is the father of zonal pressing, based on an outstanding defensive organisation. And by doing this he automatically gave a new generation of coaches stability. He is one of the managers who evolved football and brought the game to a new level. A large part of his successes came by drilling his teams and for that he will always be appreciated.

His vision has produced so many good coaches and I believe that is the biggest compliment you can get as a coach. That AC

Milan team had the same key to success as we have. Wherever we are on the pitch, we are always together, with and without the ball, which means the team has to be tight as a unit the whole time. A red block. Especially in possession we'd made big steps being together in the last few years, a better positional game. The basic idea was that this approach let us control spaces on the pitch very efficiently and counter-press the opponent in an unpredictable way. Sacchi showed how the distances between the players are important when controlling the spaces on the pitch without the ball, or being able to dictate the game with the ball. That is what characterised Liverpool in 2021 and we saw that against Leeds. Planting the seeds in pre-season was so important.

But that's enough about Sacchi or Van Basten. We were playing the Milan of 2021, with Giroud, Rebic and Ibrahimovic as the strikers. An early text from Jürgen came Tuesday morning asking if I was awake. He had the outcome of Harvey's assessment with the ankle specialist: no cartilage issue, which took the injury to three or four months out instead of nine. "We've lost an important player," I said. A badly-executed slide-tackle is dangerous while a good, technical slide-tackle is an attractive weapon to win a challenge. At 18 years old, the game didn't have any secrets for Harvey. We would miss him over the coming months and that said a lot. When you miss such a decisive quality in the game like Harvey, you can do two things: hide behind a rock, or everyone works a little bit more to compensate. We had to make sure that our midfielders against Milan would understand this. Jürgen spoke with Hendo before training to make sure he played in function and gave dynamics to the right-sided triangle.

I arrived at the AXA and did a video-analysis session on Milan with Vitor, Pete and Jürgen. We decided to have a more aggressive, higher press against them. Their centre-halves should have most of the ball, then we'd cut the connections and get 'our' ball back as quickly as possible. We needed to be intense and quick in what we do – and for this we needed fresh players. Out on the training pitch I made this intensity clear by shouting: "Each opportunity we get, we speed up the play with the simplest passes; play quick free-kicks; spot and play; first pass forward; counter-press immediately; quick throw-ins; quick restarts and play on each opportunity in the back of them!" We felt that with a single 9 like Divock we could keep the centre-halves together then create space for Mo, Hendo, Naby and Jota to use the big space between the full-back and centre-half. For us, this was the best way to respect our identity as well. Jürgen says we don't have positions offensively – we have flexible triangles, so it would be a crime not using the spaces they left with their man-marking.

After training I walked into the analyst office to see they had Young Boys v Manchester United on the TV. I say, laughing, "Here is where all the problems start! Normally you'd be watching training back and showing me two or three images, but we won a lot over the last few weeks and now you're watching Champions League football instead!" It was a joke but one to keep everyone on their toes; the next morning they had everything ready to show. The reason? Because they are top guys and an incredible asset to us.

We trained for the final time on matchday, repeating our more aggressive high press in the morning to set the tone. We took Divock to one side to show some of the defensive throw-in images from training the day before. His positioning should always be to be in advantage, controlling space and seeing the player in front of him. After this, Mo came to me and said he really liked our new way of pressing and that he felt more energetic when having the ball. I love that, it means we run more efficiently. Pete used the rest of the session to repeat our offensive and defensive set-pieces. We went for the second phase in our set-pieces offensively, loading the edge of the area with four players – a clear but out-of-the-box principle. When the ball comes out, we wanted to shoot or cross immediately again and create chaos in and around the box. Vitor took the subs for some finishing drills; I watched Ox and Curtis score so many from a distance.

I was watching, the sun was shining and it was the middle of September. These are the moments when I really feel life can't get any better.

You always try to avoid problems with your coaching by trying to be one step ahead.

At The Titanic we held the final meeting. The chairs in the room were very close to each other. When the last players sat down, Jürgen said this was pretty much how compact we needed to be against Milan. He went on to explain that the first reason we'd made changes was because we had the quality to do it, and secondly, to be able to chase them over the whole pitch. We could help the team tonight with our five subs. He told the boys his biggest worry last year was having to play in the UEFA Conference League… not because of that tournament but because it would've meant we were not playing Champions League and having nights like this, so finishing third [in the Premier League] was sensational, all things considered. Jürgen explained to the players that we could cause each team in world football problems with our counter-pressing, so let's make this the task for tonight. Put them under pressure like no other team did before. Do the quick things – it will inspire the crowd. "Jota,

Thiago, you've never played in a European night at Anfield? Fasten your seatbelts." It was a sentiment we were all feeling. I even caught myself singing, 'Walk on, walk on…' when lost in my own thoughts after the meeting. Jürgen started laughing, but I told him I'm not going to apologise for that. He said: "You shouldn't. That's the problem, when you go to another club as head coach you don't have this anthem."

When we arrived at Anfield, Lee Radcliffe took me into the Boot Room. "I've got the picture, Pep," he said. In there, I see a beautiful picture of the old Boot Room hanging on the wall. I get goosebumps and hug both Brendan and Lee. I'd told them a few weeks before that this room needs – and deserves – history. If you want to know where to go, you have to know where you came from.

Our first Champions League 'final' of the season ends 3-2 against a new, but strong, Milan. You know when you're playing against a good team when they don't need many chances to punish you. Equally you know when you are a strong team yourself if you can come back with so much fire and change a 1-2 around. This is the 'mentality monster' attitude you need from your team. We played against the second-placed team in Italy last year and, this year, a side with real merit to them, and when they come through they come through with a lot of quality. It's a great project they have with so many talented young players. Milan has the now and the future. But we attacked the game from the first minute with quick, precise passes and intense pressing. Virgil shouted constantly from the sidelines, "Wow, that's a team!" Our first goal, scored by Trent, was a superb example of mixing the dynamic between our outside triangle with Mo, Hendo and Trent. Trent ended up attacking through the centre – exactly how we'd trained that morning – and scored his goal. Although the discussion of the boys afterwards was, 'Trent's goal or an own goal?' just to wind him up a bit!

For me, the most impressive moment of the night was when Mo missed a penalty because Anfield let out its loudest roar afterwards. In these moments you know you are united. We were behind at half-time but we stayed calm, explained that we had to defend more compactly and organised to close the spaces for them between the lines. There was a moment deep in the second half where we had 73 per cent possession of the ball and seven shots to nil… it felt like we took these last ten minutes of the first half personally.

For the second goal, Fab popped up again higher on the pitch, again using the free space between the centre-half and full-back, followed by a lovely assist from Divock to set up Mo. The third goal was a classic example of our attacking set-piece idea with the focus on our second phase. Hendo was ready and scored directly from the edge of the box.

Twenty-three shots, 15 corners and almost 600 passes were good numbers against such a strong side in the first Champions League game of the season. We won almost each defensive throw-in, too. Divock was key, but you know what really won the game? Our squad, our team. We used all of them and showed that we need them all this year if we want to be successful. Sometimes the victory lies in something unviewable by the outside eye. That night, every player left Anfield with a big smile on his face. Mission accomplished. Driving home, I was reminded we've always had these sorts of games in our group at Anfield… Salzburg and PSG at Anfield were what the media would describe as 'rollercoaster' games, but this one felt different because we maintained control at all times except for a mad six minutes. In a crazy way I felt that might stand us in better stead than if we'd cruised it – which the performance deserved in truth. It's hard to plan a reaction to 'football trauma', which is what we went through in those closing six minutes of the first half. To have played like we did for 40 minutes and come in behind could easily have been a 'trauma', but at no point did it feel like it.

"I didn't see many games like it. Why? Because we mixed technique with intensity. When we have this mixture of technique and intensity we will be so hard to beat," was the message from Jürgen the day after the game when grouping together our team. There was a picture going around of the whole bench celebrating our first goal as if it was the winning goal in a Champions League final. Passion. Vitor got a text message from Paulo Fonseca's analyst saying: "Last year we didn't see ONE team doing to AC Milan what you guys did Wednesday night. Incredible. How are you guys attacking so well with their man-marking? How are your centre-halves so calm against Rebic, who is a pressing monster?" Vitor replied: "Milan are now three years with the same coach, that's not easy in Italy. They're a top team and a top project."

Away from the game I sensed the AXA Training Centre was developing an atmosphere like we had in our pre-season training camp and it was getting closer to the atmosphere we had at Melwood. There were chess boards wherever there was a spot in the lounges; we played staff football games; table tennis and foot-volley nets were set up in the sports hall. Of course, it's not about the boards or the nets or the games, it's about the better interaction and connection between staff and players which creates the harmony needed. The chess is competitive, though. And maybe to understand a little bit more about my character I bought Garry Kasparov's book because we'd started playing chess between the staff as well. I come from a chess family but if you want to win you have to study the best.

Before training on Friday, Andreas told us we had five players on the 'red list': Hendo (no real pre-season), Robbo (three international games), Joel (third game in a row), Fabinho (high outputs, especially v Leeds) and Trent (highest sprint output so far, big shift for him). We knew with experience that playing a consecutive game with only two recovery days in between had a high risk of injury. We fought for this not to happen, for the protection of the players and for the quality of the game, but obviously without success.

In the sessions we decided we would need to spend more time on our midfield press, closing the centre and pushing the red button. New coaches with real football-playing ideas always, at the start of this process, play a lot of predictable passes – so exactly for this reason we needed to press in an unpredictable manner. It created new challenges for our players but I felt we needed to challenge ourselves on the training ground – then we would challenge the whole Premier League. But more importantly we needed our team fresh and with the right mentality against a new Crystal Palace, so we didn't do too much. Also, five fresh players came into the team who would help give 'life' to the other five.

We knew Palace were a team that really wanted to play under Patrick Vieira and Osian Roberts, the assistant-manager who actually sent me a lovely text while I was in the analysis meeting. Coincidence? He is one who'd put great faith in me giving presentations and demonstrations for the Welsh FA since my time at Porto. I texted back that we would speak with each other after the game!

Palace was our third game in a short time-frame. Everyone's

body is different but the average time needed for the body to recover completely is 72 hours after a game. We had 65 hours after Milan and then only 42 once we were back at Kirkby. So, we decided to combine a tactical overview while accelerating the recovery process. No additional information or dynamics, just maintaining our ideas and correcting those who didn't move in a coordinated way against Milan. For example, Mo more front-footed, Jota closing the centre better when jumping out to press, and the others reacting better to this. We gave small doses of intense game moments with a lot of time in between – exactly like cleaning dirty pipes with short, sharp bursts of water.

Saturday morning, Vitor and I were sitting together in The Titanic enjoying a coffee. I asked him what was the one thing that could go wrong today and we were going through the scenarios when Jürgen called me. 'Shit!' I think, when the boss is calling this close to kick-off something isn't right. He told me Trent wasn't feeling well. The first thing in my mind was Joe, because of Zaha, but Jürgen and I went through each step of our game plan and decided we'd go with a more offensive approach in Milner.

Trent called me a few minutes later. "I'm not that bad, Pep," he said, with an ill-sounding voice. "When I get going I'll be fine." These are the situations no-one hears about, but this is why we think our group of players is so special. I told him the decision was made. The risk of injury is so much bigger when your body is fighting, especially after two consecutive, intense 90 minutes. I told him to rest and call Mona for the right food and vitamins. "The one thing that counts is that you get better for Norwich or even for Brentford. Don't worry now about today." I'm worrying, though, because there lies another challenge in front of us: from being perfectly-prepared to, all of a sudden, what is the information we'll need to give Milner as he always goes with full conviction? We sat with James outside The Titanic hotel, going through our game plan, and he absorbed the information and looked confident. We used the papers to make clear what we wanted before the team meeting.

Jürgen's message to the boys was that Trent was out and we'd sort this with experience. "Surprise them with energy! The ones who come in, be the energisers. Life is a constant challenge, our brain is a constant challenge. We need your legs, your heart, your lungs, your brain at top speed again. Increase the speed as many times as possible. The stands will be on fire – we give back to them with our football. Palace probably think because of our midweek game there will be problems, but not with us. You guys make the magic of our flexible triangles. You make them flexible and that's what we need to hurt them. We want to be consistent again this year. How? This starts with defending them on the highest level."

As we walked out of the meeting I heard Robbo joking to Hendo that Trent has 'Zaha-itis'! "I hope he didn't spread it to Milner," joked Jürgen. 'Final no5' ended in a 3-0 win, which started at 10am that morning. A James Milner call-up and the first time since December 2018 we'd played without Robbo and Trent in a league game – that says a lot. We saw and felt that Palace were better than last year, more competitive. It wasn't easy, but in life the only easy day is yesterday. Palace's idea was to try to play behind our full-backs with longer passes. We stayed compact and could control the movements of their strikers with a high defensive line. At half-time we gave an important message to stay flexible and counter-press with all we had to stop the counter.

Milner was incredible versus Zaha. It was a brilliant game

from him; right on the limit, but brilliant. Kostas provided two excellent crosses for the goals, there was Ibou and Virgil's first time together, and a clean sheet on his debut. Considering we changed the whole last line again, it was a good performance. Three set-piece goals, three times from the rebound. I loved it. Naby's left-foot volley… strike! Sadio scored his 100th goal and we prepared a shirt for him. One of our staff members actually got it at half-time, they had to open the shop and put '100' on the back. Jürgen handed it to Sadio after the game and all the boys were screaming at him, "Speech! Speech!" He said, "Thank you to all the players, thank you to all the staff, without you I'm nothing."

Mo looked so sharp once again. We'd brought Lena Aschenbrenner in this season to our medical department to give a new impulse in our treatment process. She was on top of his needs and you saw the benefits in how his body was moving. The 'new' way of pressing was also giving more energy for the offensive moments – you saw this in the quality of his dribbles. He had fire when he attacked. But in one week we lost two of our best midfielders, Thiago and Harvey. Thiago took the game by the hand against Palace but had to come off with a calf injury in the second half. We were hoping it would not be a serious one.

After we left Anfield, the focus immediately went to Norwich and the League Cup. If you want to be an LFC legend, I believe you need the domestic cups as well. We wanted to attack this competition with the players we had available. How could we create a team and set up to be 'collective' at such short notice with our available players? Mark Leyland had stayed home to watch Norwich instead of attending the Palace game so our analysis would be ready on the Sunday. We couldn't lose a day.

WEEK 8

IS THIS THE BEST WE'VE GOT?

THE MESSAGE FROM JÜRGEN AFTER THE PALACE game was that everyone else had issues over the weekend but we were convincing. It's not easy after a midweek Champions League game with such a short turnaround, but we had the attitude and the belief to do it. That's always the most important aspect in team sport. We weren't lucky with being drawn against Norwich in the Carabao Cup third round, a Premier League team away from home, but with the right changes and freshness we'd be able to compete.

Jürgen actually told the lads the next first 11 after the Palace game. We'd never done that before but decided to do so in our meeting, with the thinking that the starters would have the best possibility to prepare themselves to become a team right from the start of the week.

During the Monday session I told the boys each structure to high press is only as good as the attitude the first pressers put in. Ox and Taki needed to have a perfect chasing attitude. We focused on our tactical dynamics and tactical overviews offensively. We'd created so many set-pieces with shots from the edge of the box already in the season, we used them well and made them decisive. If you don't shoot, you don't get corners. This is us: one idea influences the other, fluidity between all these ideas. When you want to win championships, you need to be decisive with your set-pieces – they should influence results. We'd won the most corners in the Premier League by this point and that was the first step and a logical consequence for a team shooting a lot from the edge of the area.

I took the press conference duties on the Monday afternoon and before it started, I was asked about Mo Salah's contract situation. I said that at Liverpool Football Club we only announce contracts, we don't speak about them. Mo was one of the faces of this team, he represented our integrity as a club, our humility. For me in life and in football, it's much more important who you are as a person than how good you are as a football player. He proved this every single day. I'd thought a lot in the previous few days about what really defines quality in a cup-winning team; what were – and are – the main ingredients from the best teams of the past. I had to think it over and over because I thought I'd get questioned in the press conference about our transfer policy. So I came up with three crucial aspects of consistent teams, just to show that we had all we needed to attack this league. First, the attitude: just the attitude of all the players, the attitude to see the next game as a final, everybody prepares himself with all he has, basically the very hard work. Second, the potential to improve, the talent, the doers. Third, the team spirit, to sacrifice personal statistics or gain for the glory of the team.

As John Wooden says, "A player who makes a team great is more valuable than a great player." Those three aspects defined quality for me and, with time, consistency. I couldn't speak about the other teams but these three we definitely had and didn't need more of in any aspect. The press conference went smoothly with nice questions to answer. If you're wondering why I took it, well, we all have to stay fresh – not just the players. When I can support Jürgen by taking media duties away, it's an honour for me to speak for the club, the direct staff and our team. Also, we felt it was an opportunity to gain more responsibility with the press. I love representing this club with the energy it deserves and I'm really true to my beliefs in these moments.

We travelled down to Norwich on the Tuesday and Jürgen's message was to make clear that no-one should think the 'winners' were the ones who could stay at home. Virgil and Fabinho needed a break, he said, "I'm telling you this because it's important to stop the devil in your mind from talking." He told the boys not to make excuses, these moments were not allowed and not necessary in the game. "Because we need to create a mood, a mood to be ready to face – and solve – problems. The moments when it doesn't work, we can't lose confidence. To win football games in the first place you need to defend as a unit. That's all about attitude. Nobody knows the result and I really don't care. I just want us to be brave." The boss told Kaide to be cheeky and that Curtis, playing in the 6, had to hold his position and protect the centre-halves.

Our first League Cup 'final' of the season ended 3-0 at Norwich again, with full Liverpool debuts for Conor Bradley and Kaide Gordon, as well as Tyler Morton who came on at half-time for Naby. I'd said in the 'presser', young players never ever let you down – and not only did they not let us down, they impressed with a complete package of offensive, pressing football. We need to create a new generation of Liverpool players who can continue our project. In five years' time Mo would be 34 and Kaide 21, Fabinho 32 and Tyler 23. Curtis Jones played his 50th game for the club already. The future looked bright. I was so, so proud of them and how they performed. Kaide is just pure 'street'. A killer. And I honestly can say, if you don't like Tyler Morton, you don't like football. He is the kind of player who can make a team great because the hardest thing in football is playing simple. After the game I grabbed him in the tunnel while he was with Robbo to tell him I thought he'd played unbelievable. "I never got a welcome like that," Robbo joked.

It was great we got the clean sheet, too, especially because of Caoimhin Kelleher saving the penalty in a decisive moment just before half-time. It was crucial and a turning point in the game. It was also a second clean sheet for Ibou – as I said, he was so quick and strong. It's always a good sign when you are ruthless with the chances you have. Man of the match was the efficient Taki with two shots and two goals. I'd said in the presser of Minamino: "He can only become better. That's what we like, that's why we brought him in at that time – because we saw the potential, not the end product." This result meant we'd scored 12 goals in the previous four games. That's impressive.

As we flew back, I was making notes for this book. I looked out of the window on my left and noticed the sky was bright. I looked right and Jürgen was listening to music. Vitor, behind me, was sleeping. These are the most satisfying moments in life; it's probably the one moment you are not thinking about the next game.

Back at Kirkby on the Wednesday there was a winning lottery ticket for a lot of the young boys as they got to train with Virgil, Joel, Mo, Sadio, Fabinho, Bobby and Trent. They would create the right focus for the seniors as we had three days to prepare them for Brentford, a super high-intensity, pressing team. We gave the players an introduction to the quick decision-making needed. Each session should turn out as a masterpiece. To reach this, we brought up 12 young talents so there was no time to slow down. Barry Lewtas, the Under-23s manager, stood with us during the warm-up. For me this is how open a first-team staff should look. We discussed the progress after last night – we are creating 'culture'. First Trent and Ben Woodburn, Ovie Ejaria, Rhian Brewster, Curtis, then Ki-Jana, Neco, Harvey, Nat Phillips and Rhys. Now Conor, Kaide, Tyler and Owen Beck.

Joe Gomez told us he'd felt emotional wearing the captain's armband against Norwich and I told him it looked good on him and that he deserved it so much. What a first half he played. He is one of the world's best centre-backs because he's so good at constructing the game.

We'd rested Joel again meaning he'd had a week-and-a-half without competition. Joel is a nightmare for man-marking teams. In the identity game that day, he showed his quality carrying the ball once more, scoring a goal after outplaying three youngsters. Bobby was playing as the extra attacking player to give more creative passing options; he played on one side between the lines and on the other side as the free player behind Joel and Virgil. We wanted to create stability with our centre-half pairings now – as I've said, it's one position in my opinion. The triangle of Joel, Virgil and Fabinho should work as a 'freedom-giver' to all the others. Maybe it's better to say a stable diamond including Ali because he's on the level of an extra defender and this helped us so much against pressing teams. We'd need Ali to be this 'extra' player against Brentford's pressing. Our analysts were working brilliantly this year and I'd called to ask Mark and Greg to get a specific clip of our match against Milan where Ali did exactly that versus two strikers.

In the session on the Thursday we played five-a-side with the senior players, creating one rule that the outside space should always be covered with one player but this could interchange. The amount of coordinated attacking movements between Hendo, Mo and Trent was incredible. We'll need this at Brentford, I thought to myself.

Walking in after training, I'd never seen players changing that quickly after a session! It was a girls' night out and they all had to babysit because the players' partners were going for dinner together. Jürgen couldn't believe his eyes. He asked Trent if his girlfriend was going and he said yes. "So she's going with all the girls before you've introduced her to the gaffer?" I asked, as Jordan started taking his boots off. Jürgen asked him, "Did Trent introduce his girlfriend to you yet?" "Nope," he said. "So, you didn't introduce her to the gaffer or the skipper?" I say, with a serious tone. Trent waited and waited and then responded with just one word in broad Scouse: "COVID." It sent us all into fits of laughter.

When we'd been walking outside The Titanic the week earlier, I'd said to Millie that it was time for a night out for the players as well. When we want to be strong as a group they have to see more often that behind each player is a human and a personality away from football. Because life is two-sided, not just 'I play and you don't'. It increases respect between them and helps with reacting better to each other, especially when there is some individual disappointment. The base for team spirit starts with all players caring for each other. We considered a restaurant in Porto after the game, but Jürgen, Ray and I decided that it was maybe better after West Ham in London before the November international break.

On Thursday night I got a text from Jürgen telling me about a new TV series coaching masterclass with basketball legend Geno Auriemma. I liked the show, but nobody can out-coach John Wooden! The message was summed up like this: coaching is about creating great relationships; a team is a group of people coming together to achieve what they can't do individually; it's always about getting the best people on your team. How to coach the old-fashioned way? Make them feel guilty by asking 'Is this the best you got?' Resilient leaders have a great ability to listen. They listen more, then they speak. Then there was a part which put everything we do at LFC into perspective: 'There is always pressure when you try to accomplish something that's meaningful and rewarding. When you handle this, you grow'. Winning a game has many similarities as winning in life.

I texted the boss back to say I loved the 'feel guilty' part, the old school. In many ways we are old school, even though I'm a young coach. Jürgen said we could try it in Friday's session by asking some of our seniors if this was the best they've got. Hopefully, fingers crossed, we could help a few individuals even more to reach their potential and level needed to move our team forward. The game always turns out the best for the ones who use every session as if it's their last one. It's all about creating the right mindset to follow a path. It's a weakness to get distracted when things don't work out. It showed the open mind of Jürgen – when you are an open personality, a lot of things can and will inspire you.

Our preparations for Brentford continued on the Friday. When you play against a team you haven't come up against yet, it's important to know why they are the team they are. New stadium, a young team, a fighting atmosphere, they celebrate each challenge like a goal and now being in the Premier League. A well-drilled team, a 5-3-2 structure with clear and good football ideas, confident and prepared to make this a final. We needed to be ready to play under pressure and with this we needed to prepare direction. Against any pressing team there will be open spaces and it's these 'open doors' we needed to find. The video meeting was designed by Pete to make sure we created advantages. For a short moment Trent and Robbo would be our 'free player', so with a good orientation and positioning it would be possible to start the attack here, by cutting inside with the ball or a killer pass forward. The rest of the options would be covered with their structure. Trent and Robbo would have to make little advantages with their football brains – Robbo should be deep in the build-up, but when we attacked ready to overlap, keeping his eyes open to play convincing crosses against their three giants at the back. But this was part of our portfolio anyway. This game screamed out for a full-back-to-full-back goal. The sun was shining and Jürgen was loud as he told our boys, at exactly this moment Brentford were preparing for a final – and we needed to make sure we were ready for this. I said to him afterwards, jokingly, we should have used the sentence 'Is this the best we've got?'

After travelling down on the Friday night, Jürgen's final message the following morning at the hotel was: be prepared for problems. I think he had a gut feeling. "This is a game they are waiting for, they are in the Premier League and every fixture feels like a great opportunity for them. But when we are the team we want to be – with a top, top, top attitude and outstanding mentality – we will be able to win this game. What's important, for example, is that we run to block balls, not to show that we run."

Our sixth 'final' of the Premier League ended 3-3 in a real thriller. It was clear again that you don't win games in this league without being ready for a second-ball fight. Brentford went long immediately and our last line dropped early, which created the advantages and spaces for their second-ball game. In the first half we didn't win one second ball – not one. I could imagine waking up in a cold sweat in the middle of the night because it was so disappointing and such a long time since we couldn't control these situations. When one presses, all the others should be in a second-ball mood, we said during half-time. First, because we were dropping, and second, because all our players didn't react well enough when the ball was in the air. When you drop and are deep, they are closer to your goal; with second balls and when crosses come in, the danger is so much higher. As a player it's natural to drop but it's not the right thing to do – it was something we had to correct immediately. That's why, for example, Joel won less than half his challenges in the air. They created too many advantages with their second-ball game and with their second-post crosses. It's difficult to control situations when the ball is in the air, but what you can do is avoid these crosses coming into your box. You can avoid being so deep in the box and for that you need to have a defensive press. It cost us two points.

On the other hand, the positives were our goals, for sure. Curtis scored an absolute screamer from outside the box into the near corner and Fab's chip in behind to isolate Mo was a lovely ball and finish. We also had Jots with a great header, freeing himself at the second post when Hendo – as the midfielder – crossed. It showed we were dangerous from everywhere. We kept our substitute plan at 3-2 with Bobby coming on; it was an offensive change but the right one to do. We needed a better positional game to keep the score, and like that we were always protected with Hendo and Fab. We really believed we were going to put the game to bed with his link-up play and the fact we had him in the zone where Brentford were winning all their second balls. It hurt that we couldn't avoid their cross for the 3-3. Bobby was as close to stopping the cross as to scoring to make it 4-3 in the last minute.

As always with draws, it felt like a defeat for us but you never knew if this would be the point which made the difference at the end of the season, and so the conclusion was you should always cherish every point you win. Virgil, Ali and myself were the last ones in a silent dressing room. It would be a long trip back to Liverpool, but Jürgen, Andreas, Vitor, Pete and myself would use the time to start work on next week and planning our next training session.

'COACHES WHO WANT TO CONTROL EVERYTHING CAN ONLY BE STOPPED BY CREATING CHAOS'

WEEK 9

LFC TOTAL FOOTBALL, 2021/22

THIS WAS THE WEEK I WOULD GO BACK 'HOME'. BACK to Estadio do Dragao, the 'blue and white nation'. I was incredibly excited, I couldn't wait to go to Porto for final no2 in our Champions League group. It's the city I got married in. They are the club who took me from PSV Eindhoven when I was only 24. They showed faith in me and I will be forever grateful for the relationships forged and the experiences gained. And...it's also the only blue colour I like.

For our pre-match analysis meeting, Roberto had to tune in from a separate room in front of a TV. His daughter had COVID and we didn't want to take any risks, despite the fact he is double-vaccinated and had tested negative. We agreed he would drive in his own car to the airport… at least if he has fuel, because at this moment in time the country was pretty much without any petrol.

As our last session started, Jürgen addressed the group. "The first question we need to ask ourselves: do we want to win this competition? If so, then we shouldn't waste any time gaining points in this difficult group."

We knew we could make a massive step forward towards qualifying. For this, we'd need an old-school LFC performance. Let them feel uncomfortable with each spell of possession they have. How? With a clear game plan: we were going to chase them over the whole pitch, from all directions. When we get outplayed, we will chase them from behind. I explained this principle one more time in training: "They should wake up at night feeling scared there is someone behind them!" That's when and how we thought they couldn't handle us, especially when [centre-back] Pepe didn't play. They were a set-piece team, a quick-restart team and, when needed, an ugly team. We'd seen that at their game against Sporting a few weeks earlier. There is a saying written in big lettering at their training complex: 'We love the ones who hate to lose'. I lived their culture for seven years, so I knew all too well that they would want to upset us. But we believed we could really dominate and create doubt for them with our offensive principles.

Before the session started, Nat told me he'd been jealous of Joel having the chance to play against Ivan Toney. He's probably the only player in world football who enjoys these situations. This would have been a game for him, for sure, ending with a few bruises or with a cut. As I'd said before, he's a centre-half who puts his head where others don't put their feet.

As the session got underway I could see on Trent's face something wasn't right. At the end of it, with all the media cameras gone, he walked away from the free-kick practice and I asked him if everything was alright. "I feel my groin," he answered. That wasn't a good sign, the day before the Porto game and just six days before the City game. Jürgen was standing with Lee Nobes and the doc was waving his hands. I was already on my way – swearing as I went – to catch Milner. Coaching at this level is to make players secure, not insecure, so clarity is really important – that's why I caught Millie immediately. We went through the tactics in front of the board: this is what we want defensively, this is what we want offensively.

Trent didn't join us on the flight that afternoon, he stayed at the AXA Training Centre for treatment. Despite the blow of losing him, it felt good to be boarding a plane for a Champions League away game once again. We trained on the morning of the game at Boavista's stadium. The amount of derbies I played there with my youth teams in the past… and now it was the place to prepare for this big game. Boavista is the smaller club of the city and has this superb mentality to fight with all they have. The atmosphere was always hostile, something I didn't mind. "At this moment, everyone is Portuguese," said Jürgen. Even the biggest rivals of Porto would share information. Maybe the only Portuguese who would not be with Porto were Diogo and Vitor.

Normally we do our set-pieces on the morning of the game, especially when we have such a short period to prepare for the match. It's always a long day when you play away in the Champions League, so it's nice to be out of the hotel and go through a few details. We introduced this last year to start with our high press, just to set the tone and rhythm for the game at night. A lot of these decisions are based on intuition. This is the most important factor when it comes to making them. On this particular day we decided to go for good feeling – a lot of short, quick passes and rondos. I like it when the players have a smile on their faces.

Robbo told me he came to this Boavista stadium as a kid to watch Celtic play in the semi-final of the UEFA Cup. The coach of Boavista at the time was a friend of mine, Jaime Pacheco. The football world is so small.

The atmosphere was good, the sun shone and I felt we were ready for the night's battle, but driving back to the hotel we got the message that Roger Hunt had died. Such sad news to receive. He was the club's top scorer for such a long time and we immediately thought about how we could pay our respects to not only a legend but a real gentleman too.

Later at the hotel we were informed about a minor victory from our painful draw at Brentford: our throw-in performance was the best Thomas ever saw, not just from us but any other team.

After lunch I asked the hotel if they could get me that day's sports newspaper… maybe there was something we could pick up. Their coach Sergio Conceicao said, "I'm a realist. In specific game-moments this Liverpool is the best in the world. We have to counter these moments with organisation and mentality." Their midfielder Otavio said, "We will try to change history this time."

Jürgen and myself went through the game plan one more time just before the meeting with the team started. The gaffer was on fire that day – with his vocabulary he gripped each player: "The headline of this game is that everybody should be ready to jump. We need to find exactly this little voice in our head. We need to chase them – that's the difference. Many teams do pressing, we do chasing. Chasing when we are outplayed. A vintage LFC performance – play like a top team which didn't win anything. We talk so much about defending because that's what makes us different. When they want to come out with the ball they should be a magician, or just lucky." We were changing step-by-step the personality of this team, stimulating our old and new habits. LFC total football, 2021/22.

And the boys delivered. Champions League final no2 away at Porto ended in a 5-1 win. We were superior to a weakened home team. We showed real variability without losing our identity. I'd seen the best football both collectively and tactically, flexible but organised. We constantly made good, defined triangles around the ball. In particular the 'outside' triangle of Sadio, Curtis and Robbo consistently found spaces to progress. The analyst of Porto said after the game that it was so difficult to get close to Fabinho. This is exactly what we wanted to create:

doubt around their 'double 6', Sergio and Uribe, and having our free players to build up.

Curtis was our standout performer on the night, involved in four of the five goals. We scored 20 times in the month of September. Five wins, one draw and every time at least three goals. Pre-season was paying off. Mo proved himself as a striking machine again with his two goals. Nothing more to say. It was a big step towards qualifying from this complicated group.

After the game I immediately searched for Fabio Vieira and Joao Mario, two of my boys when they were so young. I gave them a strong hug and told them how proud I was of them. FC Porto's 'Project 611' (2006 till 2011) was still delivering talents to their first team.

After the game Milner was on the bench and I asked him with a big smile, "You still think we should have changed the team?" We'd had a big and long discussion the day before Porto and I'd told him it was time for stability. In life you deserve second chances, while he thought we should have changed more after our performance at Brentford. He is so committed and more and more was thinking like a manager – that's why we really could discuss these things.

We stayed overnight at Porto following the game, which gave me time to walk the next morning past Taylor's Port Cellars, where Danielle and myself got married. Porto will be forever in my heart, not just because of the football memories. But now it was time to go back to Liverpool and move on. It's all in the past. Manchester City were waiting. More and more, I got the feeling this year was a completely new start. A new Liverpool FC time. Pre-season felt like we had a new team. We re-introduced all of our basic principles and added new ones we wanted and needed. It's an honour to be able to document this complete process with all the small decisions around it with this book project. Fab said it well after Porto: "We have to keep this quality and intensity."

We could not allow ourselves to get distracted in these next few days – that would be a bigger enemy than Man City. I always thought: if this was our first season together, we would be so positive about our start, a new team, new style and new principles. We were in it, that was the most important thing. But games like Man City you can't prepare for in one or two days.

Back in Liverpool the weather was the opposite of Porto. It was windy, raining, but the whole building felt like we were getting close to a special game. We trained hard with the ones who didn't play – they needed attention and loads of different experiences. Naby was back and finished one and then another right into the top corner. Vitor and myself put the last line under the highest pressure – they had to play against eight but starting really high. While we were doing it, I said to Jürgen, "Here lies the key against City." We knew we needed to be so aggressive against their one-v-one players with our full-backs, Millie and Robbo, and at the same time close our last line to control the movements of Kevin De Bruyne and Bernardo Silva. Here, we felt we could take away a part of their offensive play, and the only way was to be unpredictable in our pressing. This would make sure we'd have the ball more and that's step one towards beating them. We wanted to put our game on show by dominating the ball and the whole pitch. With this came defending really well; when we defend on our best level, the more we could attack them.

We wouldn't step back against them. It's philosophical but also our main idea – and if, but only if, we had to, we'd step back as a unit. "If we try like a normal game, we shouldn't try," Jürgen said in the analysis meeting. It's the most exciting game for us coaches. I spent double the time with our analysts to make sure we were right in our thoughts. We could give City a proper knock, I believed, but we'd have to do a few things really, really well. Take their plan away with our last line, forcing mistakes and forcing long balls. Take their offensive play away by creating two-v-one situations against their one-v-one players.

"We have to become unpredictable again in our pressing," Jürgen said. How the hell will Guardiola plan against unpredictability, I was thinking. Coaches who want to control everything can only be stopped by creating chaos. The only way to press them was with our principles – you couldn't tell them like this and then that. The only thing we could control and help was making sure our line was front-footed and high. It would be impossible to be clean in our pressing – we'd have to be wild. That's why we focused on principles instead of what I call 'A-B-C coaching'.

Against Chelsea and Tuchel, it was defensively our most aggressive game. That's the bravery we needed again. Everybody had to chase in this game. And when we won the ball… first pass forward. Against City, pressing isn't enough – you will get outplayed. So our main principle of 'chasing the opposition from behind' is the magic trick. I made this clear one more time during the training session. "Jota, chase Rodri here from behind, the influence on their positional game will be massive. Sadio, chase Walker here from behind. We have to chase them so hard that even when they are completely free, they should always feel someone is close and coming." I shout out to our forwards, "You have to invest a lot!" I felt we would be fresh. We went into this game with less strategy than our last encounters. We focused on us, and I really liked it.

There was a different issue to contend with at Kirkby. Jürgen and myself sat with Ali, Fabinho and Roberto in the office. We had a situation: we spoke with Jonathan Bamber, our lawyer, and there was no way to make the quarantine easier when they came back from Brazil after the internationals. It was scheduled to be the day before the Watford game and it was not clear what would happen and where they could do their quarantine – in their own house, private residence or hotel? Then, we were due to travel to Spain three days later – what was allowed for them? On top of this, they were due to play Friday morning and we would play Saturday against Watford at 12.30pm, so that ruled them out for that game. We explained the situation to them. We spoke with Juninho about his decision around calling up Roberto, who was on standby. His wife was due to give birth to their third child and under those rules, he would not be allowed to be with her in the hospital. Also, we felt he'd benefit from two weeks of good training after his injury and missing most of pre-season. It would be a long season and we would need him.

In our final session on the Saturday, Milner was pressing like a wild dog. We had to slow him down and say maybe better not to jump on Cancelo there. 'Old habits' can be difficult to change; we'd asked him to jump in the last few games, so he continued this. Vitor joked and said when we go to Porto, the English boys ask for pasta instead of all the nice seafood. He has his own rituals and sticks with them. We joked that English people go to a good restaurant and complain there is no fish and chips on the menu. The problem is, I'm becoming the same!

The 'old v young' competition at the end of the session was won by the young. At that point in the season, it was 6-6 overall, a real competitiveness between them. In the hotel on the Saturday night, Mona brought in the birthday cakes while we were at dinner, with Roberto and Ali celebrating their 30th and 29th years. Everyone sang for them, while Virgil laughed and said to Ali, "You look more 30 than 29!" Milner passed by and Jürgen joked to him, "These kids!"

Afterwards we watched Atletico Madrid against Barcelona. On the Friday I'd sent a text of support to Alfred Schreuder, the assistant of Ronald Koeman: "Keep your head up high." They were under real pressure. Luis Suarez assisted and scored and together with Joao Felix and Lemar, Atletico opened up Barça's defence time after time. The talent Barça has is incredible, though: a new generation of La Masia isn't just knocking on the door but running through it, I believe. Pedri is the best young midfielder in Europe… only because Harvey and Curtis are Brexit players now! He designed each attack of the Spanish national team at the Euros. Then there's Fati, Gavi, Nico... can you imagine them in two years' time? These are the ones where class is the biggest indicator of their talent.

And so, on the Sunday, final no7 of our Premier League season ended 2-2 in a game with two of the best teams in the world of football. The levels we reach in these games are insane. If you don't like to watch them, you don't like football. Jack Grealish started as a false 9, Pep prepared a magic plan. But to be honest, only in the second half did we do the things they don't like. We tried first half, but only us – and only us with one idea – can do this really. We opened the centre too much without pressing them intensely enough. Jota couldn't control Rodri. Our midfield was dropping too deep. Our last line was too passive. We refocused at half-time and each block we made in the second half gave the stadium energy. What a difference in atmosphere it was inside Anfield – you could see Robbo growing with it.

Strong squad: Kaide Gordon gets a chance to impress in the Carabao Cup tie against Norwich in September

Leading the way: Our skipper Jordan leads us out for a game against Crystal Palace at Anfield; a quiet word with the boss at Preston; celebrations as Fabinho finds the net in a 3-0 win over Leeds and Curtis enjoys scoring in a 3-3 draw at Brentford

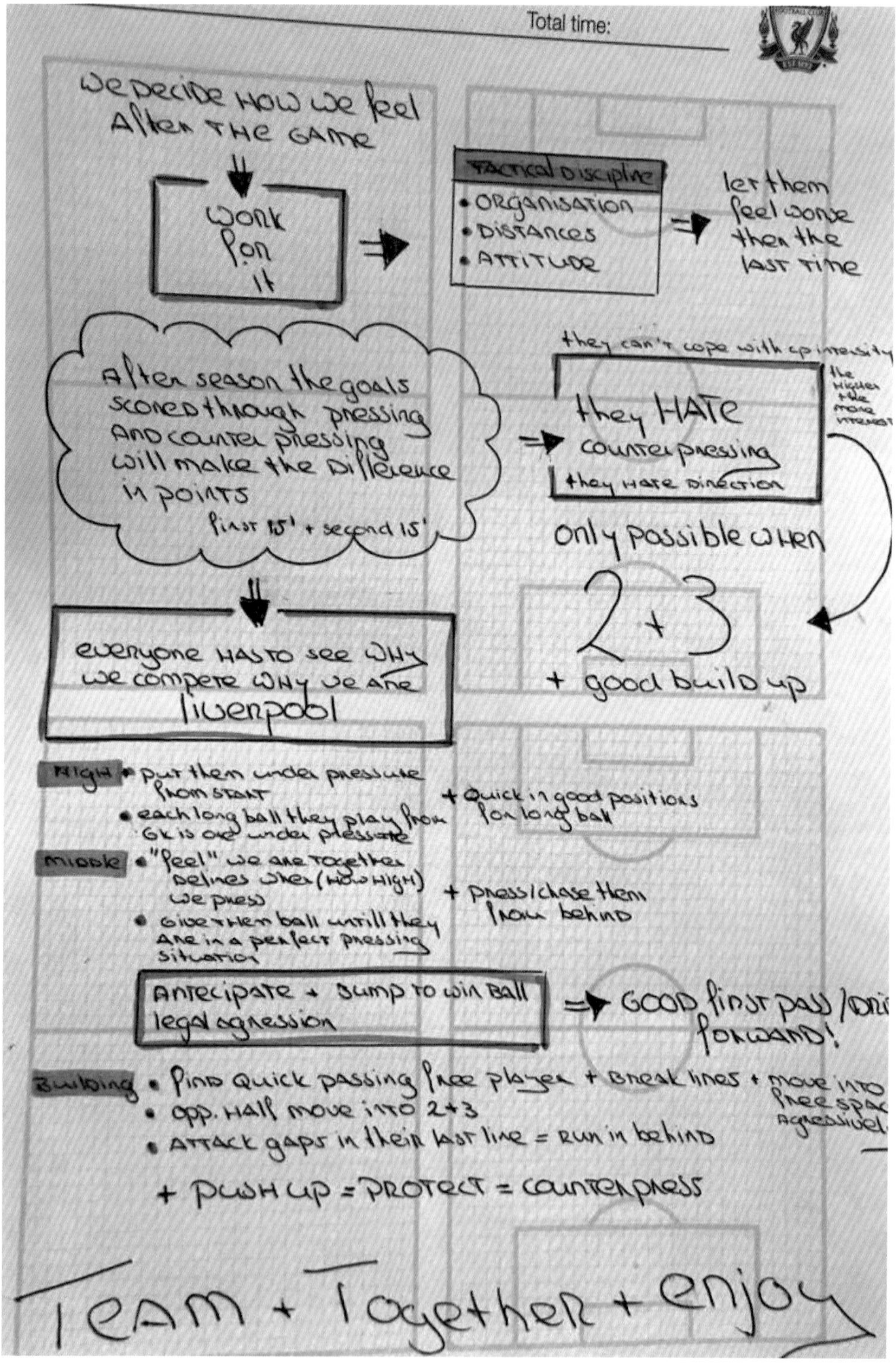

Total time:

WE DECIDE HOW WE feel AFTER THE GAME

WORK fOR it

TACTICAL DISCIPLINE
• ORGANISATION
• DISTANCES
• ATTITUDE

let them feel worse then the last time

After season the goals scored through pressing and counter pressing will make the difference in points
first 15' + second 15'

they can't cope with up intensity

they HATE counterpressing
they hate direction

the higher the more intense

only possible when 2 + 3 + good build up

everyone HAS TO see WHY we compete WHY we are liverpool

High • put them under pressure from start
• each long ball they play from GK is one under pressure
+ Quick in good positions for long ball

Middle • "feel" we are together defines when (how high) we press
• give them ball untill they are in a perfect pressing situation
+ press/chase them from behind

Antecipate + Jump to win Ball
legal agression
⇒ GOOD first pass/dri... forward!

Building • find quick passing free player + break lines + move into free space agressively
• opp. half move into 2+3
• attack gaps in their last line = run in behind

+ push up = PROTECT = counterpress

Team + Together + enjoy

Getting the message across: Putting my thoughts down on paper helps me to communicate clearly to the players so they work effectively as a team

Touch of class: Bobby in action against Porto during our 5-1 win at Estadio do Dragao. Our second Champions League group game – and our second win

Go on, Naby lad: (Above) Naby Keita's shot flies past Atletico Madrid keeper Jan Oblak in our 3-2 win at the Wanda Metropolitano. (Left) keeping a close eye on training

My ball: Diogo tangles with Rúben Dias in our 2-2 draw with Manchester City at Anfield in October

My hat-trick ball: Mo takes home a souvenir after our 5-0 win over Manchester United

It was a game where the job wasn't finished until the last whistle. We were ready to suffer but it didn't take away our belief in the game and you saw that with our second-half performance. What it took away in the first half was our football-playing. Reaching half-time at 0-0 was so important. We could show the gaps they were using at half-time and we could explain the importance of playing the extra pass to open them up. Stay calm, play the extra pass and we will hurt them. Luckily we could correct all of this easily during the interval and we didn't change a lot, we just reinforced the plan we had.

Curtis was brave throughout the whole game and the goals we scored were really incredible. There are not many good things about defending deep, but one is that you have a lot of space to exploit. You saw that with Sadio's goal, the pass from Mo was knife-sharp. Then, Mo's goal was just pure magic. Wow. A blueprint for dribbling skills. Absolutely absurd. Mo won so many balls – he plays as if he is an U13 player because he has so much pure joy.

We had an incredible chance to win it as well, three metres from the goal right at the end with Fabinho, but Rodri blocked in front of the line. Our boys were really disappointed after the final whistle – and they should be disappointed with not playing our football in the first half. When I shook Pep's hand after the whistle and hugged him, he was saying, "What a team you guys have, what a team." "Your team isn't too bad either," I told him.

Jürgen spoke after the game and said we lost a half showing the world our football. We could play much better against them when we did the things right, but 2-2 was a fair result in the end. Hendo said: "It is a little bit frustrating, especially when you go [for] the second time in the lead and there's 12 minutes left on the clock. I think we can see the game out better. But overall, we've got to learn from our mistakes. It's not the end of the world – there's still a long way to go. Take the positives and learn from the things we didn't do so well and be better in the next game."

When I arrived home, I thought to myself that we were going into the second international break and hadn't lost a game so far. Please, guys, come back safe and fit from your matches.

WEEK 10

MAKE IT LOUD

I TRIED TO USE THE SECOND INTERNATIONAL BREAK as some time to relax and recharge during the first week of our players being away from the training ground. I only visited AXA a few times by myself, using the opportunity to talk with our analysts. When football dictates your tempo in life it isn't easy when this tempo stops, it isn't easy at all. Not the physical tempo but the mental tempo, the tempo of preparation – the go, go, go.

Danielle and I visited the city centre of Liverpool a few times. You don't have a lot of time normally, so these moments are nice. The city has such a great atmosphere and vibe. I'd actually forgotten how it felt to be there, in the centre, and honestly I fell in love with it again. It was also the week in which Jürgen would reach his six-year anniversary with LFC and the club media guys asked me for a quick interview to reflect upon his time here. Normally I give interviews imagining I'm speaking to our players, or to our fans – that's why I give detail and explain. I want to take them with me on our journey. I believe that every word that comes out needs to give direction because, in my opinion, it helps us. I finished with exactly that: "This is a hungry LFC team, confident and knows what it wants. Jürgen leads and corrects. It's a beautiful time to be a Liverpool supporter. Cherish it. Make it loud." The last bit was for our supporters; we needed positivity around us in the coming period. It was my message to them. We always try to influence how people look at us because I know in football this makes a big difference.

During the week I called Jürgen to check how the [padel] racket presentation in Barcelona went. He is representing Wilson now and has his own official 'JK' racket. His heartbeat map is the logo... If anyone wonders why the logo almost doesn't fit, it's because he was playing me when it got recorded! Our passion became his sponsor, his own racket. How cool is that? John was in Mallorca, Jack was in Scotland, Pete in Germany and Vitor was in Portugal during this week, but I couldn't wait till we were all together in the office again discussing why our identity is intensity.

'WORKING FOR LIVERPOOL IS DEALING WITH HIGH EXPECTATIONS'

WEEK 11

BACK TO THE ORIGINS

BY THE TIME THIS WEEK BEGAN, THE PREPARATION for Watford had already started. We didn't know a lot about them because of Claudio Ranieri coming in the previous week. What he did at Sampdoria without money was exceptional, from relegation to 15th to 9th. It felt like this happened a lot with us: having a new manager to face...or even the opposite, a manager getting the sack after our game. We tried to prepare by watching Sampdoria and we knew his ideas from his earlier Premier League spells. As always, we tried to get all the information we could gather and use it in the right way. We knew when he took over at Fulham, Roma and Sampdoria he changed immediately to his way: a 4-4-2. He keeps things simple and clear. Isn't that the secret anyway, I asked myself. The moment the minds of the intuitive players get confused, the end is in sight. "Every disadvantage has its advantage," is a Cruyff saying. Not knowing what he would do, gave us time to focus on us and our way.

As we entered the start of a new period, we were all handed new training wear. We looked like either a captain from Star Trek or someone from Robin Hood, but it was the elite Nike line so it fitted really well. Jürgen arrived back at AXA in new Adidas gear. "Early Christmas presents," he joked, before he changed into his LFC kit.

Before training got underway, we spoke about Ted Lasso in the coaches' office. All of us watched the second season during the international break. We loved it and recognised so much. It was really well-written, so many jokes taking the piss out of everyone, especially the Dutch characteristics. One of life's most valuable lessons is not to take yourself too seriously and we've all had to learn this with time. Sometimes it can feel like time literally stands still. One of these moments is when we, as staff, are watching a warm-up game or training, just before our maximum focus is asked for and required. We talk about everything that comes up in our mind. Jürgen is a great leader – he knows like no-one else how to play down pressure.

It was confirmed we'd be without Fabinho and Alisson for our trip to Watford. They'd head straight to Madrid after international duty. We were obviously disappointed but we didn't even mention it between us. Instead, there were no distractions, just pure focus on the ones we had.

The training was spot on in the lead-up to the trip to Vicarage Road. Bobby was incredible, which was so pleasing, and I thought to myself: whatever happens, he needs to start at Watford. He was in a good moment, he played in such a way that the others love to pass to him – that's a great sign for a good player.

The boys laughed during the rondo that Trent needed a 'nappy change' because he didn't go full-in for the ball and if there is something our players – well, basically just James Milner – don't like it is when someone is not giving everything. Hendo was constantly in Ox's ear: "Support me quicker." Standards are set by the ones who need to live them, our boys prove that time and time again. Me and Jürgen observed and played with the type of rondos to make it interesting and give different challenges for the group. We chose four exercises in the start of the session where we increased the levels of concentration and interaction. This increased the right intensity.

Thomas Gronnemark was with us this week to provide extra focus on our offensive throw-ins high up the pitch as our defensive ones were improving. Thomas is a crazy throw-in genius, but I told him that we needed a more optimistic approach. We stood in front of the tactics board and moved our players around. We created one set-up for the latter stages in a game... a set-up to create chaos. We created a long-throw set-up, sending our centre-halves into the box. When Pete came into the office, I asked them to organise the exact set-up together with Thomas to be as close to our corner organisation as possible, ready to dominate the second phase – our real strength. Like this, there is fluidity and balance between our moments.

After this, Jürgen and I went over the line-up and discussed a call we'd had with Ali and Claudio Taffarel, who we were bringing in as a new addition to our goalkeeping department. Yes, that Taffarel. He has a real passion for goalkeeping and his resume speaks for itself; we believed he would bring experience and personality to all of our goalkeepers, working with John and Jack.

By the way, the ones who are most passionate are always on the end of jokes. For example, Robbo told Jürgen he always has a sore shoulder when seeing Thomas walking into the building – he knew the throw-in coach was here and he'd focus on him a lot. Jota gave Robbo stick when he walked off the pitch: "Don't throw it on the chest, throw towards the feet." They take the piss when there is no perfection. The atmosphere was great, and rondos always help, we needed these smiles on their faces while playing. Mo laughing with Sadio, Hendo laughing with Trent.

Keep simulating the origins is how I describe it; the type of training and atmosphere they had when they were kids. Love for the game, passion for the ball, ambition to play in the world's biggest games. Pressure like this becomes relative. When you were young, you would play each time as though it was the last game of your life. The good players keep this characteristic, the top ones add professionalism and don't allow one to interfere with the other. If you try to chase the players, they will always run away from you. But if you have what the players want, they will come to you. Make it interesting, go back to the origins. The exercises should attract the players.

Overall, what was most pleasing in the second international week was there was another young surprise. This time it was Harvey Blair. Everyone left the training pitch astonished, asking me how old he is. Ibou was laughing with joy watching him. You had to see it, this young boy in his team finishing from everywhere and winning the 'identity game.' I really believe there are not many exercises to make players better but a lot to make players worse. That's why we have just a few real good ones and vary from there. The identity game – three teams competing for the ball and competing to attack more – is definitely one of them.

I had a feeling it was make-or-break for us in the next phase of the season. Our injuries, which happened last year to have such an impact, meant we were now missing players again. The group needed success to believe we could do it after what happened last season. It couldn't become negative because only this is what could stop us. During his pre-Watford press conference, Jürgen was on fire, right on top of it all. This was what we meant during pre-season when we spoke of an 'us against the world' mentality. Newcastle's takeover, Watford's managerial record, Curtis' injury with England Under-21s, Southgate's selection inconsistency… they all got some from the boss.

However, the analysis meeting was all about us. Pete selected some exceptional images of our Burnley game when we played literally each first pass forward. Jürgen highlighted the threat of Ismaila Sarr and used Sadio to confirm his speed. For them it would be a new start with a new manager, so we'd need an attacking mindset and, at the same time, our front three would need to defend with all they had. The difference between a good and an outstanding game of ours is when we are ready to leave our positions to jump for 95 minutes and ready to close the important gaps for 95 minutes. When we play a positive game, we are constantly ready to accelerate.

After our final session the day before Watford, Hendo asked me: "Did you watch the City game back? Was it me and Curtis who were too deep?" I told him: "Yes, but we could correct it at half-time, so all fine. It isn't easy to close gaps and put pressure on against them, but you changed the second half with your pressing moving the team higher up the pitch." It's exactly that which we trained on MD-1. Hendo is like a sponge in training, filling the no6 position with attitude. He was top against Burnley, dictating each attack, and that's what we'd need at Watford.

Jürgen and I had discussed how to create exercises where we could accelerate the 'common plan' after our boys have been away during the internationals, so in training we took a player out to train our midfield press, with nine outfield players in our structure pressing the hell out of the second team, who on this occasion were representing Watford. It was our way of stimulating the interaction between our players and the level of concentration went up – you saw how our players were moving and thinking. These are the moments I love, the day before the game, the last bit of information and our boys reaching levels of concentration they never reached before.

First Roberto went out so we were pressing without a no9, which was designed to stimulate Milner and Naby to jump and then the others needed to close the centre. Then we took

Hendo out, our no6. This influenced Mo and Sadio's positions and behaviours, so now we pressed with two lines of four and Roberto forcing the press to the outside while still trying to catch their centre-halves from the blind side with Mo or Sadio. Every time we repeated it with one more ball. Then we took Mo or Sadio out. We needed to fill our plan with life and these exercises helped, not just because of wearing the shirt but because we needed to be together and we needed to be intense. Jürgen stimulated our flexible outside triangles in our offensive 4-3-3 structure; stimulating technique and skill instead of just playing the obvious passes. Also, we encouraged the interchanging of positions. It was the first time our boys were together after being away for two weeks, so it looked rusty, but with time the boys were speeding up more often and finding each other blindly again. Repeat now so tomorrow the mistakes will not happen. It's never easy to prepare for the first game after an international break.

But working for Liverpool is dealing with high expectations. Everything has to be perfect for us to succeed. Why? Because we need to over-perform – there is no margin. I was carrying a feeling that we were at a turning point. It was a feeling and it wasn't a nice one. It lessened after the meeting and the last training session, but it was still there. That's why I asked Mark to create a video about our chasing dynamics against Manchester City, called 'We are never outplayed', just to reinforce our togetherness. It was perfect to show our players before these difficult fixtures away from home because it focused on ourselves.

On matchday morning Jürgen started the meeting with a German saying: "A good horse only jumps as high as he needs to. But to become consistent we need to jump every time as high as possible. The second half against City should be our benchmark." Later, during the pre-activation in the small corridors of Vicarage Road, Virgil joked with Sadio that he jumped higher than him but I always gave Sadio the win. "You are the horse Jürgen mentioned," I told him, "but Sadio is the real horse." Virgil walked away saying he won each header against Sadio at Southampton. Everyone hugged each other so strongly just before we went out. Milner was loud, some of the boys were praying, but everywhere was a focused smile. It was time to go again. You saw this is a team full of friends.

Final no8 ended 5-0 against a new Claudio Ranieri team. Roberto scored a hat-trick, he was everywhere and always in the right moments. Thank you! We, as a team, controlled the ball and the space so well. We had great control of the tempo against a team with full speed in the front and built to kill us on the counter with Sarr and Hernandez. It was crucial how flexible Trent and Robbo were during the building of our attacks and how calm and patient the strikers and midfielders were in order to receive the ball in better positions, which was very important against a line of five with a deep block. Our players in the back could use the gaps, and this was also the message at half-time: we stay patient and use the gaps created, use this game like we use our 'gates game' in training. We could see that when spontaneity and creativity come together, goals like that afternoon could happen. Mo and Sadio combined to finish incredibly. Beautiful goals with another worldie from Mo and a hat-trick for Bobby. On top of that, a clean sheet for Caoimhin Kelleher. Not a bad day's work!

WEEK 12

THE ONE-RULE PRINCIPLE

THE WEEK BEGAN EARLY ON SUNDAY MORNING IN Jürgen's office. It was raining outside and we discussed our Atletico Madrid plan. 'Don't change, we won't change, the team deserves to go again after yesterday's performance', was the message. There was time enough between Atletico and Manchester United to be fully recovered again, so there was no need to make changes now. We had rhythm and we could protect Robbo and Trent by taking them off early at Watford. With this in mind, our next two days would be all about recovery. But there were three things Jürgen said we needed to do: use the images, create the right ideas, and let them come alive on the pitch.

We analysed our two games in the Champions League round of 16 against Atletico in 2020 and we really learned from the away game. Our performance had nothing to do with us being away from home – our positional game wasn't good enough to break them down. Some games are life-defining, I think. Take our game against Barcelona, or our game against Flamengo in the Club World Cup final when we became world champions. The home game against Atletico was spectacular and only God knows why we didn't go into the quarter-finals. It made me really angry for a long period, especially as it was the last game before COVID-19 hit the world, so it was stuck in my mind for a long time.

The best advice to the team was that we shouldn't let those games interfere with what we were now. Jürgen spoke to the team and explained that "the world is talking about Watford being bad, but we will never know how much that was because of us. I can tell you simply, it was a lot." We had jumped as high as we could, all our individuals were behaving and thinking in the same counter-pressing way. This is what pleased me most, I need this feeling – this gave me a little bit more confidence that we were IN IT. Sadio scored his 100th Premier League goal at Watford, so we all clapped for him before training. What an achievement. Drogba and Mo were on 104, so he was in the mix to become Africa's top scorer of all time in the Premier League.

With the week ahead in mind, I asked our ground staff to set up 'our pitch' at the AXA. We have a standard 40x40 pitch marked by the ground staff exactly in the centre of the pitch. In here, we normally play a variation of five-a-side games. The rules vary; in one game, they can only score when the whole team is pushed over the halfway line. This is to stimulate our team moving together, and pushing up to be ready to counter-press and stop counter-attacks high up the pitch. Against deep-defending teams you need to push up so far otherwise they have the chance to counter from there.

In the other game, we positioned a gate in the middle where they can score by passing through it. This was designed to stimulate defensively, closing the centre of the pitch. The 'one-rule principle', I call it. Only one rule and with this they can still play freely. As I've said, our habits become better and better and repetition of certain exercises is what makes the team evolve.

Our boys had come back from an international period with three intense World Cup qualifiers, then we went away to Watford for an early kick-off, and now we were going away to Madrid, all inside 48 hours. We only had one session to focus on us and now we were going into one of the world's toughest away games. It was a challenge accepted because we like the difficult ones. However, we needed to be fresh to be able to compete with their speed, I believed. Atletico had even been granted the weekend off by La Liga, with their game cancelled, so we knew they would be fresh and we had to be ready. This was why we made the decision on Monday morning to only do passing and rondos on our game-day session in Madrid – exactly how we did it in Porto and hopefully to create a smile on the boys' faces on matchday morning.

Pete's analysis clips to show the boys were concentrated on stopping counter-attacks and playing against a deep block. We believe the 'real training' in periods like this are done in the video meetings with the boys; we have to build more on good habits and video is perfect for doing this, for evolving the team and making the next step. We knew they were powerful on the counter, so we had to show this. In possession their strikers were very mobile, Suarez staying in an offside position, Felix moved freely between the lines and this would give our structure some real questions, so we would need to control these movements. They were capable of defending deep for long periods and still had a belief and mentality to decide games in the last minute.

They had quality and different styles up front. Correa was an animal – he went for everything. They were a team of fighters who stretched things to the limit, so we knew the referee's performance would be crucial too. They were better than us at annoying the opposition, that's for sure, but probably that was the only aspect in which they were better than us, aside from maybe their counter-press which was their biggest weapon because when they pressed they came with all they had.

As we walked out to start training, Kaide passed by. "Congratulations on your new five-year deal," Virgil shouted. "You're buying Starbucks now!" I laughed and said, "You know who needs a new deal?" and pointed at Mo. After the Watford game,

I was asked why I thought Mo was having the season he was. My reply was: "Even top players need a break, this in combination with a full pre-season created the right base. We underestimate the importance of regaining freshness after emotional, high-intensity playing periods. His mentality since the start of the pre-season has been outstanding, a true example. We all know he is a special player, and he is playing with pure joy. When top players can enjoy football and have this professionalism, they become unstoppable. Sometimes it looks like he is in the park, a young boy again, dribbling and combining to score. The team and especially our right side is connecting really well which helps his time to find good positions. This calmness in our positional game is so important for our front three to become unpredictable. The beautiful moment of football is when we see spontaneity and creativity come together and goals like today or v City can happen." I think I covered the right things with my answer.

We travelled to Madrid on the Monday. It was a longer trip than usual, so we met early at AXA. We would arrive late in the hotel in Madrid. The city and the stadium will always be a special place for us. We became champions of Europe there. I still see us wandering through an empty stadium with a beer in our hands to find the boxes where all our families were. I couldn't have been more happy to see them, it was a game that changed all of our lives. Now it was time for a big season-defining game. Not a life-changer but a season-changer. It's how I said before, these games would make us better, that was for sure. Could we put our game into place against one of the world's best defending teams? When we can do that, results will follow.

On the Monday night we sat outside the hotel on the terrace as it was warm. We watched Arsenal v Crystal Palace on our phones. We discussed Jürgen's padel trip to Barcelona, Vitor translated Simeone's press conference. Billy Hogan joined us with a glass of wine. He is part of the team.

On matchday morning we started with a meeting with Ray to plan and organise for the 2022 World Cup. We would give the boys who were not involved some days off and then meet up at our training camp. Ray did some work on two camps: one in Dubai and a second in Cape Town. We decided we'd go to Dubai as the players could join us more easily from Qatar. We then took time to go once more over our pre-season plans for 2022. We would go to Singapore and Thailand for our return to the Far East, hopefully playing a match against Manchester United.

The session in the morning was good. Everyone was together, not splitting the subs with starters, which was so important. The group was united and smiling. Plan worked. That's what I meant with football dictating the tempo of your life – you are constantly making small plans and executing them. 'Small' plan for the next training days, 'small' plan for the line-up, 'small' plan for the next opponent. After the session I remembered the first time I went to Madrid. It was 2 April 2017. The club sent me to watch Isco and Theo Hernandez, who played for Alaves at the Bernabeu. I'd never experienced something like that; a small plane was ready at John Lennon Airport and took me directly to Madrid to watch the game. Giving your honest opinion in those situations, that's pressure. I made my report and we all decided to go with Robbo from Hull.

Jürgen's last message to the boys was: "I have massive respect for Simeone – he keeps his players on their toes for such a long time now. We need to be ready for a fight. We need to have this constant offensive idea: play the first pass forward. Bravery means in this game, don't play your position – move into an offensive position, respecting our triangles. The more we have this, the more we show we are ready for this fight. This fight we play with our tools, our football tools. It's the best offensive and defensive option we have, to really play with the ball."

The boys took the message onboard as our third Champions League 'final' of the season ended 3-2 against a fresh, street-fighting team. In the tunnel before kick-off, Joao Felix surprised me with a big hug. He was my player for many years at Porto and it was great to see how well he was doing. I was really proud, to be honest. Benfica became champions in 2018/19 because of him. He decided our youth tournaments with his spontaneous dribbles, passes and smile – and we all saw in this game his influence on each attack. How can a human body feel angry and proud at the same moment?! When walking out of the tunnel, the whole stadium boomed 'Atleti, Atleti, Atletico Madrid!' The song triggered my mind, it was the one I always heard when I faced Atletico Madrid in youth tournaments. Anyone who says that with face masks there can't be an atmosphere is wrong, by the way.

The game itself started rough and tough. We had the ball and tried to find openings, then Mo created one by himself by outplaying three Atletico players, dribbling inside and shooting, with the shot deflecting off Milner and into the net. I said to Milner the following morning: "That was your goal"… and then I walked to Mo and said the same to him when Millie could hear it. "Just split the goal bonus, lads," I told them.

Atletico dropped off as expected, with Thomas Lemar, Joao Felix and Antoine Griezmann ready to counter from deep positions. The position of Joao Felix created headaches for us – this and the link-up between him and Lemar. Koke organised their whole team, when to press, when to wait. It's incredible what a leader he is – and I thought throughout the match that if we took him tactically out of the game, the castle of cards would drop. He is a no6 close to my heart.

Our second goal – another Naby worldie – opened up the game and they started coming much more. We defended poorly as a group and two goals from Griezmann got them level before half-time. The stadium was bouncing. I tried to speak to Jürgen and he couldn't hear me, it was crazy as I was standing next to him. That's how loud it was.

All their danger came from their left side. Fabinho in and Hendo to right-midfield will stop this, we thought. At half-time we showed images to be better organised deeper on the pitch to close the half-spaces better. The second half was one with so many stoppages, the game never came to life, but Griezmann's high kick on Bobby's head saw him sent off. We re-organised our offensive structure and brought Jota and Ox on for new energy. The ball into Jota created the penalty and Mo kept his nerve to score and win the game. We made a huge step towards qualification with these three points. Two wins outside of Anfield in this group. We got tested and we delivered. When I walked off the pitch with Virgil, he said: "These games you need to win as well." He couldn't have been more right.

We gave the team a well-earned day off on Thursday after staying over in Madrid, but we did a session with subs in the sunshine in Estadio Alfredo Di Stefano – the venue where we'd played against Real last season.

So it was back to work on Friday and we had our special guests with us – our free-kick specialists, neuro11. Hendo started the session in the boardroom with the guys and went directly to the pitch afterwards before the main team session started. His reaction to the drills was a very positive one; he said this was a much better way to practise free-kicks. Mo had a brilliant session because he got Alisson as the goalkeeper.

There was this sound buzzing out of the speakers and with their focus they needed to shut up this sound. Wow, that's training. It's about creating a mindset. In the meantime, Alisson had to do everything to distract him. He was jumping left and right, telling him he knew where he wanted to go. Mo said he never felt so much pressure before a penalty because it was Ali! Training with the best pushes you to your limits. I walked off the pitch with Ali and told him it was great that we organised so he could go directly from Brazil into Madrid with his family for those ten days to avoid quarantine. He said, "I paid you and Jürgen back with my performance." I smiled and said, "Very true – you saved our arses once more!" Despite the positivity, we had a feeling something wasn't right in our way of play. Opposition just came out of our counter-press too often, especially on our right side – we'd felt this many times with Felix and Lemar. We had to address it and had to address it now, without losing the determination to make it into the box with five players.

It was United next and with their individual class and speed, we couldn't make it an individual game. When you talk about United, you talk about speed. If they beat us, it should be through their merits not because we are badly positioned. It was a big game. Bruno Fernandes needed to be stopped as high as possible on the pitch so he couldn't distribute the passes that would hurt us. Marcus Rashford and Cristiano Ronaldo would be waiting for these moments. How should we do it? Follow the situation quicker so we are all in better, higher positions when we lose the ball. We had to stay together as a team – wherever we were on the pitch we needed to be together. One of our first and most decisive principles. A compact formation only works when you are aggressive with it. Virgil and Joel had stayed too deep too often recently. Against one 'lonely' striker they were always very good, but when there were two strikers deeper or floating it was much harder because they had to communicate quickly and clearly with the others in front of them, or man-mark. Secondly, we had to push up towards the edge where many times the counter-attack started because of their free players. In football you always gain in certain principles and lose in others. That's how you evolve, that's how football works. You gain habits and with these habits others become less influential.

So on the Saturday, the day before United with the wind blowing as always around AXA, we sat in the manager's office and went through our options with Fabinho missing. His knee was still swollen after the challenge in the Atletico match. Maybe we should go to 4-4-2 with our four main front players and have a 'double six' to control Fernandes' movements better. Eventually we decided to stick with our 4-3-3 structure and principles, but it was a clear option if we needed to change. We opted to change Ibou for Joel and Jota for Sadio. We kept Naby, Milner and Hendo as our midfield three.

It was getting darker earlier now; the floodlights were on and it was only 10 to four in the afternoon. The tactical meeting started in the U23 press room at 4pm and Jürgen made clear that what the media was trying to do wasn't right: because of their signings, they tried to make this game a make-or-break for them. We went through all our pressing moments on the pitch. Goal-kick press, high press, midfield press, deep press, throw-in press. The attitude and body language of our starters was aggressive. We took some doubts away for Hendo and Virgil, who would have to be man-orientated to Bruno and Cristiano. Then we focused on all our offensive ideas with extra attention to the movements of our strikers. We knew and felt it would be hard for Scott McTominay and Fred to control the spaces on the inside.

We'd spent 20 minutes showing the boys how we could protect ourselves better, quicker and higher. First we walked through it to make sure the points were clear. I love these moments of 'extra' tactical work, correcting those who don't move in a coordinated way, correcting those who don't apply our principles with all they have. Constantly stimulating the search for a perfect and connected counter-press. We have to be creative in our planning; sometimes we have one day to prepare for the game, to correct our way, to introduce new ideas. Preparing for United, we had two days to do this, but as I said, recovery and performance go hand-in-hand and our intuition was important in these moments.

Vitor is massive for us in this aspect; he controls the timings, the recovery, the planning, always with the idea that we want our players hungry for the next exercise, for the next day. Being ready to compete with full energy in the first, the second, the 20th and the 38th game. You can imagine that this takes a lot of planning and thinking. It's one thing if you play to get a top-four spot and another playing to become champions. They are really two different worlds and we need players and a style for this – players and a style which can reach consistency. I always felt that we needed to improve our offensive positional game to reach this; we played with much more patience, calmness and connection.

In Jürgen's last meeting, he told the boys that it looked like United were never happy when they played us. They always wanted to use this game to sort everything. We were different, we wanted to squeeze everything out of this amazing situation we had here. We just didn't have time to waste. We had the magical formula pressing-wise, mixing that up with outstanding attitude. Everyone should feel responsible for defending because not conceding is a very important tool for winning football matches. Because of this we should go the few yards with all we have. "That's the little contract we signed: I give you all the freedom to go forward defensively." The difference maker is to progress them to the spaces where maybe they were not as strong as other areas. All with the idea to fill the box with five players and one crosser, meaning there are four players left to protect ourselves in a very huge space. This means one-v-one situations – that's not a problem because it's our strength. But what's most important is to step up in each position, so we are protected better. Let's try to calm the stadium down with our football. It was clear we were going to compete.

"You Scouse bastards," the fans chanted at us as we arrived at the stadium. I thought to myself: but we'll leave here as Scouse winners today. And so it proved. Final no9, 5-0 on a historic occasion for us at United. A dark day for them, another three points for us. I was lost for words, to be honest. We wanted to write our own history, Jürgen said after the game, and we did. This one definitely went into the history books.

I will try to capture what we wanted and what we ultimately saw. When we practised our finishing two days before the game, this was exactly what you wanted to see, low in the corners with speed. Searching for clinical, quick finishes, always ready for the rebound. Our front three were like the velociraptors in Jurassic Park. We started the game with a real offensive plan. How Bobby connected the game inside and moved to open spaces for Diogo and Mo was impressive. Harry Maguire and Victor Lindelof never felt comfortable jumping with him, so we were always able to have an advantage in the centre and, at the same time, Diogo and Mo used the space that was being freed from Bobby to attack the centre. One goal for Diogo, three for Mo and a world-class game from Bobby. With a striker like Bobby, everything becomes easier. We scored some incredible team-play goals. The low crosses after our inside-play worked out perfectly, with Jota sliding in for the second goal.

Making it 4-0 just before half-time was a game-decider. At half-time Jürgen literally said, "What do you guys want? In five years we will discuss how this could have happened, or that they have to discuss how this could have happened." All the boys understood what he was saying: we needed to improve in the second half! We showed images where we played well, insisted in our plan to find the centre and speed up with movements and options everywhere. I was so pleased for Ibou after he had an incredible game because it wasn't easy to come into the team against United. But my highlight of the day was Hendo playing the first pass forward to isolate Mo in front of David De Gea.

The new speaker we had played music so hard after the game – as loud as the Atletico stadium after they made it 2-2. "Musica!" the boys normally scream after a big win. On the bus Jürgen and myself made a line-up for the Preston League Cup game. It meant Vitor could now organise with Barry Lewtas the game time for the following day's U23 match. We would see the surprise of the last international period at Preston... Harvey Blair.

'THERE IS NO SUBSTITUTE FOR COMPETITION IN TRAINING, IT DRIVES ALL ATHLETES TO LEVELS THEY COULDN'T EVEN DREAM OF'

WEEK 13

"ONE PLAYING FOR ELEVEN"

THE DAY AFTER UNITED AT AXA AND I WAS TRYING desperately to avoid Mo and Virgil…

Andreas told me just before going on the pitch that Virgil was asking for me. I spotted the two of them coming towards me from my right, so I quickly manoeuvred to my left. The whole morning was like a game of Pac-Man, but it was done with a big smile on our faces. They wanted to know their plan, whether they'd be given a day off with the League Cup fixture. Even when they were doing the 2 x 10-minute jogging session, Virgil called me to come over – I couldn't stop laughing.

More importantly, I went to find James Milner after he'd had to come off at Old Trafford with an injury. I found him on the bed in the treatment room. He'd just had his scan: four to six weeks, which ruled him out until after the international break. I told him in that case, he should still stay really close to the team, to the dressing room, to our games. This is how Jürgen wants it. He is our voice and our values in the changing room. My title is assistant-manager, but you could give this title to James as well.

We really trained with the subs from Old Trafford on the Monday, preparing them for Preston. We created a specific rondo to stimulate counter-pressing with following higher, quicker and better. Repetition, repetition, repetition. The boys trained really, really hard and looked hungry and confident. In our analysis meeting I paid extra attention to the details of the opponent as on Tuesday, I'd be back on press duty and would do the press conference. I always do an interview with club media half-an-hour before to give them the first answers but also then ask them to help prepare me to do a few 'uncomfortable' questions off camera. If we ask our players to train, why should that not also count for managers and coaches? "Our game needs freshness, we want our players to be unpredictable, we want them to feel free to attack," I told the reporters. "It's really important that this freshness is there. We want to attack tomorrow's game. That's the only thing that counts and the only way to press how we press is with players who are fully, fully ready to do that. I'm 100 per cent [that] in each game in this cup we're going to play our way and with the commitment of our players."

After the press conference was done, we held our pre-match meeting with the boys. It was a short one because 'It's raining inside,' Jürgen joked – there was a leak in the meeting room just in front of the first row. The boss said that if they thought we didn't respect the competition, they didn't know us, we would show what we wanted on the pitch. We had to be ready to fight, especially with the weather like this. We couldn't control everything against a long-ball team but there was always one who needs to play the long ball – that's what we could influence. Championship teams historically are good at set-pieces, so make sure we are spot on. "Enjoy and show that we are Liverpool," said the boss.

We took the bus to Preston on matchday and the mood was good. We were wearing new Nike tracksuits for this game, but they obviously sent the wrong sizes because everyone was looking like they were going to jump outside a plane. "The 80s are back," I said to Ray. Ray got a lot of stick, which is always good for the mood because he can handle it and respond with a joke like no-one else can. Jürgen and I observed when everyone was preparing to go out for the warm-up that the young boys were great in the dressing room, they put on their boots and were ready to go, in comparison to all the seniors who need much longer to go through their routines of strappings, pre-activation and massages.

It was a tough game but we saw it through to get a 2-0 win at Preston. Only the ones who've played in England know how hard it is to play in these away cup games when it's windy, rainy and cold against Championship opposition. It's one of the toughest competitions in world football, and sometimes I think these teams are made to knock out the big ones in cup competitions. We didn't play particularly well but what we did was we improved inside the game. The boys found rhythm, they needed this. What was crucial was how we re-organised our dynamics on the right side in relation to the qualities of Ox, Neco and Harvey Blair. Like this, we could create and use spaces more often and better. At the same time we were better protected with one more player inside behind the ball.

When we brought Conor Bradley on, this gave us even more energy. The difference between good and bad is many times only about five metres, which is how Cruyff once explained it. For us, Liverpool FC, it's many times five metres forward – our way, the offensive way.

We scored our first goal over the right side with a low cross from Neco towards Taki, who finished typically. Divock then finished with an acrobatic back-heel for the decisive second goal and I told him after the game that was like a scorpion-kick. In the press conference I'd said Divock is a world-class finisher and he proved that once more. After the game I asked Jürgen after he'd finished speaking with the boys, "Where is our best player?" Tyler Morton wasn't in the dressing room. I went outside and he was still talking to the press in the Lancashire rain. So great to see. He has this capacity to put everyone on the wrong foot, to mislead, to trick, to fool. He shows to play to the left but plays to the right. He shows that he is going to pass but turns out to the other side. I love it. Against deep teams this is a characteristic that makes a big difference, otherwise you will only play from left to right. Harvey Blair also made his debut, as did Elijah Dixon-Bonner, who came onto the pitch for the closing minutes of the game. We saw that Harvey needs to train more often with the first team but when he came off we said he should be proud of making his debut.

Last eight of the cup and we'd won our four consecutive away games after the international break. Scored 15, conceded two and three clean sheets. As a coach you can't wish for much more. We used the Thursday session to create responsibility in training. I spoke with Conall and Andreas about how we had to keep surprising our 'main guns' in the warm-ups. So, we started with races where they had to sprint and put a cone on top of a pole and then score in a mini-goal. There was fire in the eyes and we were only minutes into the session! Without this commitment and hard work we are no-one.

United have some of the best players in the world but perhaps not the best 'team'; for our next opponent Brighton, this was exactly the opposite. We were going to play against a team who are fifth in the league. City had only 52 per cent possession against them the week before and they had to score and win the game with two counter-attacks. That says everything. City fought for each ball with so much energy because Brighton have good technicians, they are calm everywhere on the pitch – especially from out the back – and last season we struggled with them. A lot. It cost us five points. Luckily we were a different animal now, but we had run too much without finding the chance to win the ball, not being together enough in the centre of the pitch, so the set-up of our midfield would be crucial. One part of the game always influences the other.

Because of injuries we didn't have too many midfielders left who could control both parts of the game. Now we needed these little victories by winning a challenge early on in the game, we needed these little winners in the middle of the game while being compact. We don't need to solve problems that don't exist anymore, but we had to realise and look in the mirror now facing them again. We couldn't be too open again. In the tactical training we had to correct this because we were making the same mistakes as against City, who have a similar set-up. Curtis, especially, was defending too deep. The secret against this Brighton team was not letting Yves Bissouma and Adam Lallana switch the game and Curtis and Naby would have to chase them from the blind side to steal the ball and play the first pass forward. We wanted momentum in the game and this is only possible when you steal balls. When you run a lot but you can't find the challenge, that's when you never gain momentum. You lose energy. They knew we were different so maybe they would play the long ball earlier and more often. Also, we'd changed our pressing dynamics this season, so we were hopeful that would not create the same upset.

The 'first pass forward' was such a big part of us by this point and Jürgen started the meeting with it. Even when we can't continue, it gives us direction in the game and many times we win the ball immediately back again with our counter-press. Jürgen continued with: "If we want to attack the centre we need options there." Against Man United we created so many questions for Fred and McTominay, we constantly had this natural overload behind them and we needed to do the same against Brighton's three midfielders. It's becoming a natural skill now that we move an extra midfielder between the lines; it's clear and an efficient dynamic. We'd use the width to open the centre up because in the past we were – in some games – too predictable when it came to our positional game. We trained 'surprise runs' in behind their last line. Virgil connected with Mo to play the ball over the top while Mo was moving from outside in behind. Same for Ibou with Sadio.

On the way home from training on Thursday I was stopped at the petrol station by some fans. You know that's a sign the team is doing well. One fan told me: "I didn't realise you were that tall, Pep!" I said to him that's what happens when you work with Jürgen – everything that the rest does looks a little smaller. I cherish these moments and interactions with fans because, quite honestly, you never know how long they will last in football.

The day before the Brighton game it was again windy and raining, but we had 20 people involved in the staff football game. It created such a good atmosphere. Even the Doc was in – and he scored and was so surprised by it. It was funny to see his eyes getting so big when he celebrated. We played 15 minutes longer than normal to give me and the gaffer time to create a proper comeback... It has some advantages being the boss. On the bus to the hotel on Friday afternoon we were all reading Jamie Carragher's interview with Arrigo Sacchi. I couldn't have been prouder of the words he'd chosen. It started with: "This Liverpool team is a masterpiece. You see one playing for eleven, while other teams are eleven playing for themselves. Eighty per cent of the time, they are moving when they have the ball. [Our outside triangles give this coordinated movement]. Football is about collective intelligence." About the Milan team of the past he said: "I knew it was impossible that we couldn't attack and thought it was better to attack than to be attacked. Having possession, you learn more.

You are the boss of the ball. And the closer to the opposition goal you win back the ball, the higher the chance of scoring." It could be us – LFC's coaching staff – discussing football. It was one of the best interviews I'd read in the last few years. He is one of life's biggest inspirations for football coaches.

In the team meeting at The Titanic, Jürgen started by telling the boys we were a better team than when we'd won silverware. "A clear structure plus the consistency of you guys is what made this happen. We want to go always to the next gear, always. We have to be ready to suffer, when we get outplayed we chase them from behind, which top team is doing that? When we do this, we earn the right to become successful this year. Mix our attacking tools up, that's always a sign for a good game. Don't forget our surprise runs in behind their line. Counter-press them with all we have, like a swarm."

However, the outcome of the game was two points dropped. It finished 2-2 against a lively Brighton after we lost control of it. For me, this game had two faces: before the injury of Naby and after. We had momentum during the opening stages, which resulted in two incredible goals: Hendo from the edge of the box and Sadio with a header after a beautiful cross from Ox. But we weren't compact as a collective in the second half, we weren't protecting each other, we weren't intelligent collectively, as Sacchi would describe it. And when we found challenges, we lost them. To win games you need to dominate midfield offensively and defensively, and everyone, the whole team is responsible for this. Brighton deserved a point from this game – they outplayed our midfield too often. We couldn't stop their connections and with this we opened up spaces between our lines, which they used and they overloaded against Virgil and Ibou with runs into the gaps around them.

That said, we did have two incredible goals disallowed, with Mo moving from outside to inside to reach Sadio's pass and round the goalkeeper and, earlier in the game, Sadio pressing the goalkeeper and scoring.

Still, it was hugely disappointing to have dropped points. My head was down after the game while eating some rice, salad and fish as Adam Lallana came to say hello. I asked him if he could stop man-marking Hendo. He laughed and said it was necessary. Adam was one of the fathers of our successful style by always setting standards, being vocal and giving energy to the pressing. It was really great to see him. He said hello to everyone and walked around as if he was still one of us – at least that's how it feels, I guess. What worried me the most was Naby's injury. At home that night it was causing me a real headache. In three days Atletico Madrid were coming to Anfield. We needed to find a solution to our midfield issues. We needed to speak to the medical guys to see if Thiago and Fabinho could step up and be ready. Atletico would be coming to us with a point to prove.

WEEK 14

LIVERPOOL'S LAB

ON THE DAY NUNO ESPIRITO SANTO WAS SACKED AT Tottenham Hotspur, we had our talent group training again. Harvey Blair was in. So too were Owen and Conor and so on. Vitor and I, we call it "Liverpool's lab." It gives us time to experiment with new exercises and ideas we later can implement into our first-team training. But coming back to the sacking of

Nuno, I realised more and more that if it's not clear at a club about where they want to go, it's impossible for a coach to deliver. If it's not clear what a club stands for, it's like a 'prayer without an end'. A club with the best training and game facilities in world football, the club which stood for a typical London offensive style, must be a sleeping giant. They must be. 'The king is dead, long live the king' is what they say, and yes, when I watched Sky Sports a few hours after Nuno's dismissal it said Antonio Conte was ready to step in. Conte's energy and willpower would be drilled into that team, it would be a different animal when we played them. It was unlucky for many teams who hadn't played Tottenham already.

I walked with Jürgen over to the talent group session; it was on the 'C' pitch on the other side of our complex. The U18 and U23 coaches were watching along and listening to Vitor's explanations. Like this you create a club culture: first-team and youth-team staff together on one pitch, training the best talents. Jürgen always says, "Life is about relationships" and he spoke for a while with Marc Bridge-Wilkinson, our U19 coach. He had the UEFA Youth League game against Atletico on the Wednesday afternoon, so something like this must give him a great boost. The session was quick and the exercises worked really well. We watched Luke Chambers excelling – this boy has everything to become one of us.

Later that day we worked with our team on stopping counter-attacks and following to be well-protected. Our attackers had to finish three or four balls and then react as a unit to hunt it back when I threw a new ball into the last line. The last line was waiting in formation next to the goal and they then tried with this new ball to score in a goal that was positioned on the halfway line. It's a great game to concentrate on stopping counter-attacks. I pushed Fabinho and Thiago into the session; after a little pushing, medical confirmed it was okay and they were good to go. It rained hard, it was cold and it's on these days we see who our real passionate players are, who are the real characters. In sport it's about maximum concentration and maximum commitment – these two will define who you are.

"We misunderstood our 2-0 lead against Brighton," Jürgen told me after training in his office. "We lost concentration, we lost structure," I said. Jürgen had one of his important meetings with the team and made sure everyone understood: this season was one of long steps and long breaths. I met with Hendo and we discussed how to deal better when we were in moments where we lost control; how to get the team reorganised. I told him we didn't need to be angels, there are ways to take control again to put the team back together with a common plan. "Balance the intensity," is how Diego Simeone puts it; take a moment to speak with everyone. When our forwards want to go forward and our defenders want to go backwards it's a clear sign things will not end well. They are the moments we can – and should – avoid.

Jürgen met with Virgil in his office, one boss to the other. He took him in the office to chat as he was really disappointed after Brighton, like all of our main guns were but maybe a little bit more. When I knocked on the door, Jürgen told me to come in but I replied, "I'll only come in when Virgil is smiling!" He laughed and told me, "I'm calm now, Pep. Let's get qualified on Wednesday." There is so much passion inside and outside this club for this European competition and with this comes responsibility. We wanted to qualify for the first time ever by winning all of the first four matches. We'd come close the season before but lost against Atalanta at home in the fourth game.

But this year's good situation shouldn't turn into a disadvantage. We would have to play this game with tactical discipline as though it was a European Cup final. Nothing less, otherwise we would lose the fight. We'd done the work in training, so it was about dedication now. We knew we would need to be very brave against a defensive and street-fighting side. We needed to position ourselves better and higher with the ball. When necessary we would pay back with our football, but never with emotion.

Tuesday meant we could focus on ourselves in training as we had an extra day, so we made clear to Sadio and Mo we would need them as a fourth midfielder when we needed to fill up spaces against Atletico. "Let's underline our intentions, nobody should be alone in our team," Jürgen said. "Help the guy who is under pressure. We will need to go to our limit when we are in our defensive mood." Offensively we corrected the opposite triangle to pick up higher and better positions, this was in order to break down the 5-3-2 system. A lot of things you can and should train, but it's that Einstein quote again: 'Logic gets you from A to B, but imagination will get you everywhere'. This part is what gives colour to our game. Logical patterns are so important but the spontaneous, the intuition and the talent will make these logical patterns unpredictable. Bill Shankly said it like this: you need eight to carry and three to play the piano. Pete, Jürgen and I discussed before our meeting that we had to keep giving freedom to Mo, Sadio and Jota where they can move and act. The others have to adapt to them, carrying the piano. For example, if Mo is wide, Trent then comes and plays inside next to Fabinho respecting the outside triangle.

But that afternoon our plans took a blow. I thought to myself: there must be a witch sitting somewhere and causing our injuries! It's Murphy's Law, we could be in a Will Ferrell film… Curtis accidentally got Ox's finger in his eye in a challenge and he had to go to the hospital immediately. Initial diagnosis told us he would be missing for sure for the next two games. He would have started against Atletico and was one of the only fit midfielders left, so it meant Ox would come into the team.

This part of the season is where you are creating a foundation, a base. What values are we creating? How do we respond to adversity? How are we creating a positive inner-voice within our players? That's what would be crucial when the finals came around the corner. It was the base that could allow us to go on and be decisive.

On game day, Jürgen started the meeting in The Titanic with the words: "We have to be in a mood to make our set-pieces decisive." It was two hours before the game was due to start and it was freezing cold outside. "We have to be in a mood to make it our fight – not theirs. There will be three scenarios: first one, we dominate; second one, they dominate; and the third one, it's an open game. In all three scenarios we have to defend with a tactical discipline and our emotion. Yes, we can combine these two. Not one of our front three of Sadio, Jota or Mo can be outplayed tonight. When they pass us, we chase them from behind, so not one of our team members is alone versus Felix or versus Koke. With the ball, be brave, play forward, we will be free more often than we think we will be. Use our bodies to protect the ball. Our stadium has the best atmosphere in the world but only if we set them on fire. Fireworks we need, fireworks of counter-pressing. There is not one team better than us at chasing them in packs everywhere and from everywhere on the pitch."

We later heard Milner repeating the boss's message to the

team from our coaches room when they came back in from the warm-up. And it did the trick: final no4 in the Champions League ended in a 2-0 Anfield win against Atletico Madrid. Job done, qualification secured… and how. Fabinho, back as the no6, made everything more stable; he is 'the Lighthouse', he gives direction and orientation to the others. The team was together and higher on the pitch because of our centre-backs directing the tempo of our positional game better. In the previous games we'd felt they were too deep, which, in turn, made the others be deeper as well to give them passing options. It's difficult to break down teams like Atletico, but Virgil could step forward each time he was 'free'; Joel stepped into midfield time after time. It was the 'best' game our centre-halves had had so far. I always think when our first phase of build-up is good, we will play a good offensive game. The same goes for our first phase of pressing.

For the first goal Trent won the ball, played the first pass forward to Hendo and the outside triangle combined, ending with a first-time cross from Trent, who was inside next to Fabinho. Jota headed the ball in. The way he puts his body behind the ball ready to head is incredible. "You have these days," Diogo had told me with a big smile on the Monday after the finishing session. He finished one ball after the other from the most difficult positions.

Trent played much more easily as a second no6 inside, I loved it. Jota and Sadio were constantly interchanging, which created doubt behind Angel Correa, Koke and Rodrigo De Paul. Sadio kept the most difficult balls under the highest pressure and they tried to stop him with all they had. They tried again in midfield as Sadio took the ball out of the air, in a way only he can keep it, turned away in midfield and moved the ball to Hendo, who pushed himself higher. Trent came inside and fired a shot and Sadio tapped in. Brave football. Two-nil after 20 minutes at home, Anfield explodes. Fireworks. Our starts had been incredible since the international break. Felipe stopped another counter-attack of ours, but Danny Makkelie, the Dutch ref, didn't accept it and showed him a straight red card. Only one thing could stop us in this game and it was a red card on our side. We took Sadio off at half-time to prevent this from happening. It was not that we didn't trust him to play with the yellow, but we were concerned about what could happen. It isn't easy for players when we make these decisions, but it wasn't the first time and would not be the last time we'd make a decision like this for the team. Milner, who was injured but with us, spoke with Sadio, which showed our group is so close and the respect for each other is huge.

It was fair to say our front three played the piano so well that night… and so did the eight who carried it!

There was one more game to go before the international break, but it'd be a tough one: West Ham away. As our group reconvened to begin preparing for that trip to London, the gloves and hats were on as we huddled outside the training centre. It was beginning to get colder. Winter was on the way. Jürgen always opens the first match-specific session in the same manner and this time he looked back to Madrid and immediately forward to West Ham.

We speak a lot when things don't go well, so we have to speak also when it goes well: "Qualification in this group, this early, is a big compliment to all you players. But we have to look forward: West Ham has a combination of strength and power with a few real technical players which makes them hard to beat. They deserve to be in the spot they are, they can make the game but also can transform easily to a counter-attacking side. There are two reasons why they have collected so many points. First of all, teams are getting surprised by their quality, which can't happen with us because you can't get surprised when we tell and show you. They kept the team together, added Kurt Zouma and increased their intensity. Secondly, it's their quality and variability up front: Michail Antonio is a monster in the air and quick on the counter; Said Benrahma is a superb dribbler and quick on the counter; they signed Jarrod Bowen, the Mo Salah of the Championship; Pablo Fornals is a technical Spanish international who can launch counter-attacks. As a team they have developed so much in the last two years, probably the most of any Premier League team. They improved as a group and that explains the positive run they are on."

In our meeting with Pete, Vitor and Jürgen, we discussed their build-up because it was really tricky. They opened the pitch in width with the four defenders as a line, so you could get stretched as a team when you wanted to press them early and quickly. We decided to prepare our pressing situations by luring them in until Zouma or Angelo Ogbonna really showed where they were going to play. This would give time for us to be compact and create 100 per cent pressing situations. They normally sent the passes from the back to the front-four. We had to show compactness in each line against them, especially in our last line with their different qualities. This would be the secret to having a good game: compactness in the last line so Fabinho could find and make challenges. Joel and Virgil should be as lively again with the ball, otherwise we'd be attacking with only eight players and we all knew you needed one or two of these eight to be protected against counter-attacks.

But two days after Atletico and two days before West Ham,

our session was all about recovery. When you recover your players you want them to get focused, you train concentration. Prep for the next game has started, physically and emotionally. We start with a five-v-two rondo, this is the biggest number we play rondos in. Many teams play six-v-two or seven-v-two, but we believe players don't need to move enough to create options everywhere. We continued the session with a four-v-four game with six of our starters around on one-touch. The starters who are on second-day recovery have to be at maximum concentration to create a free player in the inside. Virgil played one incredible splitting pass after another, but Hendo saw this and topped him with a killer pass taking all four players out. This natural competition between our players is what makes sure we are improving.

And if you think that we'd played two years ago against Atletico and now we'd played them twice in two weeks, you'd see we had improved. Again. Our way of play forces this individual development; our training methodology forces this individual development. We want our players to be with their whole body in training. Not just the legs and the lungs – the entire body. There is no substitute for competition in training, it drives all athletes to levels they couldn't even dream of.

In the tactical training the starting 11 was so strong that we finished training early and skipped parts. We were ready. On our pre-match walk on the Sunday morning, we walked around Canary Wharf. We had runners passing us by, some were surprised to see us but most just go about their lives. Typical London… Although one guy had us all laughing when he shouted, "Oh shit – that's Mo Salah!" as he went by. Virgil and Ali discussed if they would run after their careers are over… Jürgen joked, "Yes, to the BBQ and back!" The boys had their night out scheduled for after the game. Time was flying. We were almost at the last international break of 2021 and if we needed a little bit more motivation, Chelsea's draw at home to Burnley the day before should do that. James Milner had travelled down with us and I was sure he'd be telling the lads that on our way to the stadium.

But final no11 saw us lose a game for the first time in seven months. We had been unbeaten since April of 2021 – which was an incredible run – but it was ended by a team ready to counter-attack us, a team set up for set-pieces. They shoved their finger in the part that hurts the most and it was still painful as I wrote my notes for this book afterwards. Suffering a goal early is never easy, but how we conceded left a really bad taste. We felt again, but this time in a negative way, that set-pieces are decisive in the Premier League. Ali got blocked from a corner and then obstructed by Ogbonna. He couldn't punch the ball away because the arm of Ogbonna was stopping his, but we reacted well and played one of our better games between the lines, freeing Mo, Sadio or Diogo to turn and attack the centre. We stopped the counter-attacks with good positioning in protection and, when necessary, with our legs sprinting back 60 yards.

At the end of the first half Sadio protected the ball, turned and got a free-kick on the edge of the box. Trent got into his zone and our set-up with Hendo and Mo created the doubt necessary... Over the wall, perfectly-executed, 1-1, half-time. I was happy for Trent and for Niklas at neuro11. Hopefully more of these situations would prove decisive.

In the second half we lost so many unnecessary balls, we positioned ourselves in a suicidal situation with both Hendo and Ox being high up the pitch, leaving Fab in such a big space. This combination of missing easy passes and bad positioning is just not allowed for a team with our qualities. They scored twice in seven minutes, the second from a counter we could have stopped easily – we just needed to make a last step to create a challenge – but Bowen dribbled between three of our players. These moments are not acceptable and if you see the game as a final, it would not have happened. The third was again from a corner, which resulted from a counter-attack. It's always hard to win a game when the other team scores twice from a set-piece but it would still have been possible. We changed and brought on Thiago, Taki and Divock and went for a 4-4-2 for the last 15 minutes with Divock and Taki as the strikers and Mo and Sadio as the wingers. All in. Divock scored to make it 3-2 with a world-class finish, turning with the ball out of the air and volleying with his left. Sadio got a massive chance at the end to equalise when he came in front of Lukasz Fabianski with a clear header.

We are not silly, we know we can lose games. But it should be because the other team merits it fully and not because of us being sloppy and inviting counter-attacks. We had to learn and had to learn quickly. That said, the boys would still have their night out – and we wanted them to enjoy it because it was a long, long time ago that something like this would be possible for them and for the unity of the team, it always provides a boost. We know that in the end the best team – and the team with the most spirit – would win this Premier League. For myself, I knew a few tough days were waiting. Losing never becomes easy, especially when you have a lot of time to think during the international break.

‘WE DON’T NEED TO BE THE BEST TEAM ON THIS PLANET BUT WE NEED TO BE THE TEAM WHO CAN BEAT THE BEST TEAM ON THIS PLANET’

WEEK 15

GETAWAY

I TOOK MY FAMILY AWAY TO TENERIFE TO SPEND some real time together during the first week of the break. I believe you need to deserve holidays to be able to enjoy them – and I had hoped to go with 26 games unbeaten to deserve a celebration. Thanks for that, West Ham!

While I was there, I checked three times in which division Tenerife FC were, so you can imagine we had a lovely time together! The reason why I only went on holiday then is because we had the most intense period of games coming up. It creates balance for me and my family. But I'm not sure what's more relaxing: going on holiday with the mother-in-law or the intense game-programme in front of us!

That's a joke, I promise. She is a lovely grandmother for our children and I love and adore you, Marianne!

WEEK 16

HOW ANGRY CAN WE BE?

IT WAS MORE THAN A WEEK WITHOUT SEEING, speaking to or texting each other. It was probably the longest period in the last three or four seasons. Jürgen and I sat in the boss's office, discussing the last week and West Ham. I guess we all had to get over what happened at the London Stadium and knew some time for ourselves would work best. Jürgen started our chat with: "One of the oldest football rules, maybe even Shankly said it, is that offence wins you games and defence wins you championships. We need to show more commitment for defending." I replied: "The last step, changing a 50/50 into a 60/40. A little bit of a different attitude always makes a big difference. Consistent attitude." I always say fighting to become champions or fighting for a top-four spot are two worlds apart. Type of player, type of style, consistency. You could see Chelsea's consistency because they were defending really well. Everyone thinks about City's possession-based game but they were also defending really well.

We then went through the week ahead and the January transfer window. But most important of all, we went through the problems we had in the second half and how we can approach an immense Arsenal game at the weekend. Losing control in a game doesn't happen a lot. Even when we win we hate it, but when we lose it feels even worse. We needed five per cent more in the commitment of counter-pressing and, with this, we are the most difficult team in world football to play against. But without it we are vulnerable in the moment we lose the ball with so much space behind our last line against the better teams. We needed everyone in their best mood to stop more counter-attacks and, with this, avoid more set-pieces. We had one day to correct this in the meeting and in the training.

What we had wanted to create at the start of the season was a base from which we could attack the rest of the campaign. A foundation. We created that base, maybe not perfectly, but it was a foundation we could go with. We accepted it and we were going to use it. The rest of the season started now. Every three days was a game until the middle of January. Nine weeks, 17 games. We needed to be in it, the walls needed to stand strong after this. During a season, and especially after West Ham, we would have things we needed to improve – that's part of the process, that's always there. What attitude do we show in the challenges? Do we really commit? We needed to be good from the first until the last minute. One half isn't enough, a bad phase will cost you at this level. Consistency through organisation and commitment. So, no foul but 100 per cent challenge. Yes, if this ends up in a foul, okay, but try to challenge. How angry as a team can we be? Remember we want to be the team no-one wants to play against, legally aggressive. How could we make it uncomfortable for Arsenal? By chasing the opposition like someone desperately looking to go on a date. We don't need to be the best team on this planet but we need to be the team who can beat the best team on this planet. That's what Jürgen constantly stimulates: an angry team, a team which lives and loves to defend. We work day-by-day to sort these problems, to create this mindset again, because it doesn't come naturally. Always to make steps forward, literally and figuratively.

I was thinking about Cruyff's five metres again. The only mistake you can make many times is not going forward. Compactness is trainable, preparing pressing-triggers is trainable, closing easy-pass lanes into the centre is trainable, but causing the opposition real problems is only possible when the players want to make a difference in the last two metres of each press. Kill the pass they are playing during our press. Blocking a ball on the sideline only five minutes into the game, pressing the goalkeeper unexpectedly in the first five. These moments we have in our good games.

To be honest, as staff our own game to win is the one we play in the meetings, on the training pitch getting the right information across. If we win that game, there is a bigger chance the players will win theirs. When we started the week, we did one-touch combinations: after 15 passes they had to react on my signal to press Vitor or Pete, win the ball and finish with a quick transition on two small mini-goals. Every exercise was related to our chasing attitude, even a passing drill. We worked on stopping counter-attacks, making the challenge. I gave an example from West Ham when we didn't move forward into the challenge. I always threw the second ball around Ox and Thiago to give them this stimulus. With time, it became good. I shouted: "THIS – EXACTLY! This is the difference between winning and losing Premier League games."

We knew because of our injuries that Thiago and Ox would form the midfield, so it was great we could have them train together from the first day. The same for Sadio, Thiago and Kostas, our left-sided triangle. You always try to foster these relationships in these periods. Because it was still the international break and a lot of the boys were away with their countries, we had a big group of young guns training with us. We only had Thiago, Sadio, Ox, Ibou, Nat and Joel from our senior players. "Doubt in yourself creates more problems than going outside your comfort zone ever will do," I said to them. I gave Thiago a compliment in front of everyone about how he focuses in the warm-up. "That's the mentality and that's what makes the difference between a talent and a professional." I did it just to set the tone for everyone this week.

During training I used Sadio as the example of someone who wants to steal the ball from the centre-halves making the last step after he stole the ball from Joel's blind-side. I said to them that this was the difference between us and many other teams; most strikers of other teams just press to force them in a certain direction, whereas we press to steal the ball then and there. He did it once, he did it twice and I stopped the training and told all the young ones this is what we mean!

Sadio grew, of course. Mission accomplished. A compliment is so powerful, not only for the receiver but also to make clear to all the others what's good and what's not. The carrot is mightier than the stick, they say, and with time you hope that the seniors feel so strong that they give the young ones time and feedback. Here is how you create culture within a club. The session was so intense and quick for our young players because "a smooth sea never created a good sailor," as FD Roosevelt said. We put them 'in the jungle' is how we say it.

After training I continued to work with the young boys and encourage them to take their chances. I told them it's only possible when you see every day as a chance, if you believe in yourself, that you can do it. "Believing in yourself is a game – get good at that game because it will make the difference." I told them they earn that by working really, really hard and that this week ahead was all about getting used to the ball with the pressure and standards of first-team training and to adapt to our style again. "We have this Stefan [Bajcetic]," Vitor told me. "He is good, Pep. Have a close look. He plays with intelligence and insight in front of our defence during training." He normally played in the backline for the U18s but Jürgen immediately said he could reach the no6 for us. I was so happy because we'd searched for a while for a talented no6. Hopefully he could fill this position one day, but he was the surprise of this latest international break. You only get seven seconds to make a first impression on whether people feel positively or negatively about you, but as a footballer it's probably 70 minutes, so it was definitely a case of 'Well done, Stefan!'

On Tuesday, Pete, Jürgen and I had an interview with BT Sport about the famous old Liverpool Boot Room. It was the most interesting and pure interview I'd had for a while. Normally I would prepare for interviews, but this time I just wanted to react from my heart while talking about the club. Let them surprise me, I thought. When I walked into the cold and dark press room, Peter Hooton – the singer from The Farm and famously from Altogether Now – told me Jürgen had just called our situation here "Boot Room reloaded." We have the title for this book, I thought. We'll see, I guess. James and I were sending ideas to each other regularly throughout the season.

This week also saw two of the most talented young PSV Eindhoven coaches visit us. One of the guys, a 24-year-old skills coach, left me astonished when he'd called me a few months ago about the similarities he has nowadays to when I was in exactly the same job. We normally don't do these things but I invited them to come over. I felt I could help with the experience gained over these last 15 years away from PSV Eindhoven. Vitor talked to them about tactical periodisation, Nick Marshall and Alex Inglethorpe about Academy principles, Barry Lewtas about managing the transition process and Mark Leyland explained our analysis. Jürgen had walked in during Vitor's presentation and gave one of his strong speeches. The best moment was when Vitor started explaining the influence on team and players' performances through biological rhythm. Why I think this was the most important is because when we plan our schedule, we always search for consistency. So, for example, we try to keep a certain pattern in training in the days before the game. If we are in a busy period this is so important; for example, we had to play Arsenal and then we'd have two training days and Porto, a day off, two more training days and then Southampton, a day off, two training days and then Everton...you get the picture. So we try to find a biological rhythm two days before each game. Even if we need to give two days off, we try to find the right consistency for each phase of the season.

I also had the chance during this week to spend a morning with Alex Inglethorpe on the Academy side of our Kirkby site to catch up. Inside his office all the names of our talents are on the wall. He started with: "Pep, this Under-14 you will really like, he is quick and technical..." We know exactly what and how we want to have the Academy process – and it's proved it is working. During my year with the U16s, our team became so strong. Alex and Nick Marshall drive this Academy. Over the last eight years we made a return on selling Academy players but, importantly, we brought so many of them into our first team. There is huge respect between the two buildings and it is something we have to cherish. I try to keep this relationship strong, with Alex and Nick. We know we are 314 metres apart but together as one. Only 314 metres for players to get into our building, but for many it will take six to eight years to accomplish those 314 metres. One of the advantages of being so close to each other is that they can see it during each session they have.

The focus returned to Arsenal. They were on a strong run, ten games unbeaten, which equalled their best sequence under Mikel Arteta. [Goalkeeper] Aaron Ramsdale made a big difference with his distribution and Takehiro Tomiyasu was a great addition as a right defender. He drops and tries to attract our press and find a pass behind the last line. These two new faces plus a clear defensive structure – not as much based on the opposition anymore – made them so much stronger. The team was finally settled. A talent I really admire is Emile Smith Rowe – he has everything to reach the World Cup squad, in my opinion. We thought they would maybe change Martin Odegaard for Alexandre Lacazette to have more defensive stability, but in the end the structure stayed the same.

The night before the game during dinner in The Titanic hotel, Vitor, Jack, Jürgen and myself spoke about the most awkward situations we found ourselves in during presentations. I've had a few but the most strange one was for the Welsh FA when on the third row of the audience, with probably 500 coaches there, an older man fell asleep as I was talking. I couldn't stop noticing and thought three times about telling him to open his eyes. After 45 minutes of speaking, everyone started clapping, so I'm thinking: it wasn't that bad, then. At that moment [coach] Osian Roberts came on stage and I was desperate to tell him about the sleeping gentleman, but he started to thank me with nice words and said he had a typical Welsh present for me and the vice-president would hand it over... Next, the guy from the third row wakes up, stands up and gives me a box of Welsh cakes and liqueur. I later found out that he wasn't really a football guy, so that makes the memory less painful...

On matchday we joked about how Kostas warms up as though it's the game itself as we walked back to the dressing room. We made sure to the boys that our game plan was clear: we wanted them to think they could play, we wanted us to be more compact, especially with Jota holding the position a little bit longer which would automatically be more compact. The simple ideas are always the best ones, but it's as Einstein says: if you can't explain it simply, you don't understand it well enough. And until we can explain how we do it to the players, it takes us two or three days to find the exact right idea and words. With the ball we wanted four players in the build-up and four players between the lines in and around Partey and Lokonga. With four players in the build-up (Fab, Joel and Virgil plus one) one of them would jump to give us all the space to turn and speed up between the lines, or to switch quickly to the open space on the outside.

And we delivered. We were incredible under the floodlights. Final no12, 4-0 at home to a vastly-improved Arsenal. If it wasn't for Ramsdale the score could have been much higher. It was an outstanding performance, mature and decisive. "They looked how they looked because we played how we played," Jürgen said directly after the game. We came together from everywhere against a team that had been on a super run. They had five touches inside our box and Trent said, "This was exactly what we needed: a clean sheet and four goals. We couldn't have asked for more. First half we showed the aggression needed. It was flowing on the right side, I find myself in different positions now." His assist for Taki was the perfect team-play goal. Our pressing was from another level, it was the man-of-the-match in my opinion. Why? Because we were compact with and without the ball, it gave us time to be in perfect positions to press or to counter-press. Our front three all scored and Thiago and Ox as the no8s had shots from the edge and even inside the box. Trent and Kostas were constantly overlapping. Offensively we grew in the game. The aggression inside the stadium came from the bust-up between the benches; it made everyone want it a little bit more, I guess, and with everyone I mean everyone. The whole stadium threw themselves behind the team.

Not everything was perfect as we needed to correct Trent's positioning 20 minutes into the game – we had five players (Joel, Fab and Virgil plus two) in the build-up and only two between the lines too often. Thiago would drop to use his skillset at bringing the ball out but we couldn't take advantage with the spaces created because there were not enough options between the lines at these moments. But still, it wasn't a bad night's work.

'PEOPLE CAN RECOGNISE US WHEN WE PLAY. EVEN IF WE WORE DIFFERENT SHIRTS THEY WOULD KNOW AND FEEL IT'S A LIVERPOOL FC PERFORMANCE'

WEEK 17

"INFLAME THE STADIUM TODAY"

THE NOVEMBER INTERNATIONAL BREAK IN ENGLAND was one of many different faces. It was the week Steven Gerrard was appointed as Aston Villa manager and the red part of Merseyside was wanting two teams to win now; it was the week Michael Edwards officially announced he'd be saying goodbye; the week when Dean Smith got sacked by Villa and appointed to Norwich; the week when Eddie Howe stepped into Newcastle United; and the week when Antonio Conte was appointed at Tottenham. For us, the week presented a new set of challenges with Porto and Southampton to come at Anfield.

Ox had said after the Arsenal game, "I never thought I would enjoy so much the defensive part without playing outstanding on the ball." He was outstanding in pressing players from the blind side, counter-pressing them. In training last week I told one of the young ones, "Watch how Ox is pressing." He was really making steps and it was good he got a run of games. Everyone was so happy for him and Mark, our analyst, was helping a lot by giving clear images and corrections.

Before the first session of the week got underway, Jürgen gathered all the players and staff together outside the AXA to celebrate a special day: Ali got his 50th Premier League clean sheet against Arsenal, so Danielle – Jürgen's PA – organised a jersey with autographs and messages from all of the boys. Jürgen wrote a big '+1' on it, referring to the decisive headed goal Ali had scored at West Brom last season. I heard Joel saying, "I also have 50 clean sheets." Everyone was laughing. "Did you know, Trent, you got your 50th assist at the weekend?" Jürgen then asked. Trent looked surprised and said no. Millie immediately reacted: "He put it out there himself!" To which Joel responded with a big impression of Trent: "No, no, no – I didn't know!" As the team walked off to begin training, Jürgen told the boys: "Don't forget, when we defend like this we are a monster."

While we did rondos and the 1-2-3 game, Milner and Trent were together. The 1-2-3 game is a routine where you train your brain in relation to keeping the ball in the air. Two players go together and play the ball to each other; they tell their partner how many touches they are allowed in keeping the ball in the air and with this, they have to adapt their bodies quickly to control and return the ball. I explained to Millie we did this game after each training session during our time with the U16s and I always told Trent that if he beat me, he'd be ready for the first team. Millie responded, "So he's still not ready?" to which I laughed. I always made sure I beat him, even if it needed to happen with a little bit of cheating. He always demanded, "Another one, Pep, another one," and we played again. There were times the floodlights were turned off and we stood in the dark somewhere in the middle of the training ground.

Niklas from neuro11 sent me a text that morning to say that Trent had improved with 30cm better accuracy from his free-kicks. It wasn't a surprise he put the ball exactly on Sadio's head with the opening goal against Arsenal. I got all the reports later that night and Mo's accuracy, and an impressive consistency, was the best so far from all the takers. Probably better not to share with Hendo and Trent, I thought to myself! The perfect shot happens by itself, there is a low chance you score so don't feel any pressure. Mo, Trent and Hendo had to continue the routines three to five times after training. We were increasing the constant difficulty for them by going closer to the wall and goal.

The routines we tried, we gave them new ideas, but they took charge as the best ones should do. We gathered for the analysis of Porto after training. The best games we'd seen of Sergio Conceicao's side, they'd put their foot on the gas and pressed the opposition like mad. Raça and paixão are keywords in Porto's club philosophy, these go so well together with pressing. Raça means willpower, guts. Paixão means passion. That's how Sergio claimed results in recent years against big teams like Juve, City and Milan. Why he didn't against us, I don't know, but what I know is that the day after our game there, Sergio put the team in an 11 v 11 constantly pressing against the B team. He was unhappy with not pressing us, we heard later from their staff. What I know is that he said he anticipated it would be a completely different game, that they'd learned their lesson and improved in what was missing against us first time around. But the thing was, we'd improved as well.

Jürgen told the boys in the meeting that Porto were already 1-0 up from a motivation perspective, so not to allow them to have an advantage. "Don't let that happen that they have this advantage." It was 16-2 at this point. That's not a date, it was the score in recent years between ourselves and Porto… and probably 90 per cent of the goals we'd scored in five games had come at the Dragao. We felt Luis Diaz would be a challenge for protection and stopping counter-attacks. He is this street player who we really admired. We needed to be flexible and, at the same time, push up to be well-protected against him and the two strikers. I hoped the Anfield floodlights would turn us into a pressing monster again as that's the second-best way to stop counter-attacks.

Our approach was simple. "If we want to win, we have to win," Jürgen said in the meeting. Some had ten games in the past and some will have ten games in the future, which meant we'd rest the ones who'd play those ten games such as Fab and Virgil. We also opted for a safety-first decision with Hendo and Robbo coming back from injury... we'd have the most experienced bench ever and would use that to divide the intensity.

During this week we appointed John Hill as our new physical coach, bringing him up from the Academy. Another one from the inside, perfect. He would be more involved to control the gym programme. Vitor was still having problems with pronouncing the 'H', so Jürgen said to John: "When Vitor calls you don't worry – he can't say the 'H', so it will be John 'Ill!"

On matchday morning I watched the previous day's tactical MD-1 [matchday minus-one] session back together with Mark and discussed with him about showing Tyler a few clips to make sure of his defensive positioning when they outplay us on the outside. It's not easy to defend like Fabinho, but being in the same position should be a certainty. On the pitch it was cold, we went through our set-pieces and the substitutes did a rondo with Vitor. I always think, one of the best sounds in the world is when your kids are playing and having fun, or on game day when the players are laughing and interacting while playing rondos. This combination gives me the most confidence entering into a game.

Jürgen started the final team meeting with: "Whatever the people are saying from the outside isn't important – only what we think counts. We can surprise them. Nobody ever told us that we had to play football, that we had to win, that we had to score. We did all of this because we wanted to. We decide how we look at this game. Don't hold anything back. Commit to defending. It's Champions League, the floodlights are on, it's sold out. When we were young and they took the ball from us we started crying, that's the spirit I want to see tonight. The moment we feel it's right, we put them under the highest pressure."

And so Champions League final no5 ended in a deserved 2-0 win against my old club. We had 15 points from the 'group of death' and there was nothing more to say except it was quality. Beating Porto was a victory for our team and our squad, as well. The bench was so loud during all of the game encouraging our players, it made me really proud.

Thiago scored with a beautiful strike to get the decisive first goal and make it 1-0. Decisive because after that we felt free to play our football. It was great to see the goal came from a second phase of set-piece. We'd scored more goals from outside the box than any other team in the Champions League at that stage, so the shots from the edge of the box were paying off. In pre-season, we knew we had to improve our goalscoring variability. Tyler Morton also assisted Mo Salah, sending him into space with a long pass. Mo then netted with his typical characteristic dribble from outside going in, putting a defender on the floor and finishing cheekily at the first post. We were able to divide the intensity with our subs and rest Thiago, Mo, Sadio and give some important minutes to Robbo after his injury.

The day after the game, while Mo and Sadio were running around the pitch on their first-day recovery jog, I walked up to them and told them they were one assist away from becoming the pair who assisted most to each other in the history of Liverpool Football Club. Mo reacted immediately, saying that will be in the next game. I was happy about a lot of things so far in the season, but how these two had performed since pre-season made us lethal again. After the session we were in Jürgen's office with some big discussions going on. Tyler did his post-match interviews without a jacket on at a cold, cold Anfield. Some senior staff members weren't happy about it. Senior staff are always thinking what would be best for the young ones: spotlight yes or no, play yes or no, how can we protect them and at the same time give them the right impulses? The press office team guides this process brilliantly, I have to say. Trent did interviews when he was 18 and some players are ready for them, others we wait with. Discussions heated up but in the end I started laughing and said, "Let's put everything in perspective: if a jacket and a successful debut are our biggest problems we have (being almost in December) then we are in a good way, I think. Yesterday we inspired 200 boys 314 metres away – that's the most important victory we achieved."

But the focus now was on Southampton. We knew they played 4-4-2 – the best system to organise a defence – and that's what they did. A highly energetic team who try to overrun teams in the first 15 minutes of the game. The best example of this was against Aston Villa where they scored with their pressing only three minutes into the game and ended up getting a 1-0. They scored 75 per cent of their goals in the first 20 minutes, so our goal would be to take confidence away every time we had the ball, leading them to adjust their plan. Fabinho and Thiago would be crucial in this; they hardly ever miss the easy, quick passes and are constantly available to find or to create the free player, which is what we'd need. The more problems we could create, the more we would take their pressing confidence away. We had to force them in ugly situations, when we outplayed their press it'd feel almost like a counter-attack, so much space we would have to exploit. Ali would need to create three in the back and then quickly pass through their lines. It needed to be exactly like Arsenal, step-by-step taking confidence away from the opponent. We'd scored two goals with Ali starting the attack and five or six seconds later Sadio or Mo in front of the goalkeeper. We could open up teams within four passes, many other teams need many more passes to do that. "Knowing what they want to do gives us information about what we are going to do," Jürgen said in the meeting. "We need to increase the risk in our play the higher we come on the pitch. Making sure we push up in good positions to stop the counter-attacks."

I made sure in training Trent and Thiago knew about pushing up towards the edge when we broke their last line, but to do that it would be crucial that our no6s would attract Oriol Romeu and James Ward-Prowse to create space between the lines for our forwards to catch. Like this, our forwards could become 'snipers' again. We put two mannequins on the edge of the box during the session as a reference to push up to. Jürgen and myself simulated the positioning of two strikers and Virgil, Ibou and Fabinho had to protect while we were attacking.

Fabinho has the capacity to make the players around him better. It's really difficult to find players who have the talent to make the other ones flourish. Thiago would make sure the team would evolve and make the next step. That's what we needed because the teams around us had become stronger, they knew better how we play and they tried to destroy our way of football by putting certain tactics into the team. We'd bought a solution for the upcoming problems, hopefully.

Jürgen's first words in the final meeting with the boys were these: "Inflame the stadium today. The moment we don't have the ball we have to be intense, the stadium will need our energy. We can press longer and better than them because we mix it up with periods of real possession. There are always small margins when you speak about attitude. We don't doubt you guys, but how much are we willing to invest today? It's the third game in seven days, same hotel, same system, same message. Who should hold us back? Following up the attack is a big part of defending. We need to be smart and lively with our triangles, using our football brain to outplay them. And when we don't have the ball, inflame the stadium."

When we arrived at the stadium, Mark told us they'd gone with five-at-the-back. I immediately responded with: "Good, let them worry about us." It didn't surprise me, but it showed again 70 per cent of the teams change their system, or their plan, against us. But final no14 of our Premier League season ended 4-0 against a highly energetic Southampton. Ralph Hasenhuttl admitted after the game that we'd killed them with our moves in the first half in the centre. Our lively triangles were made to create space, to find space, independent of the opposition's structure. Robbo and Trent adapted constantly into the free spaces, inside or outside but always with a threat to overlap or to underlap. This was freedom within our principles. When both our full-backs get either assists or goals in a game, you know your positional game was right. Fabinho and Thiago were at the start of each attack, speeding up the tempo finding our forwards. We wanted active sixes and we got them; they held the key in exploiting all the space Southampton's last line left. Jota could free himself between the lines and made the box time and time again. He has this capacity to be in the right moment at the right time to finish our attacks. A 'sniper'. By this point, Jota, Mo and Sadio had scored 25 goals together so far, the highest trio in the Premier League. Thiago scored, again shooting from outside the box – a bit of a replica, again from second phase. That was his second goal in one week; he was on fire.

Jürgen's half-time talk was one full of mentality. "We need

a disciplined, grown-up game now. Clean sheet is the target. When we reach the final third, we need to have more overview and make better decisions, which sounds ridiculous because we scored three times in the first half but there is so much space we can exploit." In the second half we played towards the Kop. Sadio placed an angled shot from outside the box, but Alex McCarthy tipped it over with a worldie save. From the corner, though, it was Virgil and 4-0. Creating, using and making our set-pieces decisive, again. Shoot to create set-pieces; set-pieces to create second-phase. Our training ideas were paying off, so I was a proud man!

We also had the chance to bring Hendo's minutes up to 70 without any issues. Thiago was able to go to 60, Milner stepped up his fitness with 20 and Ox showed his discipline in midfield again with half-an-hour. Our new way of approaching corners this season was paying off – we had the second-most corners per game behind Man City with more than seven a game. Creating the highest corner-shots-per-game in the league. One goal every two games is average, but we were having one shot with every two corners, making us the highest in the league. We created a goal from seven per cent of corners – the highest in the league. And in terms of shots, the players with most in the league by this point were Mo, Sadio, Jota, Cristiano Ronaldo and Michail Antonio – three of the top five were our boys, not bad. A good day all-round.

On the Sunday we met at AXA. We were in the middle of an FSG / Jürgen Klopp club project. We had an excellent team behind the team, with clear tasks for each one, all of whom were obsessed to improve with real togetherness. We had stability in our squad, there was a core group, there was experience with a combination of leadership and discipline that creates the necessary continuity. We had talent from our own academy, a real brave inside-pathway and we always created space in our squad for young ones to make the next step within our way of football. But above all, the 'holy trinity' was installed: there was a strong relationship with the players and the fans, who all thrive with a never-give-up mentality. People can recognise us when we play. Even if we wore different shirts they would know and feel it's a Liverpool Football Club performance. It's a performance based on the '30 per cent mentality', a 'we want to have the ball' mentality, minimising the time by maximising the intensity. We want to be different than any other team in world football when we don't have the ball. Always working together and working 100 per cent with tempo and energy with only one target: creating special games and creating memories together.

But as always, we needed to think about the next step, so it was time to discuss future signings. Julian Ward, our new sporting director, Jürgen, Pete and myself met in a cold office. The lists were coming out: there were three players and one young talent we really liked. We made sure to explain what we needed, and what we wanted to make the team evolve. That's why we could be so clear in what type of player we wanted. It's all about our identity.

WEEK 18

FOOTBALL ASSASSINS

MERSEYSIDE DERBY WEEK WAS FINALLY HERE. I HAD the feeling that we should be like football assassins against Everton. Stay cool when they fight, use our football as the bullets. I was standing in front of Jürgen's desk when he spoke. It was clear: we'd need to control our emotions. Jürgen was in full spirit. Provocation only works when the one who receives it is intimidated. "It's a game where we can turn the season around," Rafael Benitez says. But not with us, I thought, because if we were intense and compact I felt they would struggle against us. "We are a better team than in the past derbies," Jürgen said, "We deal better with emotion."

Eight of the last nine games at Everton had been draws; I couldn't remember one game there – or even against United at Old Trafford – where we were really ourselves before this season. But we were a different animal now. With time we'd become convinced about what we did and who we were, the system was clear. The boss spoke with the team and said that we had to be intense, physical and emotional. In a football way we wanted to be assassins. It was about controlling the game: attack the game instead of attacking the goal; get control by putting them under pressure with and without the ball. We knew that if we put full pressure on and kept the ball in the first ten minutes the stadium could become frustrated. It's what we'd worked on.

Monday was the first official day of Claudio Taffarel as a member of our backroom team. As I've said before, at Liverpool Football Club we only announce signings, we don't speak about them. It was very important for everyone that this came out through the right

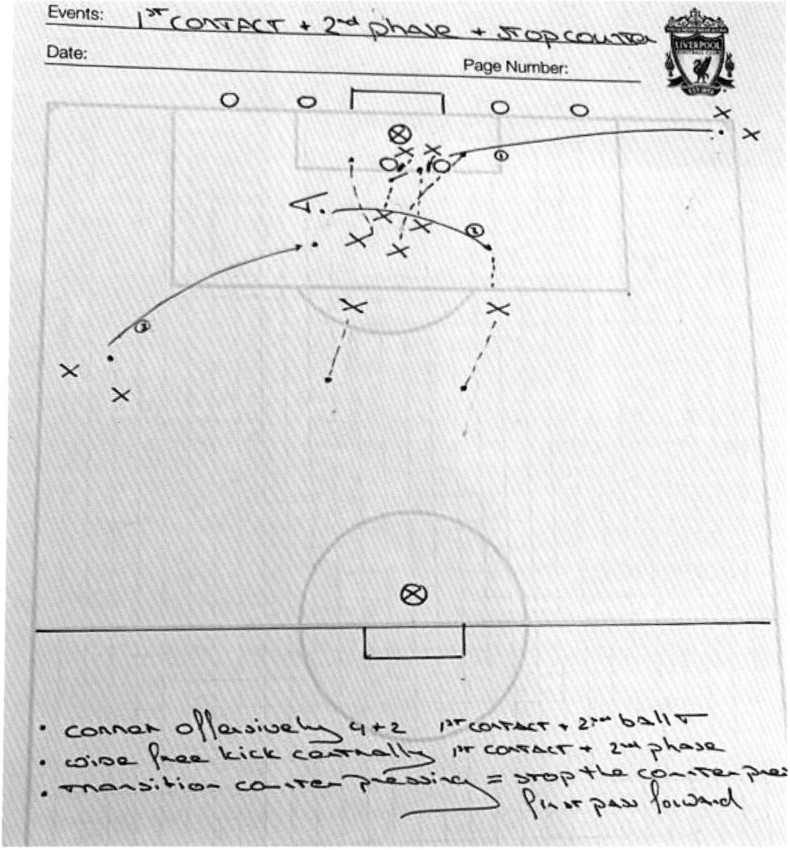

Staying alert: First contact and second phase – stopping the counter-press

Happy work: The ball only smiles when the player smiles... and the coach too!

Tak that: Taki gets on the scoresheet during our 4-0 defeat of Arsenal at Anfield in November

Marked man: Ibrahima keeps a close eye on Milan's Zlatan Ibrahimovic in our final Champions League group game and (right) coaches I love and admire – Johan Cruyff and Arrigo Sacchi

Complete striker: Diogo scores our fourth goal at Goodison in a 4-1 win. He has ability to score with his right and left foot, and his head

That man again: Divock's late goal at Wolves was so typical of him. He has scored so many 'deciders' and 'season-changers'

Body work: An important stretching routine during training at the AXA Training Centre in Kirkby

Two legends: A handshake between Steven Gerrard and Millie after our 1-0 win over Villa; a hug for Trent after his goal against Newcastle; Caoimhin was the hero in our Carabao Cup penalty shoot-out triumph over Leicester and Robbo celebrates a goal at Tottenham

channels. Taffa is a legend, he was here to assist our goalkeeper coaches, John and Jack. I didn't have the greatest memories of him because he saved two penalties in the semi-final of the World Cup against Holland, the decisive ones from Ronald de Boer and Phillip Cocu… but okay, we had this idea that we never want to stop developing, so I accepted and he got the benefit of the doubt! For all the young goalkeepers it was great news – we had three high-profile goalkeeper coaches now. Adding a staff member in the middle of a season is never easy but if there is one group who can deal with this it's ours. A few foot-volley games between the coaches and goalkeeper coaches would do the business!

Jürgen, Pete, Vitor and myself discussed that our front three needed real energy when chasing Jordan Pickford; we wanted him to feel under pressure because when he's calm he starts attacks really well. Our last line needed to be compact and steady because they'd put four quick players against them, but if we did this well we could take 60 per cent of their threat away. They didn't have more speed in their first line than we had in our last – and we had more speed in our first line than they had in their last. Football is a collective sport, so this wasn't a guarantee of anything, but it was a good indicator. Also, we needed to follow our attacks toward the edge of the box and our centre-halves needed to be really active in organising protection because the counters were something we felt they'd be waiting for. It was a real weapon: Demarai Gray, Andros Townsend and Richarlison had this direction in their game and Salomon Rondon could hold the ball well to give them time to move into dangerous spaces. The better we talked in protection, the less we'd need to run.

Teams were trying to use the space on our right side and we assumed it probably would be Gray. Virgil and Joel would need to be very loud to put Fab and Thiago in the right positions.

Jürgen and I went through our offensive set-up once again when they would drop off. We put on the tactics board the situation we were afraid of: Joel and Virgil too deep, Fab coming too much towards the ball, Trent and Thiago both deep in build-up and Mo and Sadio too far away from each other, leaving just Jota in the centre. "This can't, can't happen," we said to each other. We couldn't make the mistake of not being flexible nor together when we had the ball. How could we attack the centre when we didn't have many movements between the lines? In the session, we gave the boys the tactical overview. We told the boys, "When you are here, you move there." We explained our small plan to try to cause Everton big problems.

And it paid off as final no15 ended 4-1 away at Everton. Snipers we wanted, snipers we got! Three massive points. In the one moment our last line wasn't compact, they punished it with Gray's aggressive movement between Trent and Joel to make it 2-1 after Hendo and Mo had put us two goals in front. Following quickly and keeping our team together was key in this game. They pressed very aggressively with the consequence of leaving a lot of space when we outplayed them. Especially in the first 25 minutes, we recognised and used this almost perfectly, searching early for our attackers. Sadio, Jota, Mo and Hendo were so dynamic picking up these spaces and gave life to each attack. The outside triangle of Trent, Hendo and Mo moved and inter-changed fluidly. In the end, we scored four incredibly well-executed goals, each one with a different complex story. But all of them finished so confidently, strongly and into the corners.

On the staff bus after the game Billy Hogan jumped on and shouted, "Love you guys!" What a guy! Winning again away at a difficult ground, we drank our one beer while driving back to celebrate. It was four games since the international break;

14 scored and just one 'suffered'. We had momentum, but how could we keep this? Just by focusing on us, our way and on the next game. We could not make things complicated. I was in love with how our outside triangles were creating and evolving. Organised chaos, we called it.

However, the morning after the derby I got a text early on from our analyst Mark asking what time I'd be in. That's strange, I thought to myself and asked if there was a problem. I tried to call but he didn't pick up. When I finally met him at AXA, it was clear to me what was happening because he was wearing his normal clothes. "You have an offer, correct?" I asked. "Yes, Newcastle," he replied. We headed into Michael Edwards' office to talk calmly. The analyst guys are superstars in my eyes, the amount of work behind the scenes to facilitate our work is incredible. You have to be careful with analysis because the more you look, the more you find, and so in the end keeping things simple is key. The best analysts think like coaches and Mark was thinking like a coach. I was angry and proud at the same time. He is someone who I knew would be very difficult to replace – which should be the target for everyone in our organisation, by the way. Eddie Howe made a great call in hiring Mark, in my opinion.

But we had to continue to focus on ourselves because the upcoming period would be the decisive one and so we decided that against Wolves we would not make any changes and we'd keep the momentum with the team that had won the derby. We knew it was impossible for the boys to be completely recovered in time for the trip to Molineux, but Wolves were in the same position. "When you want to evolve a team, you always have to build on what you did. Consistency in messages. Why do you win football games? You are doing the right things often enough to dominate the opposition when they have the ball," is how Jürgen started the meeting with the team. "Your defence is organised and with a plan to take away options. This plan changes in detail game-by-game. Taking their plan away gives us a better feeling and them a worse one."

It'd be about closing the options to the two real good no6s, Joao Moutinho and Ruben Neves – closing the route to Hwang Hee-chan, Francisco Trincao or Adama Traore.

Speaking of Traore, because of the way we defend corners, it can happen that Trent and Robbo are in each other's position for a short period of time on the opposite side of the pitch. Robbo laughed in the build-up and said only when we play against Wolves is Trent immediately back to his own position!

I felt Wolves were a similar team to Chelsea in terms of organisation and ideas. I still had our first-half pressing against Chelsea clear in my mind. We were incredibly brave in that game, many times leaving only Fabinho, Virgil and Joel one-versus-one at the back and that was fine because we knew it would happen. When you know things are going to happen, you don't need to panic. The key lay in the fact that the passes played in these areas were not the best ones. We would need to be brave in our push-up as well at Wolves to have complete freedom in the final third. "Not only to be closer to the celebrations when we score," Jürgen joked at the end of the meeting. I'm perched on an uncomfortable chair in the hotel in the Midlands as Jürgen starts the team meeting by saying: "We have the right tools, it's about using the right mind to give everything. The derby was easy to focus for, but now we have to put the same intensity in." Our small pressing plan, with Mo, Sadio and Jota controlling Neves and Moutinho before starting the pressing machine towards their three centre-halves, was a crucial one. The headline of this game was: 'Be super brave'.

Before we went out at Molineux, we were in a small coaches' dressing room. On TV, West Ham against league leaders Chelsea was on. Just before we had to go out, West Ham scored the winner. Anyone who needed a little push got it now. We took the team out for the warm-up and the Wolves team went just before us. Ruben Neves passed and gave me a big hug. He was my captain in the youth teams for many years at FC Porto; he played as the no6, connecting and playing incredible passes over and over again. Our relationship was – and still is – very strong. Ruben became Porto's youngest club captain and I love him to bits.

After the warm-up Vitor worried me by saying, "It feels the same as at West Ham." We needed to give them energy before we went out. Final no16. Brave and 'big belief' substitutions created a 1-0 win away against a tricky Wolves team. Divock Origi showed once more his legendary characteristics, scoring in moments when it really matters: deciders, season-changers.

Five games in 14 days had taken its toll and we all looked tired in this game. We missed more passes, always took an extra touch, never made the runs needed to open up decisive spaces and waited a second too long with our decisions. I spoke with Jürgen at half-time to think about changing our system more offensively and bringing on Divock as the striker to push Conor Coady and their line backwards. We kept Thiago and Fabinho on to always be protected against their dangerous counter-attacks. Sadio and Mo could decide to use the inside or the outside space, which helped Trent and Robbo to stay fresh for the decisive passes or runs. In my mind I had the 'mistake' we made against Chelsea. The plan – or rather, the idea – was so long in place but was never needed because of the amount of goals we'd scored since then. Now it was time. But you need guts to make these decisions because it creates instability defensively for a short period. These are the moments I love Jürgen; he is responsible but so receptive to these kinds of changes.

After our change we created chance after chance, moment after moment, stopped better and better the counter-attacks. Finally we could impose attack after attack and push them back. We brought Ox on with his energy and movements to open up space between the lines, but it was only in added-time we really fired. Origi the legend, against Coady deep in the box, turned and finished after a brilliant assist from Mo. It was a sublime pass from Virgil that isolated Mo immediately against Ki-Jana Hoever. It really was such a smart ball from Virgil. The bench went nuts when it went in, everyone in ecstasy. Jürgen and I were discussing the last sub a few minutes before and we'd decided to hold the last sub for if we would score. So, after Divock's goal, we immediately brought Millie on. When Jürgen walked off the pitch after the final whistle, he whispered in my ear, "The old-style way." Then, when we walked into the dressing room, the boss said: "Welcome to Disneyland, Origi you are a legend."

To the boys it meant so much. They immediately played Whigfield's Saturday Night – you know, the Origi song – on the speaker. The 94th minute… there isn't a better time to score a goal in the world of football. You never knew how much these two points would count for in the end. The only thing I knew is that it would create belief the next time we found ourselves in a similar situation. The inner voice of the boys would say to them, 'It's possible'. Also, changing to a 4-2-4 next time will be an easier decision!

In the end it was a vintage 2019/20 Liverpool Football Club-style victory with Divock Origi once more the King of the Kop. He did it against West Brom in injury-time, he did it against Everton to win the game in injury-time, and now he did it again. Unbelievable – a Liverpool legend.

‘WE DON’T COMPARE OURSELVES WITH ANYONE – THE ONLY WORTHWHILE COMPARISON LIES IN US YESTERDAY VERSUS US TODAY’

WEEK 19

PLAN A WITH TEAM B

WE STARTED THE WEEK BY FOCUSING ON DRILLING our last line again. It was two days before Milan and we knew we would change the whole defence at the San Siro. Neco, Nat, Ibou and Kostas would have to hold the line high, control the positioning of Zlatan Ibrahimovic and the offensive movements of Brahim Diaz and Junior Messias. We repeated, corrected and repeated again, Vitor and I shouting over and over again, "Hold", "Push up", "Close the gap", "Find the challenge" and "Block!" "Well done, Kostas! That's closing the gap. Nat, now you need to push up and leave the striker." In the coaches' meeting we decided we'd go 'all in' – our way, our plan, we would not change our ideas to chase them high and intensely. We believed; now it was up to us to convince the subs to believe as well. Plan A with Team B. Nobody can do this better than Jürgen.

But I had the worst night in Milan the day before the game. I'd not been well since Everton. Headache, shivers, blocked nose and ears. It wasn't coronavirus, I knew that because I was getting tested each day. But the travel from Liverpool to Milan didn't help. At least I could sleep a lot in the hotel. "There is a reason why Italian managers don't stay long in the Premier League," Vitor joked while we had some cakes after our morning walk in Milan. The food is just incredible in Italy and we always have these kind of moments with the staff on matchday. Sometimes we win with fresh English pastry, but many times we get a scone you could smash a window with!

San Siro. It's a colosseum, this stadium. It felt like the stands went right up into the clouds while I was checking out the pitch before the game. The last time I was there was with PSV Eindhoven as a fan, but now I was standing in the middle of it as the assistant-manager of Liverpool Football Club. Pride. “It’s a monument,” Vitor says while walking back into the tunnel. The fight we would face on the pitch that night would be one of belief. The team rotation would say to the outside world that Liverpool gave up before the start, but we needed ‘a mood’ and new players would give us this. “Enjoy yourself out there,” Jürgen told them. “It’s good fun if we press them with all we have.” We were really positive about our changes because if they did similar things to what they’d been doing in training, we felt they would create real problems for Milan – and with Mo, Ali and Sadio alongside them, it’d give this extra push for them. We focused in training on habits so in the end the habits become us. That’s why training is so important… and in football you have to prove yourself each and every single time. History doesn’t exist on the pitch, so preparation is what counts.

And boy, did they deliver. Final no6 in the group of death ends in a 2-1 win at the San Siro against a Milan side who had to win to have a chance of qualifying. We finished Group B with maximum points.

Arrigo Sacchi would be proud of our last line that night and we became the first-ever English side to win all six group-stage games. History. Milan were first in the Italian league, we made eight changes, but after 45 minutes we’d had 60 per cent possession and created nine chances against the three of Milan. It says everything that Divock had more shots than the whole Milan team combined. We moved the ball so well using the width with Neco and Kostas. Tyler, Ibou and Nat could identify really quickly the free player in our build-up. Tyler orientated himself throughout the whole game and completed all his passes. It was

1-1 at half-time after Mo scored from a rebound from Ox's second-line shot; we'd conceded with a simple in-swinger corner, which was really painful. But in the second half we scored with Sadio stealing the ball after pressing Tomori from the blind side and after his shot was saved, Origi headed it into the back of the net. We could take Sadio and Mo off and give Naby and Joe their first minutes back after injury. Fabinho, Conor Bradley and Max Woltman also came on, so it became a night for the Academy as well.

When we got on the bus afterwards, Ibou was standing in front of me. I opened the pocket on his jacket and he gave me a strange look. "I'm trying to find Zlatan," I told him. He and Nat led the line, were vocal and gave direction. 'The bald Baresi' is what we called Nat in the dressing room afterwards. Jürgen hugged him and said, "I didn't lie when I said you and Lewandowski are the two players who improved the most." I added, "Many people say we talk nonsense until time shows we are right – sometimes there is only a result between in the football world." I told John Achterberg that if he clipped up all of Ali's passes on the night, you'd have the benchmark for all our Academy goalkeepers. He plays passes like a traditional no6. When our team can do this after so many changes, away at Milan, it's a compliment for everyone involved keeping them fit and involved throughout the season. It's a proof of the stability and quality of the training process. It's proof our squad is evolving.

"The positioning of the last line defines how small you make the pitch," I explained to Virgil, Joel, Robbo and Trent as we restarted work at AXA. "We don't have these moments a lot, so we can really train you guys. Two weeks ago we did, now we build on that. You know how important it is to be vocal, to lead the line Virgil. You guys know how important it is to make life easier for the six in front of you by keeping the team compact." They had all the tools in their locker but even with experienced players, training the last line is like a plant: it needs watering a minimum of one day a week. We gave them a whole watering can during that training session! Jürgen observes with open eyes. You saw against Milan that an organised and disciplined team can win against the best players in the world who don't play as collectively – this is the result of training. Can you imagine top players playing collectively? It happens during some periods and results in winning Champions Leagues, in winning Premier Leagues.

So we started the training with our three midfielders – Fabinho, Hendo and Thiago – supporting a four-v-four in the centre-circle to keep and move the ball quickly. The only rule: ten passes = one point. This normally increases the speed and quality of the decisions. Vitor searched long this particular afternoon for an exercise that stimulated support on the outside but forced the players to find the free player inside. The circle forces these kinds of behaviours. When he suggested it, I said, "Perfect, I love it!" We knew Aston Villa played in the figurative Christmas-tree formation: a 4-3-2-1 that opened the width of the pitch and closed the centre. In order for us to use the width but open up and attack the centre by finding free players inside (like in the centre-circle exercise), we had to avoid playing just around them where they had the advantage. If we did this, we would lose the game. I was convinced about this and that's why it was so important after a day off on the Wednesday to immediately force them to concentrate to find and solve specific solutions. The speed of how the ball moved was the best I'd seen so far this season. Being quick and confident in mind obviously makes a simple exercise beautiful to watch. Coaching is nice when top players play and act collectively. We changed Hendo with Trent and Thiago with Robbo to make sure both know they can move inside as well.

After the session, Jürgen and I drove back home to our families together. Those journeys are always a very nice, relaxing 30 minutes just talking about life. The session is done, job done and no need to stay any longer at AXA. Football life goes on. I'm now more than 20 years in football and that's the only certainty I have. It goes on, with or without you. As Graham Carter said to me when I was the only one left in the building on his final day with us: "Pep, this club will still be here in 20 years, but your kids will not be kids."

On the Friday I walked into the office to find a chestnut on my desk. I started laughing, I knew what this was about. I immediately walked into Jürgen's office… We'd spoken the day before while driving home about a new Danish thriller I'd found: The Chestnut Man. The series is based around these chestnuts… I will not explain further so as to avoid spoilers, but it's not good when you see one of these! Jürgen had followed my recommendation and watched the series and then had this idea. I love a Danish series like The Bridge, The Killing or Borgen, which is a more political drama. When we have a day off it's great to relax and between our staff, we always share our binge-watch experiences.

Focus shifted quickly back to the following day. Steven Gerrard was coming back to Anfield to cause problems – that was his message in the press conference. That's a sentence a lot of people thought would never be said, but it's our home and he'd done a lot of good so far with Villa. We didn't want that to continue with us, regardless of how much we love Stevie. Jürgen gave clear instructions to the boys that they would 'offer' us pressing moments, which was good news for us. It would be a massive advantage if we closed the centre and pressed. Each team would have problems with our front three chasing opposition aggressively and influencing their passing game. The main message in this game was: 'Don't slow down.' "Our identity is intensity and with this we'd create 'presents' in the box," was how Jürgen finished the meeting. Our plans took a blow when Divock left the training pitch while doing the set-piece routines, saying he felt his knee again, so we needed to make a quick decision and go for Ox.

On game day, Jürgen and I discussed the change with Ox and I gave him a quick tactical overview of what would be the plan when we had and when they had the ball, but above all we wanted him to be himself. He'd played many games very well in pre-season as the false nine. "Be cheeky with the ball and create, create to score," I told him. We went through the defensive parts. Again, Einstein came back to me: 'If you can't explain it simply, you don't understand it well enough'. There couldn't be a better saying to capture coaching in this complex game of football. All your brilliant ideas as a coach only have merit if you are able to explain it clearly to the kit man!

We were able to edge the game against Stevie's side – final no16 – 1-0 at home, but I felt a lot of tension that day. A strange atmosphere in the stadium, as if it was something bigger than just the game. The crowd, the amount of former Liverpool staff on their bench and behind the scenes, Stevie, as well as the whole media circus about who should succeed Jürgen in 2024. What a time that was to discuss 2024, by the way, especially in the world of football where the only thing that counts is winning the next game. I don't know what it was that day, but it felt different, but what I liked most was how aggressive we were with the ball; we attacked the open space they left with each opportunity we got, replicating the circle exercise in terms of speed of passes. We just needed to be more calm and smarter playing the last pass. We did that in the second half, though, and had so many good finishes. I joked to Robbo afterwards that our two full-backs could have two days of ice baths after their overlapping that day.

It was Mo who sealed it in our favour by getting into the zone and scoring a penalty he'd won by cold-bloodedly firing it low into the corner, despite any efforts to put him off. We sent Milner on to control Emi Buendia and Matty Cash's side and give power defensively again. Taki then came on late to give us new pressing energy to keep influencing Douglas Luiz, who was playing as the six and starting their attacks. Afterwards I felt that last year we wouldn't have won a game like this – we would have lost control in the last 15 minutes – but the whole last line performance was outstanding. Playing this type of game improves and gives life to our team. Good games always do.

By this point it was 37 points collected so far. City had won, Chelsea had won and then we won. Two points separated first from third at the top. We came back in the dressing room and Jürgen complimented the team, saying intense games like this deserve maximum recovery and because of that we'd give the boys two days off with only one rule: they couldn't leave the country. We told them to be safe in their decisions because by now, the Omicron mutation of COVID was aggressively taking over the English health system. Most of our boys actually got their booster jab after that game. We had 100 per cent full vaccination at that moment, and 80 per cent booster. In a crisis situation, you have to act before you are right – and this pandemic was still a crisis situation. A health crisis situation.

WEEK 20

A SHOAL OF FISH

"PEP... THEY MESSED UP THE DRAW!" THE WEEK BEGAN in interesting fashion: a phone call from Jürgen on our day off on the Monday. "Huh?" I replied. "Why? How? What?" I'd only followed the draw for our Champions League last-16 tie on Twitter and knew we were down to play Salzburg. "No, no, Pep..." the boss said, before he explained the situation to me. "So two scandals in two days?" I said. "Yesterday, Hamilton v Verstappen..." The Formula One really had been incredible television the day before. We'd actually had an electricity problem outside the house, so the engineers who came out to look at it were so surprised looking through our window on an otherwise peaceful Sunday afternoon and seeing my whole family screaming at the TV for 40 seconds. "Come on Max, let's go, this is the moment!" It was Dutch confidence and great tactics by Red Bull. I have huge respect for both drivers, both are just simply really good. Lewis Hamilton is such a steady driver and deserved to overtake Michael Schumacher for Formula One championship wins in my opinion. But back to our matters and the conclusion was that we wouldn't play Salzburg in the last 16, we would instead go back to the San Siro. It was Inter Milan who'd be waiting in February.

On the Tuesday the boys were back in. Jürgen spoke with the team and told them, "This season will not only be decided by how many goals we score or how few we concede, it will also be decisive [in terms of] how our discipline off the pitch is. Avoiding a COVID outbreak will be crucial to following our route." Testing had now been increased to every day and we had to wait in our cars for the results before we could even enter AXA. More and more games were getting cancelled and it was bringing back ugly flashbacks to the start of the pandemic for me.

The Champions League draw was a topic of discussion among the boys. We were heading into the 'finals' now, a winner-stays-on concept but with the away-goals rule now scrapped. We were anticipating more penalty shoot-outs, so we were preparing to be busy for a while to create ideas of how to approach these moments. At the time the first leg was two months away, but as I've said, finals you prepare for in the 51 weeks before, not one week before. Create a habit and perfect it each day, so when the time comes you don't even have to explain things. We needed to know the personality aspect of the boys who wanted to shoot, the courage aspect they had to put it without the distractions of the opposition goalkeeper into the trained corner. Milner, Mo and Fabinho were clear and so was Trent. A questionnaire was created by neuro11 giving more insight into the personality of each player around set-pieces. In combination with this, we created a six-step process to train penalties while telling the goalkeeper where they were going to hit. This prep is crucial because when you see the keeper go into your corner, you know that when you hit with power he is still not able to reach it.

I spoke with Millie on the training pitch and asked him to take responsibility helping to define the takers, to help define the side they should go, and their discipline to train. The good thing with James is that if you say it once, he is still repeating the message even if we forget. I planned to sit together with neuro11 and implement a proper pre-shot routine, specific for each player which we'd train under different physical and mental conditions. Social hierarchy is a key element for inducing social pressure, so we'd define who would be the takers and in which order. We still needed to identify a few others. The first step is to define where the player wants to shoot, so we would assess and clarify the ideal target for him. It depends on his personality. The ones who have this natural confidence should define their shot high in the corners – it's the biggest chance to score. We would train this during the second step without a goalkeeper. Then it's about understanding the importance of accuracy; four shots they would do without telling the goalkeeper and then four shots telling him. After that, it's about eliminating social pressure, so we'd train with other players watching and throwing balls away. The player had to tell the coach where he'd exactly shoot the ball to be clear in his mind. Step five was about gaining confidence and eliminating distractions. The player had to tell the goalkeeper where he would shoot the ball exactly; the goalie and other players could distract the taker while he stepped up. Step six, the ultimate training, after a game in the stadium. With a keeper we'd use the vibe still hanging around the place, but the taker doesn't tell anyone where he will shoot the ball to replicate game situations. The conclusion? We wanted to create confident penalty-takers who could eliminate distractions. Habits.

We had Mo, Sadio, Bobby and Fabinho working on their penalties – at this point, we were only on step three. Ali shouted to me after he saved another good hit, "Do you want me to stop, Pep? I'm taking all their confidence away!" It made everybody laugh before he accused Sadio of turning his back before he took one. There's no messing about with Ali. It's incredible how he reads and has the speed of reaction to save a well-taken penalty. It showed that we needed to practise more, but we had the advantage of the best goalkeeper in the world. Best with best creates excellence.

The main session was about creating energy in the final third, so we introduced our 'finals' exercise again, where the better you play, the more you play. Four teams competing and trying to earn the right to stay on the pitch, each game as a final. Goal on, goal off, maximum one-minute games. We defined the teams by the triangles so there is a logic in relationships. 'Specificity'. The ultimate goal was to win four games in a row. If that happened, the finals then stopped and we had a winner. Sadio, Thiago and Robbo won four games in a row early, so there the finals then stopped. Not all the players were happy, but I told them if you are not immediately ready in this game, you don't play a lot of games. "I'm so sorry, Fabinho!"

The idea of these games was to simulate play inside the box, combinations and third-man movements. I like to put floaters frontally to stimulate these kinds of habits. Creating habits, using each minute to train the way we want to play. For example, by this point, Jota had scored 100 per cent of his goals inside the box, Sadio 97 per cent and Mo 92 per cent. Our first idea should always be to come into a one-v-one situation with the goalkeeper, so we tailored the sessions to be dedicated and specific, always relating to the team. It forced individual initiative and responsibility.

"What's good about a banana skin?" Jürgen asked the players when they finally sat down in our meeting room to look at Newcastle together. Nobody responds. "If you see and recognise it before, you will not slip. With this meeting we show you the banana skin. The public perception expects a result, but we should expect problems. We have to be in the right mindset to cause them problems." How did we plan to do that? By pushing them in counter-press situations. With everything we do, we put pressure on. They needed to feel we were constantly there, with bodies, movement and counter-pressing. We'd win this game if we had full energy in the final third. Do what we were good at then they'd have more problems to deal with. "But guys, they improved under Eddie Howe and the 4-0 loss against Leicester doesn't reflect their performance," the boss told the boys. We'd noticed since Howe came in they'd had more chances created, more possession and were more aggressive defensively as a team. Jonjo Shelvey was the passer: "Chase him from all over the pitch and from all directions." Allan Saint-Maximin was a fast, skilful one-v-one dribbler: "Don't let him be in a one-v-one." Callum Wilson wanted those channel-balls when they won it back: "Protect him but more importantly, avoid these channel-balls with all of our guys up front."

"Put them under pressure high and with the highest intensity." This is one characteristic of our good games, how intense we were when the opposition had the ball. We felt this would make us able to attack Newcastle time and time again. Press them at each opportunity; constant threats to penetrate them through the centre; attack the centre with come-and-go pure striker movements. Pete showed images of where we'd done this really well. We'd trained these striker movements to go against their pushing-up movements, although the thought afterwards was if clubs could see Caoimhin Kelleher in training, they would try and sign him as their no1 immediately – he is an Irish cat! Jürgen ended the meeting with: "We need the 2021 LFC version to go into these five games over the next 13 days." We showed images when we played against Howe's Bournemouth two years before. We were a different animal now – the 2021 version is top-class football mixed up with an attitude to win each second-ball fight. Adventurous and active centre-halves, our triangles dynamic and connected, having the maximum players needed inside the box. There is always a solution with our football, but we have to work for it.

The final session before the game was great: 100 per cent attitude from the starters, with the subs and staff all involved. "Curtis is baaacckkkhh in trainin'!" I said to him as he walked back inside. He laughed so hard – he knew that was my Scouse attempt at 'back in training'! The preparation was going well until a 4.30am text on the Thursday morning arrived as Virgil messaged Jürgen: "I've tested positive twice." He hadn't felt great waking up in the night, so as a precaution he took a lateral flow test. The boss and I called each other early as we faced up to another challenge. Two challenges, in fact: winning the game and stopping the possible spread. I had a call with our doctor, Jim Moxon, to make sure we organised PCR tests that morning and we went through all the scenarios. Sitting in the office that morning, normally we speak about the press, the team and life in general, but now it was only about Virgil and testing – and trying to control the uncontrollable. The testing procedure we'd put in place on arrival proved right as Virgil would have been detected as positive before he'd gone into the AXA this morning. It also showed that Curtis was positive, too. If it was the new variant Omicron, which had proven much more contagious, it could have spread yesterday. For Curtis, it was sad after such a long time on the sidelines, after getting an awkward eye injury, and now he was not able to train with the team because of COVID.

We called Billy Hogan to update him and make sure he was our voice directly to the Premier League when things weren't good with the test results. We were doing the right thing by testing everyone but it brought uncertainty as well. We saw on the TV at the training ground that Brentford had reported 13 cases that morning and Thomas Frank said they wanted to stop the league the coming weekend. He couldn't have been more right in my opinion. We found out Tottenham v Leicester had been called off as we walked to the team bus to go to the hotel. COVID had hit English football. We were all healthy, young sportsmen who were vaccinated and most of us had had boosters, so hopefully it was just a case of quarantine to stop the spread and with this protect the elderly and more vulnerable people. But now you could see how important it is to be vaccinated because there are many examples of sportsmen without it who really got hit by the virus.

Later, when I was resting in the hotel, Jürgen called me at 4pm and woke me up. It was clear something was up. "Fabinho is positive as well." My first thought was: okay, we've lost two of our best players but our line-up will be strong enough. We decided Hendo would go to the six position and Ox would come in on the eight. Jürgen called both of them and I let the staff know. The good news was the rest of the tests were all negative, so we hoped we'd cut the chain… we did everything we could in our power. When Jürgen began the final team meeting, he said: "Life is a summation of challenges. We always learn. The public will say it's a problem losing two of our best players. The answer to this problem is our squad. Nobody will decide for us how we deal with this situation, nobody. We have everything in our own hands to put them under more pressure than they can imagine. For us it's much more important to know how we play rather than who will play, because the power we can create with the 'how' is special." He told the boys they'd have to work really hard when we played through and chasing from behind, and that when the ball was in the air we needed to win the second ball. "We are recovered and ready, we all slept this afternoon… Ox did for sure because he didn't pick up his phone!" Jürgen joked. We told Hendo he needed to be more supportive than dominant; Joel needed to be in charge of the last line and make the team compact; Ibou is quicker and stronger than Wilson but he had to be ready for channel fights. "I want us to be quicker than them today, we change each 50-50 into a 60-40, because that's how we play football, we don't slow down," Jürgen finished.

When we later arrived at the stadium we saw another five further games would be postponed. 'Breaking news' it said on the TV, but to be honest we'd all seen this coming. It felt exactly like the Atletico game two years before; a different situation but the same feeling. The problem for most teams who got hit was that with now having ten days' quarantine – as it stood at the time – Boxing Day would be out, the huge, traditional matchday in English football. I felt they could prevent this by stopping the league for one or two matchdays. Half of the table had a squad health crisis and some teams had only played 14 games. Our game was on, though, and we knew Newcastle now had Mark Leyland on their team. Mark could write a book about us; he knows everything and all our secrets. He was such a help bringing the team to where it was right now. But I felt it was an advantage and a disadvantage at the same time for Newcastle. Firstly, I believe that the more you know, the more you worry; the more you adapt, the more you lose your habits. That'd be a good thing for us. Secondly, you can know but for a certain intensity you can't be prepared until you feel ours. The speed will always be the surprise. It's not a secret that you can still surprise opposition in 2021, even with all the data and analysis that exists. We surprise with our intensity. And that's what we did with a 3-1 win. After the most difficult morning of this season, this was a top win – we wanted those three points and we got them.

Having to change three positions on matchday will never help the fluidity but we had energy in the final third. Jürgen told the boys directly after the game: "The important thing is that it's clear why we wear this shirt: we fought with all we had. Maybe we were not perfect but we fought against a strong physical counter-attacking Newcastle." We recovered well from the early setback of going behind and Jota and Mo put us in front before half-time, but the highlight of the night had to be Trent's screamer. "Under-16 style!" I shouted to him as he walked off the pitch. What power and technique he has in him. Some players are born to win, some players are made for the Premier League and Trent is one of them. When I got home I was sitting in my kitchen alone with a cup of tea just thinking about what a day it had been. Jürgen was right, discipline off the pitch will have a huge impact this season. Hopefully we won both challenges today, I thought. Cutting the chain and winning the game.

There was no time for us to take a breather, though, and on the Friday we were back in to look ahead to our trip to Tottenham that weekend. Greg, one of our main analysts, started the weekly opposition staff meeting. Their strength was that it was a classic Antonio Conte team: the system is everything, the passion is everything. We all knew that at Inter he played in a 3-5-2, then at Chelsea he started with a 4-2-3-1 and changed into a league-winning 3-4-3 structure. "He knows well how he can use the strengths of his forwards and adapts his system to it," Vitor said. Pedro, Eden Hazard and Diego Costa were the front three of his title-winning Chelsea side. At Tottenham he was still fine-tuning the machine, which was not easy because a COVID outbreak had interrupted the training situation a lot at the club. We didn't know who was available for them. Our understanding was they were missing key forwards, but we would only probably find out 75 minutes before kick-off. What we did know is they didn't play a lot of long passes; they were 20th in the league for these kinds of passes, so we could expect a build-up team with clear offensive and defensive patterns. Italy-style coaching with a lot of passion. I felt he would make a machine out of Spurs, for sure.

Offensively they would attempt to find Harry Kane between the lines, while Son Heung-min and Lucas Moura would try to attack the gaps in our last line with aggressive offensive movements, but again, we didn't know the players who would be available due to COVID. Nevertheless, the same dynamic counted for how we had to stop their counter-attacks. We'd need to push up to Moura and Son, who drop deep and are ready to counter. It's something we didn't do well enough against Newcastle and we believed if we left the same spaces inside we would get punished this time. They have more individual quality than Newcastle did, but not one player plays the same football with and without pressure, is how Jürgen always says it. Our analysis was to show how to avoid these one-v-one situations, to correct those who didn't move in a common way. One-v-one situations will always happen but then we needed to solve them with quick legs. Ibou had to show this too many times against Newcastle. We needed to protect Kane with both our centre-halves to intercept the passes in to him. Kane had the advantage because he could use his body to protect the ball, but in a two-v-one situation this advantage disappeared. The other key player was Eric Dier, who played in the system as a libero.

The session on the Friday with the non-starters from Newcastle was incredible. We practised our corners and free-kicks in combination with counter-pressing. Four players got a corner to finish, a wide free-kick and a second ball; after these consecutive finishes they needed to counter-press four players who were waiting behind the goal to create a fast counter-attack. Vitor made sure balls would be brought quickly into the right places, while Pete would focus on the specific runs. Neco, Kostas and Milner would practise their focus and their deliveries. For Joe, Bobby, Naby and Taki, they had to quickly change their mind after scoring from the set-piece and then immediately stop the counter. I focused a lot on the first-pass-forward principle, not just the one player who wins the ball but especially the forwards who need to give an immediate solution forward so we can take advantage of the open spaces. Pressing is the most offensive idea in the game of football, but only when you take advantage immediately. Jürgen and I discussed that we had to improve the whole idea again, we missed so many opportunities for playing forward immediately during the Newcastle game. The intensity in our counter-press and the attitude and concentration was like pushing a red button – devils chasing the ball – but the fluidity between these moments is what makes a collective team. Everything needs to be connected and clear, so when 60,000 people are screaming in the stadium and millions more are watching and critiquing at home, when the emotions go up, when the stakes are so high, the boys can grab onto what they've practised each day. They can grab the inner voice created by Jürgen, the images in their mind by Pete and the principles of Vitor. Clarity just kills anxiety.

In training we always try to stimulate the 'fast fibres'; everything we do is in the highest gear so we can always play with quick decisions and actions. We had to improve in making first contact closer to the opposition goal when we had attacking corners. We created so many with our open play, but we had to make them decisive again. If you think set-pieces are important, practising them once before a game isn't the right message nor the right repetition. That's what I liked about today: extra focus, extra repetition, but within our way of football with counter-press as the main ingredient. This exercise had been lying on my desk for two weeks: making first contact into second phase into counter-pressing into our offensive organisation against a back line. The whole is bigger than the sum of its parts, is what they say – and this couldn't be more right in terms of how we practised our way of football while working on set-pieces in this session.

If you want to understand our training methodology, you have to understand first our way of football. That's how I create and contextualise the exercises. We don't compare ourselves with anyone else – the only worthwhile comparison lies in us yesterday versus us today, that's what we always tell the boys. That's why the exercises need to evolve as well, it is the only way to keep improving. This is why we are a hungry team, one full of confidence which knows what it wants. As I left Jürgen's office I told him we should play a padel tennis match on Saturday, just to clear the head. It was the best thing we could do to create focus on what was important again. I'd thought about it when we were sitting in the manager's room after the Newcastle game. So much was happening and it was taking its toll; so much so, we were fighting not to look like pessimistic zombies after those last few days. Sometimes in a season it can feel like it's slipping through your fingers, moments when you lose control over the process. Most of the time this is because there is negativity around us, so it was also here we had to cut the chain! The staff game was the best thing that had happened since we'd moved into our new training ground from a social and bonding perspective, Jürgen said. It's the padel tennis atmosphere, but for everyone, not just coaches. It brought people together and gave life in our new home. After this we'd be ready to pick the team, prepare well and attack matchday. That's us.

On Saturday morning, just before I was leaving the house, I got a whole package of papers from [Portuguese academic] Vitor Frade, all with notes and football poems written over it. Twenty pages of it. It reminded me of the first time I entered Porto's training facility, it was just full of papers all marked with yellow and blue pens... red wasn't allowed inside! It looked like you'd walked into a detective's home from one of my favourite Danish thrillers! The texts were about the brain, about everything that relates to tactical periodisation, a column from Jorge Valdano. Frade is 80 years old and still inspires all of his students. He is the one who gave Porto's youth identity. He would always say: "Maybe I'm not that intelligent... but I'm right many times!"

When I drove into AXA I noticed I had two missed calls from Jürgen. I opened up WhatsApp to see if I'd missed something... Thiago now positive. Shit. That's number four. Where will it stop? I thought to myself: five days ago I sat with Virgil in the canteen talking in Dutch about our families and Christmas. "We are getting better and better," I said. "If we can keep these two fit we will have a big chance," replied Virgil, pointing to Fabinho and Thiago who were walking in. "And you," I said, to which he smiled. Now, four days later, Fab, Thiago and Virgil were out...and we had to travel to London that afternoon, the epicentre of the new variant. It's in times like this I wonder to myself why not one scientist is listened to in these moments; they warn of the danger so many times, but only political and financial decisions are made. It's no wonder we go from one health crisis to another.

Jürgen's meeting started by asking the team: "Do we want to

play?" One of the big guns asked from the back: "I just want to know if we are safe." Jürgen explained his vision, but it was difficult to answer correctly because of the information that was available at that time about this new variant.

"If we agree we want to play, we need to create a mindset," Jürgen continued. Before we set off, we got the news that Hendo wasn't feeling well. It's a heavy cold, thankfully, not COVID and his tests are negative, so he would travel but it was highly unlikely he'd start. If that proved to be the case, we made the call that Tyler would play again in the six position. Matchday morning was a 45-minute drive from the hotel to the stadium, so we used a video we created about defending at the highest level in our midfield pressing zone. Jürgen compared it with a shoal of fish, a swarm of bees, a flight of birds who all move so coordinated. Because of this compactness, it already makes it difficult for the opposition to find ways to hurt us. Jürgen suggested we all watch it on the way to the stadium on our phones, so I sent it to the boys in our WhatsApp group. We still didn't know the players Spurs would have available, but we knew the system Conte would play. He had told the media it was hard to press Liverpool because we like that, so we expected them to prepare for counter-attacks. The boss finished his final words to the boys by saying how he loved so many things about being a part of football, but the fact you can leave everything behind the moment you go into a game was so nice. That's what we had to do: leave everything that had happened the previous few days behind.

The game ended 2-2 and our full-backs were decisive. We felt it was an important point gained; you never know if this point would be the difference-maker come the last matchday of the season. We certainly hoped so. To be honest, before the game

I would have signed up for this result because we were forced into changes – we were in the middle of an LFC health crisis, day after day, 'new' news coming through, ending that morning with Hendo being ruled out. A midfield three which had never played together before was not a good starting reference for such a big occasion. We gave easy passes away which were really not necessary, but fatigue from the last game and this whole situation of COVID and midfield changes could explain it. Tottenham surprised us with playing an 'extra' striker; a strategic 5-3-2, with Kane and Son both up front hunting to exploit one-v-ones against Joel and Ibou, many times in big spaces, exactly what we wanted to avoid. Entertaining for the stadium, yes, but the last thing we wanted. We needed ball AND space-control, and the moments we had the ball for longer than six passes in combination with controlling the movements of Kane and Son, we created our first big deserved chance, which was a little chip from Trent in to Robbo, who came in front of Lloris and missed not by much with his header. This was us. I loved this about our team, we could play these passes and come into these positions with both our full-backs.

Two shots followed from Milner and Trent, both saved. The first moment our midfield was disorganised they punished it with a through-ball for Kane. We can avoid these situations much better but you can't be perfect each time; what we can do is react better to the disorganisation by filling up these spaces. Robbo sent Sadio in behind Emerson Royal and Davinson Sanchez with one of his signature passes. Sadio crossed but the ball came out of the box, but Robbo followed his pass aggressively and took the ball into the box with one touch, lifting it over for Jota, who timed his jump well, turned his body in the air and headed in with so much technique and power beyond

Hugo Lloris to make it 1-1. The beautiful thing was that Trent was on the edge to finish it off if Jota hadn't got there. One full-back crosses to our striker to score while the other one is on the edge to finish. The reason we could play with both our full-backs in a constant attacking mood was the way our midfield was constructed, but that was something we missed here without Hendo, Fabinho and Thiago being available.

During half-time we spent time reorganising our protection. Ibou and Joel had to take charge, our midfield had to be more together inside because we could switch the game easily. In the first half we'd had 70 per cent possession and 12 shots compared to five from them, but in the second half we came under more pressure. We changed the second-yellow-card-risk situation with Tyler, bringing on Firmino with the indirect message to our team: 'Let's go for the second goal again'. We needed the ball more because you don't need to defend when you have it and obviously this midfield is better with than without the ball. Naby and Milner would help to stop counter-attacks and protect the inside-space better. We scored the second goal with Trent crossing during a second-phase attack directly on to Robbo, who headed it in. What a connection these two have... what monsters we'd created! But for the second time in the game, our midfield press was too open inside and they played through us exactly like in the first half. Two-two via Son. Different system, same problem.

I have to be honest, I lost my mind there for a moment that day. I don't like to speak about refereeing decisions, but on this day I felt the referee was wrong twice on the big decisions. First, the tackle from Harry Kane, who put a bad one in on Robbo. Second, the moment Jota wanted to finish our so-well-executed counter-attack until he was run over when he went to shoot.

Two big decisions that influenced this result. In the last four years we'd been second-last in the table for free-kicks received. Only in 2018/19 we were 14th in the league. I think these stats said a lot when you realise that we also had 70 per cent possession most of the time. In the end Robbo got sent off for a wild challenge. Yes, it was absolutely the correct decision, but Kane shouldn't have been on the pitch anymore, especially if you want to be consistent. When Robbo went off, we went with the mantra: if you can't win, you have to make sure you will not lose. So Joe came in for Jota. We were defending the width with five now, three in front to control the centre space and Mo up front to keep players from them back. We got the draw and even had a half-chance right at the end.

Heading back after the game, there was some doubt about our flight being able to land in Liverpool because of fog, but luckily we were able to arrive back into John Lennon Airport. We decided we'd give everyone an extra day off the following day, but at 10am there was a Premier League meeting scheduled, which we hoped would provide some clarity about the impact of COVID in the coming days. Not only that, we had Leicester coming to Anfield in the League Cup in just three days.

'THE POWER OF LFC IS THE COLLECTIVE, WE ALWAYS DO EVERYTHING TOGETHER – THIS IS OUR POWER'

WEEK 21

WOW – ONLY US!

AFTER THE DAY OFF ON MONDAY, THE WEEK BEGAN with a press conference day for me again. It was a tricky one this time. The refereeing decisions at Spurs, COVID, the Premier League CEOs meeting to discuss the schedule. AFCON. VAR decisions… But with each question I just gave my honest opinion. As soon as I'd finished, my phone pinged with a text from Billy: "Just wanted to say how impressive your 'presser' was. Completely calm, rational thought. Leadership position that we will deal with what we have in front of us – we're not happy about it, we think the situation mandates a different approach, but we will get on with it. Really, really impressive, Pep. Great leadership & great job." It meant the world to me coming from him.

After that, I headed outside for our tactical session. "Billy the kid is no more," Jürgen joked in reference to Koumetio, who was making his way past. "It's Billy the teen from now on!" Billy smiled in a way only he can smile. He is maturing like Tyler. For their age they play with tactical maturity and that's so important if you want to make the next step with us. As we walked into Jürgen's office there was some good news. "The gods are with us," I tell him. It looked like we'd cut the chain as all PCR tests had come back negative. It felt like a crucial moment in our recent outbreak. It felt like a miracle and we just smiled together. Jürgen told me he'd been up since 6am watching his phone for each result to come in. Crazy times.

Our desks were full with Christmas presents that morning. To be honest, it was a bit of a mess but great for the atmosphere with wine, whiskey and chocolates. Billy Hogan delivered a proper present, a CEO-level present. John Achterberg is always the first one to give his out, but it's the same wine each year. I think he bought a container of Rioja a few years ago – the Dutch way! Jack chose a very good wine, he knows his wines that's for sure. Mona made sure there were some home-baked delicatessens. Jürgen planted 20 trees for all direct staff in Formby nature reserve, such a wise present. Also, he gave vouchers to the whole AXA building, who were all so grateful for it. It is the small presents that make the big differences.

"Different times ask for different processes," Jürgen started the meeting on game day. "We will do a short set-piece meeting. We played through our ideas in the 11 v 11 yesterday – we will not repeat these ideas in the meeting," he continued. It was clear to the boys, I'd explained our set-up on the pitch using our tactical overview training papers. I started with how we wanted to make it an LFC pressing and counter-pressing game, to try to shock them. I told the boys, "One reason: we want the ball." This is the mentality we wanted for this game against Leicester: we want the ball! This is always a good idea against a team who wants the ball as well. A typical Brendan Rodgers side, which opened up the pitch, with technical players centrally and real speed up front. They'd had a long time without a game so would be fresh coming to Anfield. They probably will go strong, the boys were saying. Jürgen responded: "What's strong? We will change, but we are stronger than they expect if we use our patterns and our love for counter-pressing." "We can surprise them with our intensity," I added. We went through each game moment and the boys gave it life during the session. It was such a positive session, with Conor Bradley showing incredible passion. We finished with some penalties. Don't make it a piece of art, strong and confident and to the sides is what we instruct. Jürgen joked to Joe when he missed his kick: "You can just tell us that you don't want to take a pen, Joe!" Everyone laughed, the pressure was really off.

Sitting on the bus, Sky Sports was showing short images and quotes from my press conference… welcome to the world of discomfort! I had been asked if our team still had this 'greed' after us winning so many prizes. I just responded with: "If you would watch one training session of ours, it would directly answer the greed question. We have James Milner who is 35 and still dreams of winning cups. That says everything. He is on top of everything." Discipline yourself and you don't need to discipline others, is the perfect saying to underline James and his influence on the whole squad.

If you want to become a Liverpool legend you need to win domestic cups as well, I believe, and that's what we were going to try. But we'd do it our way, including our biggest talents in the line-up against Leicester. It was a line-up we loved. What I was sure of was that we would give the fans a cup night full of desire, create a special game and new memories together. It would be incredible if we could reach a moment in the coming years where we could line up a whole Academy graduate team, as a club statement to show the Liverpool Way and our progress over the last few years. A healthy club is the one with a powerful inside pathway and most of our icons come from within. For each club, it should be the target to increase the homegrown talent in their squad step-by-step. It's a process of bravery and patience of the leaders. It was some of this latest crop of young guns that created the special night we wanted. What a night it was. Wow, wow, wow, wow… just wow! Only us! I'd said in the presser that we wanted to create special games, to try to create an LFC cup night full of desire. I think we can say that we did that as we came from behind to beat a strong Leicester. We want to create new memories together and being 2-0 down, 3-1 down at half-time and then reaching and winning on penalties is only possible with a real belief.

I'd sought out Milner directly after Diogo's winning penalty because he played such a good second half. His last-minute assist to Taki was decisive to reach the penalty shoot-out. I told him: "Millie, we are going to win this one. We need to, we didn't win it yet, so we will put it right." I said this with what had happened in the final in 2016 in my mind. Then, the moment I saw Jota, I became emotional. He scored penalty number six, stepping up and taking such big responsibility in the whole game. You can just bring him into whatever position and he will play well. The key in this game was helping the team by bringing Ibou, Milner and Jota on at half-time. The five-subs rule really helps to manage game and recovery time, but it also gives chances from the bench to make an earlier impact. Jota was on the right and he scored our second goal after combining through the centre with Firmino and Taki. Milner came on in the six to take charge and guide the team emotionally. Ibou was brought on to control the movements of Patson Daka and Jamie Vardy better. We'd told the others at half-time that the most important thing was to believe that we could do it… and stop losing balls in the build-up! "We play towards the Kop and you all know what's going to happen when we score the second goal," we told them.

I sat in the canteen afterwards to make my notes for this project. I spotted a big quote from Oxlade-Chamberlain on the wall that said; "Everyone feels part of this special club." He'd played with so much technique and overview in this game and scored from the edge of the box with a clinical, confident shot.

He knew the whole game, exactly what was happening around him, and above all was counter-pressing as if his life depended on it. "The power of LFC is the collective, we always do everything together, this is our power," is another quote I spotted, this time from Sadio Mane. I have to put this one in because this is the reason why we won this game: the collective. Also, it has to be said, Naby is the best substitute player you can imagine in these kinds of games. Everyone in the opposition is tired and he can dribble past them as if they are mannequins. He started so many dangerous attacks. "This is our first decisive penalty shoot-out, but we need to practise more," Milner told me after the game. He was right – we needed more players who really wanted to take them. We scored five of our six and Kelleher saved two. He was like he always is in training: a cold-blooded Irish cat. Niklas from neuro11 sent me a text: "I really have to be very thankful for all the work and effort you put into working with us, you are clearly an innovator, very inspiring!" I responded: "I just want to win!" Begin with the end in mind.

WEEK 22

MO AND TRENT'S UNIVERSE

IN FOOTBALL THERE AREN'T QUICK FIXES. IDEAS need time. Or even better, they need consistency to become habits. Or even better still, to become consistently efficient under the highest pressure. But there is always a start-date needed; a point where new ideas gain clarity. Creating 'new' habits was the underlying message of our pre-season work, and the decisions we'd made since then were really paying off. It was US. The boys absorbed it, wanted it, and showed so much dedication to improve. I had not forgotten during the start of 2021 we faced one of our biggest challenges of the last few last years at Liverpool FC with our form and injuries. But in this time we became more complete, in my opinion, and we adapted to a new way. Our way. A common new plan. Growth. Every session, the boys were so motivated and greedy to win.

As we got closer to 2022 it was nice to see we had improved more than we ever could have imagined. It was like art. Only when others see what you want them to see, then you know it is definitely working… and most of the people only see it when you collect the three points. Our target was to play as many games as possible this season, so remaining in all competitions moving into 2022 made me really happy. I'm not that much of a football stats guy because I trust in my views or my feelings, but when stats can confirm what you're seeing, it confirms your feelings are correct. Like art!

This team was designed to shine. The right-side adjustments were designed to shine. By this stage of the season Trent had created the most chances in the league (51) and Mo was third (37). I felt those adjustments on our right were working out with having Trent as the extra midfielder. We had the first and second-highest goalscorers in the league with Jota and Mo. We had the first and second-highest assist-makers in the league with Trent and Mo. It was looking more and more that we were in Mo and Trent's universe. Salah alone had scored more goals than Brighton, Burnley, Wolves and Norwich. At this stage we'd scored the most goals in the league with 50. Across Europe we'd scored the most goals from outside the box. Our variety is unpredictability; we'd increased the amount of weapons.

We'd become, again, more complete, always with the idea that everyone is responsible for everything – one of the first messages Jürgen told the team in 2015 when he arrived. There is nothing more I love than when growth is paying off.

For me, though, this week was a strange one. I can't remember the last time I'd missed a training session, certainly not during my time with Liverpool. But it was naive to think the stomach bug that had affected my two boys would avoid catching my wife and I. As I'd said in the press conference, in life you want many, many things, but when you are sick you just want one thing: to be better. It's moments like this you quickly forget you'd just eliminated a strong Leicester team from the Carabao Cup with a much-changed line-up.

On 23 December, while at home, I received a call from Jürgen early in the morning. Leeds was to be postponed due to rising COVID cases within their squad. The traditional English fixture was off for us this year. No Boxing Day game for LFC. But even with no fixture to prepare for, the boys were in on Christmas Day to continue to train, as always. Jürgen began his talk with them by saying: "Twenty years ago when I became a manager, at Christmas I wished I would one day have a team who could beat the best teams in the world. And now, here you are, guys. It's not the first Christmas this is the case, which makes it even better. Our present today for you guys is a brilliant, planned session. Pep stayed home yesterday especially to create this new exercise for today!"

We would have three more training days before our next game, which was great for Fabinho and Virgil having come back from COVID quarantine on the 23rd. They needed these sessions and the cancellation of Leeds made sure we had real time for them. The session we'd planned for Christmas morning, after a late finish on Christmas Eve, was perfect for the context we were in: play and play again! We played an eight against eight on an octagon pitch shape, with two free players (our six and nine – Fabinho and Bobby – our connectors). Both outside triangles and the centre-halves made up the team of eight. 'Use the width and attack the centre', was the name of this exercise. The pitch size forces the players' behaviours to create and connect chances through the centre of the pitch, where they can use the width to move the opposition. It was our idea set within a 'new challenge' for the boys.

After two eight-minute games I screamed, "Winning goal!" when the red team had scored to make it 1-1. This was exactly what the team needed, there was something at stake. What was it? It's pride, the best 'teacher' for elite sports. Immediately Milner, Kostas and Taki combined again and finished with a shot from the edge of the area. "So deserved!" I shouted as they were the team with most inside play. We then played two lots of eight minutes of our 'identity game' where three teams fight to earn the right to attack more often – the 'wave' game, the game that makes us US. Vitor counted the points; the better you defend the more points you get, the better you attack the more points you get. It's about the levels of concentration you reach in training which defines the quality of training.

Trent shouted, "Merry Christmas!" while walking off the pitch after his team had won, while Virgil bellowed, "Enjoy the day, boys!" A few boys walked inside immediately. Their silence is a lovely noise, their competitiveness is from another planet. Mission accomplished. The boys trained with maximum concentration and intensity without us coaches having to correct a lot. The creation of the exercises made sure the 'correction' was when they were playing. Earn the right to attack more. As we'd set out in pre-season in Austria and France, we'd have to earn our target of playing the maximum amount of games this season.

I couldn't wait for 2022, I was so excited by the prospect of what this group could achieve once again. But first we had Leicester away in the last game of the year. It brought back memories. The King Power Stadium will forever remind us of coming back from the Club World Cup in Qatar in 2019.

We beat Flamengo in the final, lifted the trophy, travelled back and then played Leicester there in a massive game. It was almost two years to the day. It was a statement-win in our march to the title, featuring three assists and a goal from Trent. A historical moment and utterly decisive in becoming champions that season.

The day before the game, Jürgen picked up his phone when the team meeting started and read out: "Total shots, 17-14. Shots on target, 9-8… Which game am I referring to?" Hendo straightaway said, "Man City v Leicester." "Correct," Jürgen replied. "You would not say it was a 6-3 result if you only knew these stats and not the score." The boys had gone out to train on Boxing Day with City 4-0 up before half-time against Leicester, so we felt it was important to mention it was tighter than the final score showed. For ourselves, we needed to make a decision on how to approach this game. Not make a mistake in how we prepared because they played only a day ago, not make a mistake because we beat them in the League Cup with a much-changed side, not make a mistake with thinking that Man City didn't have to work hard to get those three points. Leicester are a really good offensive team, and if we didn't defend against them by cutting the inside pathways to Maddison, we would suffer offensive counter-attack situations. Our idea was that we should make it incredibly intense, make the pitch small and go all over them; we'd need to throw in everything we had to get the ball and stop the counter-attacks. By this point they'd scored 33 goals so far, so it showed their offensive strength. We wanted to keep the rhythm high, go for each back-pass. We didn't know how they were going to structure themselves, but what we knew for sure was that we had to protect against their quick strikers in a smart and brave way.

Video is a great tool but can also be a real cheat. The only 'honest' clip of a football game is the 95 minutes from front to back. What's important is that whatever you decide to show will, in the end, define you. You have a huge responsibility; be wise and smart because the power of the imagination can't be underestimated. You can increase clarity, you can instil confidence, but it's also way too easy to create doubt. How can you expect players to be creative when you are always changing strategies? Their focus goes into doing the strategy right, so why even think something new? Unpredictability, the spontaneous moments, is what we search for – and it comes from our clear and consistent ideas. It's so easy to take this part away in football. 'Strategy gets you from A to B, but creativity will get you everywhere', should be Einstein's quote if you adapt it to the game of football. Don't fall into the trap called 'strategy'.

As we headed out to train on the 'C pitch', Sadio told me he didn't really like training there. I said the reason we were using it was because it was exactly the same size as the pitch at the King Power Stadium. We have three training pitches all designed for the different-sized pitches in the Premier League. 'Ah!' Now he got it – and I hoped he liked it a little more now. During that last session Mo and Sadio found each other time after time. A good sign, I thought. "Unlucky Pep," I heard Mo say, "Better luck next time." The 'old team' were winning 4-0 against the 'young team' in one of our drills and if they got 5-0, they'd get double the points in the 'old v young' competition... Mo crossed to the back post, Sadio headed in. Five-nil. Job done. Everyone knows now I'm the coach who wants the young team to win, sometimes to create the right atmosphere and, on other occasions, pressure, because I just love our talent.

As we walked off, Jürgen said to Robbo, "Life punishes." We still had two more games to go without him after his red card at Tottenham. We missed him, but he was lively in training and supporting the team, just as a real leader should.

After the session I called Andreas to give him an update. He too was at home with COVID, though thankfully he had no symptoms and was still in full command of his physical department. The passionate ones always find a way. The biggest difference in working at the top or just a little bit below is you will not find one individual inside our building without this maximum passion. And I'm not joking. Even our security-gate team execute their jobs as if it will decide the three points at the weekend.

That night I watched as 'Mark Leyland's Newcastle' played with more intensity than Manchester United in a 1-1 draw, a spectacular game. It was great to see, I am very proud of him. But with eleven points after 19 games, there was a huge task in front of him. That said, I think it's never done and if points are the by-product of performance, I felt they would have a huge shot of staying in the league.

On matchday, Jürgen addressed the team for the final time before we left the hotel for the stadium. "Of all the things I expect us to be good at tonight, it is that we counter-press them with all we have. We will have the ball a lot – that means we will lose the ball. This will make it a high-energy game and we want to be on the same level so that when we get outplayed we chase them from behind."

"Big performance incoming," Robbo messaged the team WhatsApp group as we headed for the bus. With an hour until kick-off, Virgil was on the massage bed, Kostas next to him. "Diamond again," I told them. Smalley, our masseur, and Chris, our physio, were making everyone perfectly ready, as always. "Maddison as the 10, Iheanacho and Vardy as the two strikers," I explained. "Kostas, you will be free for short periods, orientate your touch forward so we can take advantage."

But final no18 ended in defeat as we went down 1-0 at the King Power Stadium. And we lost because we deserved to. Not because of the fact we could have shot much more often, even if it was 21 shots for us to six from them. Not because we missed a penalty and put the rebound against the bar. Not because Kasper Schmeichel made some incredible saves. Not because Ali didn't have to make one save until their goal in the 60th minute. Not because in the last ten minutes we could and should have scored three times. No, we lost because we didn't reach even close to our potential as a team. We never found rhythm, our positional game wasn't fluid at all and when we lost the ball they had a phase where they could counter each time. We didn't attack well enough and with this we lost all the advantage of being fresher than them. How can you play like this when you train like that?

Something we did wasn't right and we had to find out quickly. Tactically, we knew we didn't switch the sides often enough, we knew we didn't have the extra and crucial player between the lines and we knew we could have done so much more with all the balls we won high up the pitch. We didn't shoot once from outside the box in open play, against a deep-defending side. But my feeling was also that we never should have travelled on game day. We never do usually, only in extreme situations – and when we prepared the logistics of the game, it was an extreme situation with us having to play two games in three days. We never changed back to our normal routine after the Leeds game got cancelled on Boxing Day.

The next day I spent time watching the one clip that made the difference at the King Power Stadium. It was a 95-minute clip. 'Never point a finger', was something I learned when I was young. My mum would always say, "When you point, the three other fingers are pointing to yourself. If you blame, blame yourself." And on this occasion, I did.

'WHEN YOU DON'T SMILE, THE GAME DOESN'T SMILE'

WEEK 23

A DREAM CAME TRUE

ONE DAY OF GRIEF IS ENOUGH, ONE DAY BEING IN destruction mode is enough. Sometimes it's good to have problems – we needed this to get angry again. Watching the Leicester game back, we saw our mistake: misunderstanding. We became frustrated about things we would never get frustrated about when we would see this game as a final, I think. In a final you don't get frustrated when something doesn't work; you focus on the next situation and the next situation only.

Jürgen and I discussed and both agreed our message should stay positive but also honest. Unconsciously, we went into the game thinking: we were fresher so we would win, but the Premier League doesn't work like that... and if after a while you feel it will not be like that, the opposition has the momentum. If you only have a hammer, all the problems are a nail – and we tried to force and score each single time. We didn't enjoy it, at all, and when you don't smile the game doesn't smile. "We became desperate instead of convinced," Jürgen told the team. Against deep-defending sides you need to play the extra pass in and around the box; force shots but don't force passes. Against deep sides you need to create shots from the second line.

So, in training, we introduced the rule that you are allowed a second touch to shoot from distance. We played five-a-side games on a 40x40 metre pitch, always with the one extra rule to stimulate the team-tactical behaviour we wanted to see. Robbo took the ball and fired right into the top corner... Milner shot, it got deflected but went in... "You need to shoot before you score!" I shouted some of Cruyff's wisdom. The exercise stimulates this extra drive to finish with our players combining freely. We always believe nobody wants to be chased down by us in a race. We needed to create this mood again and we had three days to let the boys believe, I said to Jürgen and Vitor. The season wasn't over, being six or even nine points behind City. We had this game-in-hand against Chelsea. No matter what anyone said, especially in the media, we were only halfway through. We had to go to Stamford Bridge as close to who we were as we could be. If we lost at Chelsea, we should only lose by playing our way.

With the transfer window reopening, Jürgen, myself and Vitor began to seriously discuss the possibility of trying to get Luis Diaz in now. It had become apparent a deal might be possible in January, rather than in the summer of 2022. The club had established a good relationship with Porto through Marko Grujic's loan move there and believed they were under pressure to do a deal now. We had heard we would have an advantage because the boy wanted to come to Liverpool; he had rejected a Premier League offer last summer because he wanted us. We were also confident with Julian and our scouting department that we'd be able to get it over the line. Something our club and the best ones in the world all have is an alignment between ownership, manager and sporting director. Luis was a fighter, a winner and someone who could play immediately for us. We needed players with energy. There was a second player we were thinking of who had goals, speed and skill, but I wasn't really sure about the mentality, the 'survive mode' they needed to have going to a big club. Luis had technique, overview and goals. But above all, he had fight and drive to survive. Julian was convinced and Jürgen wanted him NOW. It was a statement if we did it then, a message to the team. When you have doubt, just ask 'the game'

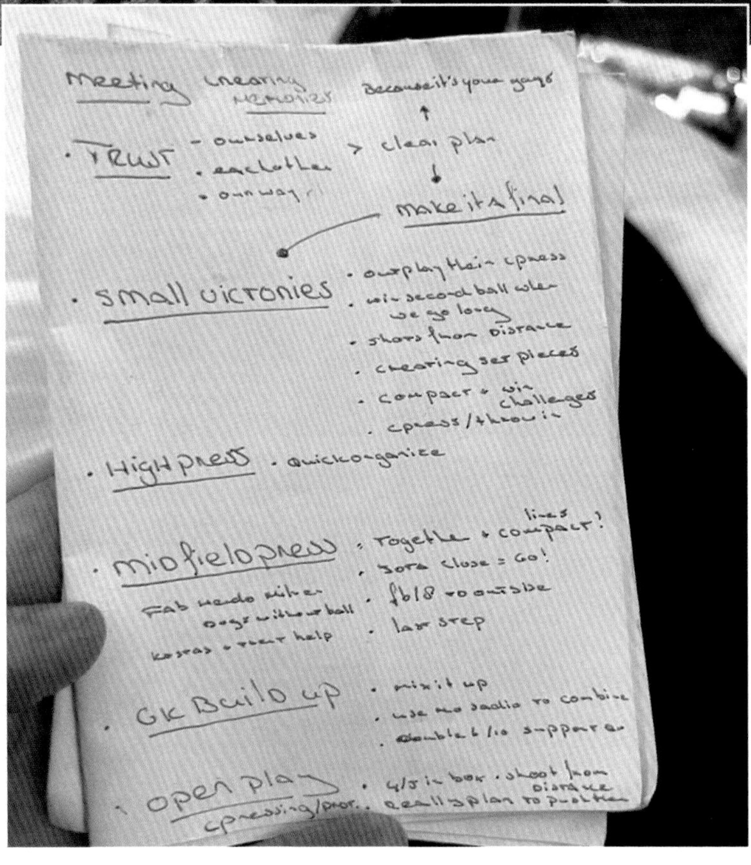

Battle plan: My notes ahead of taking charge of the team against Chelsea in Jürgen's absence in January. (Top) the team behind the team relaxing after an enjoyable staff game at Kirkby. I also enjoy padel tennis games with Jürgen

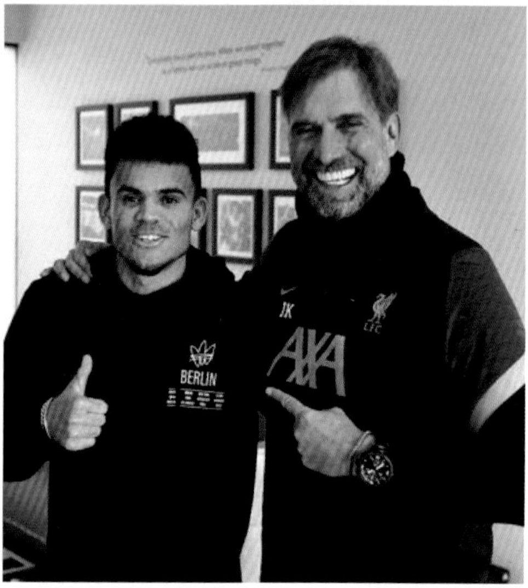

Taking charge: (Clockwise from top left) Action from Stamford Bridge with me looking on from the touchline; Jürgen welcomes Luis to our club; Harvey Elliott gets his first Liverpool goal against Cardiff; Bobby scores our first in a 2–0 win over Inter Milan and celebrations after a Fabinho goal seals victory at Crystal Palace

Wembley roar: Caoimhin (top) was one of our heroes again as we won the Carabao Cup final penalty shoot-out against Chelsea and lifted our first silverware of the season. (Above) I celebrate with our fans

Freed From Desire: (Top) starting the dressing room sing-song at Wembley and (above) celebrating our first Carabao Cup trophy with Jürgen and the backroom team

– watch him and you will get your answer. And the games of Luis were the answer: threats from everywhere, connects well with the ones around him, which is a huge plus for such a quick, intelligent, skilful winger. We needed to be smart. The player really wanted to come to us, we believed.

Back to more immediate matters, Jürgen opened the final session of 2021 by telling the boys that even with a boring lifestyle you can get COVID. Jürgen, myself and so many of the staff live like monks, but nobody is bigger than the virus. "Even Joel Matip caught COVID, boys. Please make sure you spend tonight with your family."

"We will not lose two games in a row," I told the boys during the session. "What I'm trying to say is that if we lose, we lose playing our way. That you lose on the scoreboard, it can always happen, but you don't lose yourself." You can explain it like this. There are two games in football: one is reflected on the scoreboard; the second is your way – your identity. The first one you can lose but the second one never, ever. It's the identity that counts. That's something every coach learns the hard way. After the session, I watched it back with the analysts; we started with our counter-press rondo. People underestimate the pressure our guys get from the outside world. We can't add pressure as well; we should aim to take these pressures away. How? Going back to basics; 'keep the ball and counter-press'. There is no better exercise to force the impulse to get our ball back and do the things we are good at. Focus and stimulate attack. Stress the defensive part but encourage playing really quick, simple and easy decisions.

Chelsea played counter-pressing at a very high level so we needed boys who took risks, who weren't afraid to make mistakes, to outplay this counter-press. Then we'd get Mo, Sadio and Jota in one-v-one situations with so much space. Against Chelsea we needed to play – really play – moving the ball constantly and swiftly, supporting each other quickly in well-defined triangles. With this they orientated themselves to man-marking, which opened up spaces and free players we had to exploit. 'Exploit gaps' was the final part of the training session, a finishing drill where Mo, Sadio and Jota had to create, find and use the gaps. With time they 'understood' and improved their timings, their connections and, with this, their relationships. They started improving the exercise with their own imagination and I had to say, well done boys.

But that night, the bomb dropped. New Year's Eve and my phone goes. It's a message from Vitor. I don't pick up because Danielle and I are with friends and in the middle of a great talk. But then it goes again, immediately. I open WhatsApp to see his messages: "Positive" … "Jürgen." A hundred things raced through my head at the same time, but then the boss called and told me he felt okay. We'd exchanged text messages earlier that night but I left my beer and headed straight home.

Waking up the next morning, more messages. More positives. Now it's John and Jack. It meant now we had Jürgen, Andreas, John, Jack and Taffa all from our coaching staff with positive tests. Bobby and Ali were also positive, as well as Joel. The timing could not have been worse, but we had to think quickly. I made sure we got Mark Morris over from our Under-23s to work with the keepers. He'd worked for a long time with Caoimhin, so that wouldn't disrupt things too much, but it really was not cool that our second goalkeeper had to play in such a game without the support from our main goalkeeping coaches. Our coaching group was getting smaller and smaller but losing our manager the day before our away game at Chelsea was a blow. "The last ones standing, the survivors," Pete, Vitor and I joked before our meeting. Our office felt empty and lonely, but our togetherness couldn't have been bigger.

Trust your instinct. Training has to be intense. Prepare well. These three things were in my mind. Our boys shouldn't have time to feel there was anything different. Vitor, Pete and myself prepared the meeting, we made a few key points and the videos Pete selected really supported our ideas. I expected Chelsea to really come and press, not like in their last game against us where they dropped off. "Make it a final!" is how I started the meeting with the boys. "Outplay their counter-press! Really play quick together! We have nothing to lose! I love our TEAM." We prepared the final session with a focus on our high press, on our midfield press, on our build-up with Kelleher and our open play. I shouted constantly, "Really play! Exactly like that! Well done! Look for the spaces! Outplay their press!" Hendo, Fab and Milner needed to really play but when we lost the ball they needed to be the 'dogs' they can be. Every ball we won in our midfield press would create the counter-attacks we wanted, needed and what I felt would decide this game.

As we stepped onto the plane to head down to London, Jürgen sent a message to the team's WhatsApp group…

Good afternoon
How you have heard and realised, I am positive
I feel fine
Little flu symptoms
Nothing else
So…
Use Pep as the energy source he is and GO FOR IT!
How he said in the meeting
Let's make it a final

Play our football
Enjoy
I'll watch it
Happy New Year
Boss

He is our boss. Going to a concert without the *dirigente* isn't a pleasant prospect, but there is a difference between a good and a top manager. The top ones have prepared the team for moments like these, moments where they have to become autonomous. We knew it would not be easy at Stamford Bridge, but with support and energy from everyone we will have a chance to overcome all of our problems. Our structure around this team is so strong, Vitor, Pete, Ray, Andreas and the rest of our staff. It will be incredible when we make a new memory together with our fans. Everything is nicer when you can share. On matchday morning I held the final meeting at the team hotel. It was one about trust. "Trust yourself boys, trust each other, just look who is sitting next to you and we know how much quality we have, how strong we are. Forget everything that's gone through your head in these last days – ignore it. It's only because of you guys we can DO this. And trust our way – we have a clear plan. The plan is to make memories. The plan is to make this game a final. To make it a special game together with our fans. A final is won by making small victories. Overplay their counter-press, win second balls when we play with direction, shots from distance, creating set-pieces, winning 1v1 challenges."

It was after this game we'd say goodbye to Mo, Sadio and Naby for a short while as they went to AFCON with their countries. I wished them all the best in front of the group; they deserved to fight for each prize and for them this was a big one. "A career isn't that long, you should use each moment you can to win a cup," I told them later, after the game in front of everybody. Everybody knows what kind of pride exists in playing for your country. They were African legends already, but being able to win it would be incredible for them. It's one of the most interesting tournaments in the world, so much passion and culture.

We were ready. I was ready. Final no20 ended 2-2 with Chelsea at the home of the champions of Europe and without our manager. I would say, therefore, it was a point gained. The intensity and rhythm of this one was from a new football world. They tried to find all the dynamics that hurt us. If you look at all the teams we play against, all the structures we play against, all the styles we play against, it feels like this Chelsea is the one which always finds our weak spaces, or better the open spaces when we are not quick enough against the ball. It's a real complicated team to play against for us, that's for sure; when you leave space between the lines, they use it. When you leave space around their 6s, they use it.

However, the amount of balls we stole with our midfield press chasing them all over the pitch was almost close to perfect. We forced so many Chelsea mistakes. We scored two incredible goals from Sadio and Mo, the kind only they can score, class and determination at the same time; one with our pressing, the other one playing really well and using Fabinho and Jota to overload our right side. But just before half-time Kovacic scored a screamer out of a deflected save from Kelleher, so we weren't covered nor organised on the edge of the box. Before this we'd been in a phase of complete control. Kelleher played a top game, by the way – we were so proud of him. A few minutes later, they made it 2-2 when we didn't close the gaps in our last line well enough.

Half-time came and I ran inside where Pete was waiting with

our analysts. I watched the clips and at the same time I called Jürgen. It's strange because the roles were completely opposite to how they usually were – Jürgen told me his views and gave some real input. I headed into the dressing room and immediately told the boys, "We are going to put a big line here and now over this first half, I couldn't care less if it's 0-0 or 2-2, it's the same thing. We know we can play better, we feel this, but what we definitely have to do better is defend their double 6." We showed two clips, one of how we had to close the passing options to Kante and Kovacic better, the second was how the spaces open up when we outplay their press. When we were clear, clear in mind, then we knew where to go with our passing. We had played so well and we created incredible spaces for Mo, Sadio and Jota. "Let's go and attack the second half!"

We created three big moments where Mendy had to make three incredible saves after the restart. The highlight was when Fab played a pass over everyone to Jota, who volleyed it directly towards the far corner. I think I would have ended up in the away section if we'd have scored to make it 3-2. Anyway, there was no doubt we could have played better but I was proud of how we gave our everything. If we kept this spirit, and added our football creativity, I was in no doubt we would come through this difficult situation. Personally, I enjoyed our preparation. I enjoyed our team spirit. I enjoyed the support of Jürgen at half-time. I enjoyed thanking our fans and showing them what it means to me. A dream came true without realising. To be honest, if you made a five-minute compilation of our quick breakaway attacks in this game you would see football at its most purely attractive.

After I got back into the coaches' dressing room after the game, my phone did not stop. I'd just like to say thanks again to everyone who sent me a message of support, it truly meant a lot to me. As you can imagine, it was an incredibly proud day for me. It was strange being in London, having a pre-match walk with the team into St James' Park, the gardens of Buckingham Palace and around the Churchill War Rooms, knowing at night I would lead the team into the home of the champions of Europe. Basically, in my opinion, you have two different types of coaches, two extremes: the ones who play to win and the ones who play not to lose. Or rather, the coach with guts and the one without. It's dead simple but only when the floodlights are on and the cameras go at you, I believe you will be defined as one or the other. I'm proud that in 20 years of coaching, with or without the cameras, I've always set my teams up to play to win.

'Despite everything, we came here to win', I was thinking with each step. It was a final, but it was just minutes before our walk that we'd lost Smalley, our main masseur, as his lateral flow test was positive. It was a mind-fuck for the players he had treated the night before. We shouldn't underestimate this effect; these things make me proud of the players. They don't whine, they don't make excuses, they don't blame. This mentality is what gave our team a heart and will continue to do so.

WEEK 24

IMPOSSIBLE TO PLAN

A NEW WEEK AND COVID-19 WAS CONTINUING TO test us. All of us. This virus really doesn't like our world. I pray for the ones who lost family members and friends. To be honest, nothing could have prepared us for this virus in my opinion, but hopefully it has now prepared us to deal much better with a future health crisis. For sure we've got new mental baggage with us, but we've learned in crisis situations you have to act before you are right. Nothing else. It has taught us life is a team sport.

By now, Mo, Sadio and Naby were away with their national teams. AFCON has so much creative talent and passion; they express themselves through football. Their journey helped them to own their pathway, they know how to survive and get the best out of themselves. They invest in themselves, searching for constant improvement. The only ingredient they need is trust – from the club, from the manager, from the staff.

I will give an example of something that happened in the lead-up to Chelsea. It was two days before the game and we were focused on 'feeling the net' exercises. I tried to give them 30-40 shots in and around the box from all different angles, all different situations with a high scoring possibility. No doubt, strike strong and confidently in the corners. It's a typical matchday-minus-2 [days] session; the problem is that we don't have many of these with our front three in our busy periods, but when we have the time it's like expensive fireworks. I always try to adjust the exercises to what they need, not to do what they want. When we went over to the right side of the box, Mo was constantly finishing first-post. With time I asked, "Did you try one time to the open side?" With his last one he went second-post, but in my mind I was thinking: why is he trying to go first-post? Then in the Chelsea game, 26 minutes in, Trent played one of his better passes and isolated Mo one-v-one against Alonso. Mo dribbled past him with a simple feint and finished for an incredible goal. And guess what? First-post. He surprised Mendy.

That tells you to trust your creative players, give them space to express themselves, even when it 'looks' wrong. Trust opens up creativity, I remembered again. But, ensure loyalty. How can you ask for unpredictability without giving freedom and trust? How can you expect unpredictability when you constantly change strategy? For example, I told Sadio in the tunnel in front of all the team just before going out to start the game at Stamford Bridge, "You are going to score today but it will not be a beauty. It will probably be an ugly goal, like a deflected ball from a Mo shot, or a bouncing ball from a set-piece, but you will score today." And then I said to the team, "Guys, when Sadio scores, celebrate all together with the fans as if it is the winning goal in our Champions League final." He hadn't scored for nine games at this point, the media were all over him and I hate these doubts. The creative players need trust, they need to feel we trust them with all we have, especially in moments like this. That's the only way he can play with intuition. Sadio played one of his best games in a while that afternoon and he scored. Another example is something I said to Mo: "Be the leader you are, show everyone the leader you are." With trust they have the characteristic to change difficult situations into beautiful situations. As I said earlier, at Liverpool we call them the 'piano players' after that Shankly quote of needing eight guys to carry it and three to play it. When your piano players have a world-class attitude, your team will become scary, I always say.

By this point, it had become clear to us that we were unable to plan properly in this period. It had become a mess with the COVID situation. We had been in a great position to fight for the Premier League title, so this was my idea of a nightmare: losing our position in the league table like that. You can almost compare it to a train crash happening inside our building.

Wagon by wagon crashes into COVID. Who would have said three weeks before that we'd be in this situation? No-one. But we were. We had to deal with it. We proved we are a club and a team who want to keep going. It's our challenge, it's our job. If people want to underestimate our players, or our staff, then they can do so. We went to Tottenham without Virgil and Fabinho and should have won – maybe if more decisions had gone our way. We went to Chelsea without Jürgen, Joel, Ali and Roberto, yet their best player was Edouard Mendy – and that for me says everything.

We lost Trent to COVID the day after Chelsea, meaning we would lose some of our most creative passes from deeper. He already had more goals and assists by this point in the season than in the whole of the last one. Mo and Trent not being available was hurting; I didn't know if the headache I had was because of this or because of COVID. I believed I had it too. My son had a fever and tested positive from a lateral flow test; he must have got it from me because my family didn't go anywhere during this school holiday. I was waiting for the PCR tests to be delivered to see if the rest of the family had it. Our house looked like a lab with the amount of home tests on the kitchen table. This virus variant is like Lionel Messi in his best times; it will find a gap to dribble through, even if you are brilliantly organised. It's just not to defend against.

With our cases rising, we decided to cancel training, do a new round of PCR tests and inform Public Health England. Together with our lawyer, sporting director and CEO, we prepared a submission to ask that our first semi-final leg against Arsenal in the EFL Cup was postponed as we didn't see how we could fulfil the fixture safely. I texted Jürgen to suggest we cancel training. If you know me and our football staff, you know how much we value training. It was not a decision we took lightly and showed how concerned we were.

Late at night on 3 January, very late, I got the result. The doc called me… It wasn't Mo and Trent's future absence that created my headache after all. Nope, the virus had got me as well. Our press officer contacted me to set up a statement for 9.30am the following morning announcing my press conference for Arsenal was cancelled. The AXA was closed for around 48 hours and the EFL granted permission for the first leg of the Arsenal game to be postponed.

With Shrewsbury coming, we took 23 of our players from the U18s and U23s into our Saturday morning session, while Pete took care of the press conference. Roberto and Joel were also coming back from COVID, so could train, with Vitor taking the session. We prepared as best we could, not thinking about anything beyond our control.

Saturday was also the day I did some more work on our attempt to sign Luis Diaz from FC Porto. Our scouting department makes very useful videos about the players who could be interesting for our team. We know the ones we really like a long time before it's in the media. The videos contain 15 minutes of analysis about their strengths and weaknesses, but on top of this I always want to watch full games of the ones I really like – the full 95-minute clip, the truth, the phases, the reactions to phases. This was my very last report about Diaz when Porto played away against Estoril…

'While preparing pressing, he reads where the next pass goes to intercept, runs with all he has in these moments. He smells these chances to intercept close to the opposition goal. Never stops. Wants to defend forward. Love that…'

'Can move more often without the ball in behind when the ball is 'free' from out the back. Moments he does that are with good timing but can be with more surprise. Great touch and control of the ball. Inside the box skill to create shots. Can dribble, goes easily, outplay/ slides left and right passing the defenders. In a small space with full speed tries to find the better option to pass. Love that. Always overview. Love that. Always in relation to score. Love that. Goes one-on-one to shoot from distance, what is good for our game…'

'Positions himself naturally in respect to the outside triangle. Adjusts easily to positioning of others. Ball opposite side can be more active finding space behind the last line. Needs to add idea to attack through the centre as well, more active to attack through inside. This will give him more striker movements as well, with this more goals…'

'Counter-press impulse will improve easily within our style and training. Will become more intense with this. More aggressive with this. By FAR the best player. I HAVE NO DOUBT…'

Jürgen responded to this report with: "He is a game-changer." I texted back: "Absolutely, literally for them and figuratively for us." We hoped we could get the deal done.

It was strange on matchday to be sat at home. At 10am, while I was at my kitchen table drinking a proper English tea out of my Ted Lasso 'Believe' mug, Jürgen called me. "Meeting at AXA went well with the boys who stayed behind, I'm on my way to The Titanic now." He was back in business. We made a few jokes, I told him just before we hung up that I would call him at half-time! I was so happy for him and I was happy for the boys who stayed behind to train, they needed some clarity and leadership after this last week.

I watched the game from home. The FA Cup, the soul of football. Anfield, the football temple. A final, the third round of the tournament. Max Woltman was starting, dreams can come true. It was just great. When I came from Porto, he was in the U12 team and Alex and myself coached him each Tuesday and Wednesday on the day-release programme. There is no bigger glory for the club than these moments. We want to create players who will win cups for the first team. Not just young players but young winners. He himself had only trained once after coming back from COVID but was making his first start. The Academy should be proud – we started with six graduates that day. It meant we could not lose because we gave an opportunity to talent, which is the right thing. You can lose the game, yes of course, but we will win 'new' players, we win experiences. That's the worst thing that can happen. Fifteen minutes before kick-off I was wishing I could watch the game from the Kop; if you can't be on the bench, that's the place you want to sit. I began to get excited, so I sent a text to the boys: "Anfield, vamossss, good luck guys, CHASE them."

Our first goal was set up by Conor, Kaide turned inside the box and finished well. The ages of these two players combined does not even make the 36 of James Milner. Incredible. During the first half I made notes: 'We can attack much better. We pass way too early to the outside, there are so many gaps and spaces in front of their centre-halves, especially when we move more, but we don't try, we just switch. Virgil and Ibou need to step in when they have space, show more initiative to play with the idea of breaking lines. This will push the other into the right positions. Our counter-press is good but we have to use this to play first pass forward and attack...'

I counted from home how many times we lost the ball but won it back immediately and how many times we attacked directly. But we slowed down in these moments instead of speeding up. Nevertheless, we were through to the fourth round with a 4-1 win. Bobby did Bobby things, Kostas did Kostas crosses, Fabinho scored his penalty with Mo and Milner not there and then another late on. Jürgen called me afterwards and told me we'd drawn Cardiff at home. "This has been a good day," I said. "It will only be good when your test comes back negative," he replied. We'd wait…

‘THE WAY YOU TRAIN YOUR PLAYERS BECOMES THEIR INNER VOICE, IT BECOMES THEIR GPS’

WEEK 25

ORGANISED CHAOS

I BEGAN THIS WEEK WITH THE THOUGHT IN MY head: why did I get so sick from this virus, even with the booster, even at my age? Maybe it's because my body is in stress mode too often? I don't know, but for four days I was a disaster; the headache behind my eyes was unbearable. I'm just very grateful for the vaccination process because this virus is showing its middle finger to a lot of people. Jürgen called me while I was doing my daily 'COVID hotel' routine – my family and I had been isolating in the house for nine days by now. I was doing laps, walking back and forth over our driveway for an hour while speaking to him. We discussed the line-up and the ideas for training for Arsenal. We decide we will go strong, our strongest. I see the neighbour's builders watching me and laughing – they knew who was going to play against Arsenal now, I guess! AirPods create the feeling that nobody is around you.

When I got off the phone from the boss, my mind turned to how important it would be if we could sign Luis Diaz during this transfer window. My feeling was we needed the boy like water in the desert. He would come here and he would play, and we felt we needed this boost. He was the best player in Portugal in that moment and all the top players from Portugal come to England and make an immediate impact at new clubs. Getting him in January would be such a lift, as we had with Virgil when we brought him in during the winter window in 2018. I knew it would be difficult, getting deals done isn't an easy process, but with our outstanding transfer team led by Julian, I also had hope.

I'd sent videos over to Vitor so he knew exactly the ideas behind the training plan. Tuesday's session would focus on 'organised chaos' and finishing our attacks. I told him the most important thing was to create an atmosphere to chase and make sure they created many finishes by creating spaces and using them. We'd implement the rule of having a minimum of one player asking for the ball behind the last line, believing he will get the ball. This would open up spaces and gaps we needed to use. Then it's about playing these passes through the gaps, because when we don't, we will stop running, and when we stop running, we are lost. We'd seen this in our last game against Shrewsbury, so it was a case of here is where we can improve, here is where we must improve, creating one-v-one situations for our technically-dominant players high up the pitch more often. This exercise is perfect to stimulate these kinds of one-v-one situations. Winning a one-v-one offensive situation is almost always at the beginning of each goal. A moment of spontaneity, a moment of creativity, doing something nobody from the opposition is expecting. This is always important but especially against someone like Mikel Arteta who will come with such a clear game plan. We felt everything that could be a little bit different could unbalance them. Playing a one-v-one with movements makes it so much easier, that's why you need players close to each other and they can decide to combine or to dribble. This is what we try to stimulate because creating a shot is always easier with movements around you. Finish with open eyes, go strong and confident for the corners.

The exercise I created is one where the players shouldn't be worried about their defensive position – you can leave your offensive position to fill the box, or to fill counter-pressing with life. With the videos and pen and paper, I explained to Vitor the finishing dynamics of the four players who are highest and most central on the pitch. That's why we call this exercise 'organised chaos' because our players need to react quickly to defence and create confusion when losing the ball. If you want to explain Jürgen's football ideas in one sentence, this is probably it. They have to react faster than the four players of the opposition. Try to think one step ahead, react faster and create a counter-press situation. It feels like chaos but it's controlled because we train it each single day. The way you train your players becomes their inner voice, it becomes their GPS, this is what I like so much about drilling players. Two ideas of this creating-chaos concept are first we stop the counter-attack of Arsenal (where they are strong) and second, we create this possibility to attack once more but now with this emotional advantage that the opposition lost the ball three or four seconds ago. Nothing feels worse for them than when we steal the ball back immediately, so here was where we had to make it really intense, here was where the session becomes US, here was where our focus lies in training – becoming US. Clarity and repetition, creating a specific focus for a collective display. The two or three closest players have to lead this hunt. We can only trust – or better still, rely on – our attitude when we show this each day. Vitor called me afterwards and said he deserved four days off after the session! The analyst later sent me it to watch at home and everything went to plan, as confirmed by a text which followed from Jürgen that night that simply said: "Top session."

Being back at the AXA the day before was a great feeling, I have to say. I couldn't wait to get back to work and continue the prep for Arsenal. Our MD-1 session was about making sure we'd be a team with a common plan. The first – and our best – football rule is that what we do, we do together – and we do with 100 per cent. Press smart and press intense, never make just a little bit of pressure. We search for energy, our type of energy, always within the right distances so we can create two-v-one situations. It keeps coming back to the same thing: our process. How do we want to attack and how do we want to protect ourselves to apply maximum counter-pressing? Counter-pressing isn't problem-solving but problem-avoiding… and it for sure avoids a lot of running! So, if you want to convince players this one always helps… running avoids running! We tell the boys, create a 'chasing party'. Don't speculate – GO. Don't hesitate – GO. Don't hope – GO. That's why each game we have to ask ourselves the decisive question: how badly do we want it?

Our common history wasn't a good one in January, but now we had two legs of a semi-final that could take us directly into Wembley. With Mo and Sadio missing, our message in this period was that we needed everyone in their best finishing shape. We had an opportunity to make a big step, so we needed everyone to step up with goals. Ugly goals, set-pieces goals, whatever – let's show how resilient we all are without two of our stars. Jürgen said it like this in the analysis meeting: "Everyone is invited to get on the scoresheet." We knew we would have to show a real winners' attitude, it's such an important attribute in this beautiful game. The will to win, the will to finish attacks. I like when we speak a lot about finishing and train a lot of our final-third behaviours because it gives the right mindset before a game. Everything we do is – and should be – with the goal in mind.

Jürgen and I actually decided to stop the tactical session after a discussion on the pitch. Our build-up from out the back should be to provoke, to unbalance Arsenal, to create and find the free spaces they leave. So we wanted to show the boys how we shouldn't be positioning ourselves. "Not like this," we told them. Trent was deep, Milner was deep, Robbo deep, Taki and Jota wide, Hendo high and everyone far away from each other. We brought a ball in and they had to adjust quickly to our offensive 4-4-2, with four players in build-up, four players between the lines and one open on each side, making two. It was a new, offensive Liverpool FC 4-4-2 where we were always close to each other, where we were flexible and where we had 'perfect' access to attack through the centre of the pitch. We used this session to make clear what we wanted for the whole of the month of January. Virgil and Joel looking to break lines, looking for the centre first, stepping a little with the ball to attract. Consistency started now with intense defending and creating clear pathways in attack. "Our biggest surprise against this Arsenal should be our intensity," Jürgen told the lads.

That afternoon I watched our Premier League game with Arsenal at Anfield. Little things in football make big differences, I thought as I watched the goals we scored. Take, for example, Roberto, who can keep the ball in a difficult situation while the opposition is pressing, can find his way out and create a new, better situation with his individual possession of the ball. The difference couldn't be bigger if he lost the ball in a similar situation and we would be open to suffer a counter-attack. That's why good players, coached well, prepared well, become unstoppable. We also knew we had to find and win the one-v-one challenges as we'd done that in all the good games we'd had against Arsenal. In those matches we'd always made them look a little poorer than they actually were because they'd always had good players. Now, though, they clearly had a good team and had matured under Arteta.

Everything was prepared, we'd be hunting for uncompromising challenges with our midfield three, the same midfield as at

Chelsea, the same midfield as against Barcelona in one of our most beautiful games. No dirty challenges but fair challenges for the ball, bringing our legal aggression to the next level. The moment you get passive against Arsenal they will punish you – exactly in the same way Chelsea or City do. So our message was: give them pressure everywhere and from everywhere, high and in the highest intensity, and give them pressure in an unpredictable way. Not A-B-C pressing but with the principle that our front three have to defend five or even six of them – and in training this looked really good. We had to become consistent again in the amount of work we put in, it would result in stealing many balls high up the pitch. Our attitude and our organisation can create problems for the best teams in world football, but without these we will struggle against every team. We work on this each MD-1. We are a team that is organised to be able to fight, but we are also a team which has improved our positional game so much over the last few years. It made our defending even more intense because we were fresher. This is what we needed to keep up: improvement, not perfection, just being a little bit better than yesterday. Applying our new 4-4-2 offensive system, it would give us access to attack more often through the centre; it would open up the pathways we wanted and needed, to take our positional game to unpredictable levels. It helped in these moments to get Bobby on the ball so he could link up and connect more easily. Only to get the best out of our players and have a clear common plan.

Matchday morning and 'Taffa post' arrived bang on cue, as we'd started to call it. When Danielle comes into the coaches' office with five envelopes, we say sarcastically, "Just put them straight on Taffa's desk!" It's fan mail, of course, and he'd got more already in three months than we had altogether. That's what happens when you bring in a legend, I guess. One thing is for sure, he'd improved the level of the staff games… But more importantly, Ali had told me he was happy with the work being done on the pitch. "Enjoying it?" I asked Ali as I walked past a session he was doing with Taffa, flying from left to right across the goal. "This is my beach," he replied, which sounds better in Portuguese and is more logical, I came to realise, when I wrote it down.

Jürgen's final message to the boys in the team meeting began with another question: "What was the last semi-final we played at Anfield?" He continued: "Exactly, Barça. If we can't use this game as a life lesson, what game can we use? It was a similar situation that night in terms of missing key players. Missing Bobby and Mo at that time felt as if they'd cut a leg off us, but the moment we had our meeting nobody had doubt and Divock did superbly. Tonight, we can't win the semi-final but we can lead it in the right direction. We decide if the pressing works for Arsenal. We have this quality. It's about us, only us, if things work. We need full conviction to become consistent and that only works with being defensively solid. Our football is front-footed, our football is being in an attacking mood defensively. If we show US, then we show the world. I can hear the roar already, Robbo, when you overlap. I can hear the roar already when you underlap, Hendo. We are one of the few teams who have all the tools needed to compete in all the competitions we are in."

The game itself was a strange one as it ended 0-0 against Arsenal's ten men. Our first one without Mo, Sadio and Naby. A game has two halves but this one was a game before the sending-off of Granit Xhaka and a game after it. The final 15 minutes was the part I liked the most. We brought Curtis to the left wing and Neco on the right. It was clear we created one-v-one situations for them with Robbo on the one side overlapping and Ox on the other underlapping. With this we created great moments where we could have won the game, but what I liked the most is that we interfered and changed to a clear set-up. Our new 4-4-2, but with offensive players on the outside, that we had prepared months ago. It's something we can keep for the future, I was convinced, but now I was sure it would win us finals. We'd obviously have liked to have won the game, but everyone could now underestimate us for a week. They could write us off now for a week. Then we'd go there and play a final. I couldn't wait. First we had Brentford to think about, but what I liked most is that we were talking about – and now preparing for – finals in January. Finals are what our team needs.

Friday was back to work at AXA getting ready for Brentford. Since we'd played them earlier in the season, they'd had some mixed results. They were struggling with injuries and obviously they were in a challenging period. They play, and play well, but against City and against us they'd set up mainly for long balls. They were not the first team and wouldn't be the last to change their complete approach against us. It's easier to set up to destroy than to set up to create. Carlos Carvalhal explained once that a Ferrari in traffic can't be quick. One in four passes they played against City or us was a long one. The advantage we had is that we now knew how they wanted to play against us and that it would be a second-ball game in the moments they could decide. It was a similar style to Burnley, with the only difference being they played with a line of five. What they did was planned and executed very well, making it difficult to play against, and we'd felt this during our first game. Play passes on the outside to cross to the second post; win the second ball to move behind our last line in the channel; set-pieces. They didn't have a second plan – this was it against us. We would need to avoid this plan as many times as possible to be successful against them. The challenge would be to switch quickly from an aggressive mood to a playing mood when we won the second ball, or better when the ball was in the air. Use our skill, orientation and calmness to play good passes. "These moments should feel good because it is good," Jürgen said in the meeting. It was the right way to avoid their strengths because they proved they were better than us in the second-ball fight.

The first adjustment we would make was to put Roberto in the space of [defensive midfielder Christian] Norgaard, who won so many second-balls the first time we played them. We adjusted this little detail in hoping it would take a big influence away, allowing us to be able to control the game better. One of their weaknesses was the flat line of five, where with good timings we could really get behind them, but it was clear we'd need to be aggressive in our movements when we switched the play from right to left. Our analysis also made us decide to go with six in the box at offensive set-pieces instead of four. When we show images in our tactical analysis meetings, it isn't to show the mistakes we make, it isn't easy to see the options when we go up and down the pitch – it's to show our options we have in these situations, it's never personal. "You need 20 feet and two gloves to avoid a goal," I once said in a press conference. It's important for our players to get this. Defending is firstly attacking with a perfect protection, secondly it's pressing the opposition, thirdly it's avoiding the progress, and then, only fourthly, clearing balls, winning challenges and so on. We always show the collective possibilities to avoid these kinds of behaviours, these kinds of 'situations' where there is a bigger chance to make a mistake. But it was also important we balanced our information as the analysis meeting was only 42 hours after we finished our game against Arsenal – and we'd play again the following day knowing the boys would not be fully recovered from that. We didn't give them too much, we followed our ideas, otherwise it would only cause more fatigue and this would influence the spontaneity. The body is fatigued but the mind is as well, so that's why we chose to explain our ideas in terms of 11-v-11. We'd need moments of high IQ on the pitch to break down the style of Brentford.

That Saturday was the day 'The Little Magician', Philippe Coutinho, announced he was back in the Premier League with a goal and an assist for Aston Villa on his debut against Manchester United. It was also the day Mo scored a superb volley to get Egypt up and running in the Africa Cup of Nations. We watched it all unfold at The Titanic that night.

It was Jürgen's final speech to the boys on matchday and I was thinking I needed a chamomile tea after it! We'd said we wanted to go and lift the mood and we did. "This line-up will create a thunderstorm for Brentford," Jürgen started the meeting by saying. "Twenty games played, 42 points, 18 games to go. Our target was to squeeze everything out of this season, in each competition. Can you imagine if in 30 years we tell our grandkids that we had to win 18 games in a row to become champions? It's not impossible. We need more optimism in this room. There will be difficult moments in the game, as in each Premier League game, but we need to see them as a hurdle. The only thing we need to do is jump over them. For me it's not over. The outside world doesn't expect anything at this moment. A high-energy performance is needed. Spot and play, don't wait for anyone. When we play like this, they will need breaks. There are so many teams in the world of football who see us as role models for what we did and how long we did it. Let's give them a new chapter."

And final no21 ended 3-0 at Anfield in a difficult game against a Brentford side who had come to fight their way into the game. But we executed the game plan so well, avoiding their idea, dealing better with their set-up during the second balls and so many aggressive movements on the outside. Trent and Robbo were constantly involved, starting our attacks, quick switches, balls behind their line of five, resulting in Ox scoring from Robbo's cross for the second. We used their weaknesses and it gave us 68 per cent possession, 27 shots and 13 on target. Fabinho scored his third goal in three games with our first in-swinging corner to set us on our way and Taki finished it off after Bobby's pressing. If we want to achieve big things, we have to start scoring from corners more often. Our new set-up is built for this. Today, a first glimpse of it. Jota showed again he is such a complete striker: left foot, right foot, header. Inside the box he is 100 per cent lethal. He hit the post on this day but was constantly involved in all dangerous moments. "A good start to the mission," Jürgen said, walking into the dressing room. Our mission: 17 more finals.

We were unlucky, though. Just as we'd had Divock in a good moment and then injured, we also had Ox in a really good moment until he got an ankle injury. That hurt as these were the times we needed them most.

WEEK 26

WARRIORS NOT WORRIERS

MONDAY MORNING, JÜRGEN SENT ME A PICTURE OF us two celebrating the Premier League title: "Men on a mission." "That's it," I texted back, "A new and a better one is coming I hope!" I had a great morning on the Tuesday, spending it with Alex Inglethorpe, Nick Marshall, Matt Newbury, and Tosh [Farrell] on the Academy side. We discussed talent, training, game-coaching, everything that is likeable when you're a coach. Academy football is the purest, the people are the purest. I love it. They are the heart of our Academy, they made it happen.

"Different competition, same mission," Jürgen opened the training session with, later that day, with the boys having had a day off the day before. "It's clear, we need to win away at the Emirates." Thomas Gronnemark sent us his report from Brentford: we had an incredible defensive throw-in game, our best in four seasons with 12.5 per cent ball-retention for them. We were good – really good – at defending throw-ins. For every game we got a detailed analysis from Thomas of each throw-in that occurred.

The Tuesday was our second recovery day and we used a simple rondo to get their bodies and minds up to speed again. Jota said to Robbo in the rondo while chasing his socks off, "Just because you are screaming doesn't mean you are running more than me!" "He wants to scare the others," Diogo then tells me. With the subs from the Brentford clash, we play six-v-six games in a space of 40x40 metres, and with Harvey as the extra free player. Each team had to make five passes before they could score – it was the 'pressing and counter-pressing game' and

Harvey showed he didn't lose his football brain. Then we drilled our last line and we did an offensive exercise of eight-v-six. The one rule I gave our offensive players (without the defensive team knowing) was they could only score when they moved the ball clean over the lines of the box. They needed to break the lines of the box with a dribble or a flat pass.

That night I watched our U18s play Burnley in the FA Youth Cup. Stefan Bajcetic, Bobby Clark and Luke Chambers were the standout players. They should be with us next pre-season, Jürgen and I agreed. Kaide [Gordon] was the player who impressed during our training camp in Austria and he would be starting in the second leg of our semi-final against Arsenal at the Emirates. These processes, as you can imagine, make me so proud. I said in the pre-match press conference that a coach should be judged much more on the talent he brings through.

In the analysis meeting Jürgen started by saying: "We will need to play more – and better – football. How? We need to position ourselves better." Arsenal's pressing style was that they were clear in their tasks; for example, Gabriel Martinelli defended Hendo and Trent with the 'one can defend two' principle. We would need to open the pitch more when they pressed us and support each other quicker in defined outside triangles. We would try to open up the pitch at the back with Robbo dropping on the left side. His superb left foot should give us more options when we were building. I told Joel and Virgil to drop off to open up more so we could switch over the last line easier when they came and pressed us. "Football doesn't need to be perfect," Jürgen continued, "The pass we play is the best pass we play. React." He lectured the team, giving clear instructions that we needed to play by being orientated and controlling the ball better while outplaying their high press. With time the boys get it, the seeds are planted. This is what training is all about: you have a problem, you create a solution, start training and see it isn't working but insist and keep repeating and correcting behaviours until everyone gets the point. You create trust with this. And we all know trust is what matters in finals. Arsenal tried to find the space behind Trent and Robbo, so they should be really focused to control the movements of Bukayo Saka and Martinelli.

On matchday morning I took a long walk through London with my mind going everywhere. It was sunny but cold – typical January. Wembley was waiting but it would come down to just one aspect that night: who wants it more? We had to show how much we wanted it. Football isn't perfect, the team that reacted better to mistakes would win, I felt. In the final meeting Jürgen spoke emotionally with the team: "We are still in this nice London hotel… Show how much it means to us when we counter-press them. Earn the right tonight that we can go to Wembley. It's an opportunity, no pressure. It would be great if we can fill Wembley half full of red – our red. Feel the opportunity by grabbing the counter-press moments. Be aggressive and creative in our way. One more thing: if Bobby drops and Gabriel follows, the closest player needs to run into this gap. Kaide, Jota, Hendo."

When we arrived at the Emirates Stadium on the bus, we saw all of the fans and it brought a flashback to the last game I'd visited as a supporter. It was in Kyiv, the Champions League final in 2018. Despite the result, it was an incredible feeling finding the stadium together with my wife Danielle. I visited Jürgen and the staff the night before the game on the roof of the hotel they were in. Seeing them there was emotional. It proved that coming home has to do with people and not with the location. But it was soon back to the present… and what a present. What a night! Semi-final, second leg and a 2-0 win for us at the Emirates. We did what we did before, we do what we always do. When people say it will be impossible, we reach another level. This is what we did that night. The performance reminded me of the Bayern Munich 3-1 win after drawing 0-0 at home in the first leg. Wembley would be red. Our red. We stopped their plan with our high last line and the focus of Trent and Robbo when they played these long balls in behind them. Martinelli played such a good game for Arsenal, what a player he is.

For our first goal, our right-sided triangle was flexible with Trent moving inside and Hendo dropping, opening up the pass to Bobby. It wasn't Jota, Hendo or Kaide but Trent who used the space behind Gabriel. It showed our flexibility. Bobby flicked the ball to Trent, who put Jota into a one-v-one. He outplayed one, he outplayed two and even a third one before scoring. The second, there was a lot of fight for the first and second ball before Fab won it, making a challenge behind Milner. Trent played 'first pass forward' into Jota, who moved and had an almost perfect first touch with his chest before lifting it over Ramsdale. Only Jota can be quicker with the ball than without, he has this natural capacity to control the ball while being at full speed.

Two more assists for Trent. He was giving a new dimension to what it meant to be a right defender. Kaide played a super game. He hugged me after full-time and said, "Thank you." "We should thank you, Kaide," I told him. "Keep up the passion and everything will be good." It was clear we had a new diamond on our hands. He is exactly what we need from our talents, a combination of bravery and humility.

Afterwards, the staff drank a beer on the bus as we made

our way to the airport. It's a tradition when we win. Today it tasted like having a dessert. Wembley. Finals. Bring it on. "It's a completely different feeling waking up knowing you will play a final at Wembley," Vitor tells me the day after the game. Jürgen met with the team back at AXA and started with: "Our special mission continues... Recover well in the coming two days because Crystal Palace is waiting." Walking up the stairs, Jota asked me if it was true I wanted him to do some work with neuro11 that day. "Yes," I told him, "I wanted to put your feet immediately back down on the floor!" He laughed and told me he was tired. "All good, you are conquering the world. Take this day for recovery, it's like a sabbath to Liverpool supporters."

My thoughts going into the Palace game were that we'd have to be warriors and not worriers. It was the best way to describe our situation heading into the Premier League's winter break. Most of the boys would be travelling with their families directly after the game to the sunshine. There could be many things to worry about but we should block these distractions out. Our team manager is the best one I ever saw in helping players to focus on the game and training programme. Avoiding distractions is his task in the same way our medical department should try to avoid injuries. "Prevention is better than a cure," is what the Dutch philosopher Erasmus said in 1500. The problem is that no-one sees the effort professionals put in to prevent things. I really believe our team has this character and maturity to block these 'distractions' but it isn't a bad thing to mention. Hendo told me, "We are not that team" and I love it, but we put them on their toes. No excuses. I told him: "The only one who knows whether you give 98 per cent or 100 per cent is you, nobody else will see the difference – only you know." For Palace it would be a war, and 98 per cent after travelling to London and playing a semi-final 40 hours ago would not be enough. We needed 100 per cent of the energy available.

Palace had improved so much under Patrick Vieira and Osian Roberts and had brought talent in. We knew we'd have to break them with quick switches because eleven players can't cover the size of a football pitch, at least not quicker than a ball can move. The ball always moves quicker than the player – that's why we could try to attract one of their midfielders with the positioning of Hendo or Curtis next to Fabinho. This would open up the space for Roberto, Jota or Ox, who had to use it to really speed up the game, turn with the ball and GO! Palace's biggest strength was how quickly they recovered their defensive positions, Vitor tells me; immediately, ten players behind the ball. When we wanted to switch quickly we had to use Fab (the free player) to create a two-v-one situation on the wing. Here was where we were going to try to break them down; aggressive underlaps or overlaps would do the job, aggressive one-v-ones would help. Our game plan: press and play, as Pete says. Jürgen explained and showed the team that good pressing needs triggers, and triggers need a starting position. Triggers only work within a compact formation.

If you looked at the Arsenal game we were incredibly strong and wherever we were, we were together, in the right distances, with the right attitude. All the ingredients of a clean-sheet team. What we do, we do together and we do with 100 per cent effort. Every day more and more I believe that a tactics board doesn't create this type of team. It helps, but the character of the coach and his charisma to convince is what will define the level of team spirit. We decided we would give the boys a week off after Palace because of the winter break. Most of them would travel to have a deserved holiday, so there were a lot of things to worry about. Suitcases, family travels, possible injuries. Only Alisson, Fab and Taki would have international duty. Jürgen explained in the team meeting that in the first week he came to Liverpool and realised someone had given the boys three days off he lost his mind. "Three days off? I never gave anyone ever three days off!"

By the way, that person who made that decision was... me! You need time to really understand the demands of the Premier League in combination with the cup competitions and Europe. That's why Jürgen decided three years ago to give the non-international boys and travelling staff a week off during international breaks. I think that shows how much impact English football has on foreign managers. Not many get the time to make these kinds of decisions, but it's the right thing because life is about balance, top sport is about balance; you need to recover physically and emotionally from tough periods and that's what we try to do. We believe it's the only way to play our style over long, long periods and still be creative and decisive in the final phase of the season. That's why, for example, Jürgen and myself play padel tennis, to create balance in our lives. A distraction: you relax a certain part of the brain and activate the creative part and so sometimes the best ideas are born in these moments. Okay, maybe not born, but moved to the conscious part of the brain as it was probably already there in the subconscious. By relaxing the state of mind from the game of football and the leadership, padel creates this increased dopamine flow. It's basically the 'warm shower' principle: we have the answers, it's just that the mind needs to find them. Many times this only happens when you relax the mind, like in a warm shower.

It's the same reason I can write more easily for this book when we are travelling with the team; travel creates this dopamine flow as well. What I can say is that we learn a lot about ourselves in these padel games and there is no place to hide. You need to take initiative and read the play well to be successful. On the Saturday we played again – Jürgen with his own 'Kloppo' racket, me with my own passion making sure the heart-rate on his racket is just an average one! A few days before, Jürgen had forwarded me an incredible video of him playing padel with Fernando Belasteguin, the world no1. I'm not a jealous guy but only Cruyff had his own shoes! I tried to bring the boss back down to earth in our game, but it ended 1-1.

We headed down to London once again that night and on matchday morning Jürgen had a clear message for the team, comparing our mission to a marathon: "Two athletes who get the same information will be influenced by it completely differently. You have the one on top who hears that the no2 is getting closer with 10km to go. The chaser from this moment on has the advantage. You don't need a rocket scientist to explain who we are in this race. The only way to do it is to focus on one step at a time, literally in the marathon and figuratively game by game. We need to give everything, there is no pressure, just opportunity. When you are in a high-performance industry, the most important thing is the information you get. The right information. What is our football? It's about creating a counter-pressing festival. We want to finish our attacks but when we don't, the ball is free, we should be like sharks. We just need to grab inside our pressing toolbox. You can only 'win' by taking this risk because you are 80 metres away from your own goal. This is our race – we go for it with our football."

With the boss's words ringing in their ears, the boys delivered. Final no22, a 3-1 win away at Crystal Palace. What a week we'd had… Sorry, actually what a two weeks we'd had. We had silenced the doubters. Five games without Sadio, Mo, Naby, Thiago, Harvey and Divock and we still won four and drew one – and how. The best thing about this day? The chase was still alive because Man City drew at Southampton and we won. In truth, at Selhurst Park we showed both sides of our season: exceptional for one half, feeling completely under pressure the second. Walking back in, Virgil said to me, "Pep, it can't be beautiful each time," and he was right. I like his Italian side. In some games it's important that you play the result instead of the game and this one was a good example, but we can't lose compactness and that's what happened here. That's where we could improve, something that had not happened at Arsenal. Luckily we had a moment during the second half where we could speak calmly with Hendo, Curtis, Fabinho and Roberto to make sure we closed the centre together better.

And let's discuss the good situations of this game. Firstly, our high press during their goal-kicks was perfectly organised and gave us the ball back quickly on multiple occasions. Secondly, Virgil's header at the near post with the corner was what opened the game. We improved with our deliveries, with our target area and the amount of target players. It was paying off now. Thirdly, Curtis was changing into a press-monster – the shark Jürgen was referring to. The amount of times he started the hunt or chased and surprised from the blind side, and his energy level, was unbelievable. Fourthly, we moved the ball quickly with intention during the first half-hour and created so many underlaps and overlaps. The second goal was a good example of this, team play at its best: our right-sided triangle passed the ball quickly to each other with the support of Fabinho and Roberto. With this, we attracted them and we switched at the right moment to Jota on the other side, who found Robbo who played a cross to Ox who finished cool-blooded. Just before that cross, Curtis underlapped, creating the space and time to pick out Ox.

About our compactness, it's never a good sign when your front-line is moving forward and your back line is moving backwards. We have to be inside three 'stripes', but we were in five or even six at times. The Premier League is too good to come away with such open spaces to defend.

After the game I spoke for a long time with Osian and Patrick. They are doing an incredible job, playing so much better, with young talent.

The winter break started now for us. Balance. Distraction. Loading the battery to full energy levels so we could continue our chase when we resumed in February, as well as the Champions League knockouts and a final at Wembley.

‘PLAYERS CAN ACHIEVE SO MUCH MORE WHEN THEY FEEL WANTED, TRIGGERED AND INSPIRED’

WEEK 27

SNOW JOKE

OKAY, WHERE TO START WITH THIS ONE... DANIELLE and I headed off to Austria for a ski trip for our winter-break week. Our boys were all over the world, some in the Maldives, others in Dubai, but most of the staff were skiing in Austria. I loved cruising over the blue pistes but one day in particular ended up being pretty adventurous. At the highest point of the mountain in our resort of Lech, we got stuck on a 'black route' and I survived a 'free solo' when I left my skis to help Danielle. When I got close to her, I slipped and fell probably 30 metres down the snow, with my wife panicking up in the mountain. My helmet went another 50 metres. Very dangerous! I've no idea how we ended up off-route on a black diamond but in the end we were saved and went directly back to our hotel. Crazy.

During our dinner, our sporting director called me: "You and Jürgen have to speak with Luis Diaz in five minutes. We've just agreed with Porto but Tottenham are all-in as well." Jürgen and I had been pushing really hard for Diaz, so when we heard Tottenham had made an offer we had to act – and Mike Gordon couldn't have handled it better. I joined the call and Jürgen was explaining to Luis how he would fit into our style and that we would help him. He said in reference to me joining [the call], "But you will hear this guy much more often!" To which I immediately said, "But I will explain things more calmly than Sergio [Conceicao, the Porto manager]!" To which Luis laughed. I told him: "We want you desperately and have been pushing for the last one-and-a-half months with our owners and our sporting director, but you know that these kinds of transfers are not easy to accomplish. The good thing is you will train with Virgil, Robbo and Trent and they will make you so much stronger. Our idea is to create and score; you will have to tear these guys apart each day in training, which will make you better."

His agent translated Jürgen's message and Julian Ward said, "These two will make you a better player." I told him there were not many clubs with more history and culture than Porto but Liverpool was one of them and he would feel this. Julian then walked with his phone to the trophy cabinet at AXA and finished with: "We want to add to this and that's why we want you."

If the boy wasn't convinced, he would be now. What started as a bad adventure on the slopes ended with an incredible signing. We signed the one we wanted. My crazy day couldn't have ended better. This talk face-to-face was important because players are emotional human beings, not logical human beings. Players can achieve so much more when they feel wanted, triggered and inspired. 'A player doesn't care how much you know until they know how much you care' is the best quote to explain the type of leadership needed to create this type of emotion and relationship. This is what makes Jürgen and Liverpool Football Club so different at this moment in time. It's not rocket science. The mutual respect between staff and players is the foundation of a successful journey.

The call ended with Luis set to do his medical that night… if it went to plan, I intended to order the most expensive bottle of red wine on the list!

On the Sunday I was a little bit poorer… the deal was done. Luis was ours. I couldn't wait to begin work with him. Would he be the difference-maker for the rest of this season? We hoped so.

WEEK 28

BACK TO BASICS

BECAUSE OF THE ONE-WEEK BREAK, WHICH WAS SO important to us for a lot of reasons, now we had to adapt the players again to our game idea; adapt their bodies and their minds. They had to readjust to our pressing and counter-pressing dynamics, finishing attitude and ball-possession style. So, we started from the first day back with the core principles of our identity. In five days we had to adapt to our style again – and in five days we had to prepare for Cardiff City in order to try and reach the next round of the FA Cup. It felt like five days to prepare for the rest of the season and it was five days before we had Ali, Fabinho, Mo and Sadio back. And, of course, it was five days before our new signing, Luis Diaz, joined us. So let me put it like this: these were five important days to get the team playing like us again. After a week off we like to put our players into the adaptation to our style of play, with short timings but high intensity. I put eight pieces of A4 paper next to each other on Jürgen's desk, they covered the whole width of it. "Is this all for today?" he asked, with a smile. "No, no… it's for the next two days: MD-4 and -3," I replied. Each single paper explained a specific exercise and how it related to our way of play. Most of them were new variations of our best exercises which improved our ideas. Like this, I can explain much easier the 'who', 'what', 'where', 'when' and 'why' we are doing these things. Like this, you easily see the connection and logic tactically between the specific training days and the exercises. "I love it!" Jürgen responded. "Exactly like that, Pep!" Our mini pre-season was up-and-running. Only in these moments I am 100 per cent clear of where to go. The coming days would be incredibly intense for both players and staff. We, as staff, had to stay curious and energetic and, like that, the desire of our players would follow.

I love football. I love the game. The game of winning and losing. I'm at home at Liverpool FC. My family is also at home. There are places where you just feel you belong: I had this with PSV Eindhoven, I had this with FC Porto and now I have this with Liverpool FC. I have to be honest, though, I never got this feeling with NEC Nijmegen, not even for one second. I felt the people didn't want me, I feel I should have known, but it's good it happened because in life you learn the most when people try to bury you.

"One of the problems in the football world is that the more successful you are, the less time you have for training," were the words Jürgen kicked off the session with. "Now we have time to train and we will use it, we see it as a mini pre-season. But first we sing for Curtis because he had his 21st birthday two days ago! After that we will chase, we will counter-press, and that isn't a proposal but a law." We would go back to basics, back to consistency and the players had to increase intensity at every opportunity they got. We don't want a linear or mechanical style. We want unpredictability; we want flexibility in our ball possession. We want more ball possession, we want to dominate the game, we want more capacity to create, more goal opportunity and more initiative from our players. Attack. Creativity. Our idea forces this individual development and this is the reason that our players are constantly improving. We develop.

I told the boys directly after the first session of the week that if we trained the whole week like we did that day, with such speed and passion, we would be ready for each final in front of us; success would come to us instead of us having to start searching for it.

One of the first drills of the week was the 'gates game'. I felt the chaotic atmosphere would be perfect to end the start-up session in order to create focus and combinations we could take into the rest of the week. It promotes connection and interaction between our players; it creates offensive aggression. We played three four-minute games. It ended controversially 17-16 with the white bibs (Trent's team) stealing the win, combining through a gate while Milner was putting the pole back into its place. There is just no replacement for competition in training. I love the moment we can shout "Winning goal!" in training; this shout reflects so much more than just a game which will get decided with the highest emotion possible. No, it means we reached maximum concentration and with this we reached evolution. Adaptability of the human body, of the players' bodies, adaptability towards our game, to the one rule in place. Evolution. The amount of times I told Trent's team after an evening session during my Academy days, "You guys surprised me again, I thought I would never say it but you reached another level." Every session we would finish with finals, winner-stays-on, or our identity game. Sometimes the Academy would shut the lights off and we were still playing. I need winners around me, you need to give your players the chance to get this winning voice by speaking to them. When teams show this, when the players train with big, big, big hearts, I'm a happy person. Because we all live and love the journey, but we want titles, we want cups and we want to be on top of that bus.

You know why I mention the bus? COVID took lives away as well as taking 'life' away. We won the Premier League, the first time for our club in 30 years. Think about how many coaches and players had tried to do that before us. But it was us that did it and we could not celebrate it properly with our fans. For this reason – and it's one of the main motivations for me – I hope we get the chance to do it properly at some point. And I can tell you one thing: I will feel like a fan that day. My emotions would not be limited, even if it was the League Cup that was coming up. Start with the end in mind, start with the cup in mind, and that's why this week we didn't do a 'normal' rondo, we did the intensity rondo. We didn't do finishing but we did finishing with sprints and one-v-ones over 50 metres to end with five players inside the box. We didn't do the identity game but we did the identity game with counter-attacks over half-a-pitch. We didn't do the pressing/counter-pressing exercise in the middle third; no, we did it box-to-box and exactly because of this we started the week with the gates game. A mini pre-season but a pre-season much closer to the titles.

I was wishing I could relax more but this year started with do-or-die and has to end with 'we did'. The boys have the mentality to achieve, they prove this each training session... "especially when it's a midday start!" some of the seniors joked to me. "How long will training take today?" I'm asked as I walked into the player liaison office to see if Hendo needed some help organising Wembley travel for players' families on Wednesday morning. Hendo, Jane and Danielle are looking at me. I say, with a laugh, "It depends how many he hits in the top corner today!" to which Hendo smiled. I had gone into the office to try and ensure Luis Diaz would arrive on the Friday to begin training with us. I knew he would get his visa in Paris, but I wanted him here ASAP. I then went to the coaches' office to explain to Pete, Vitor, Andreas, John and Jack the session plan and the ideas behind it. They began to organise the players in the right positions and teams, so it meant myself, Jürgen and Danielle could discuss the organisation of tickets and travel for the players' families and our staff for Wembley. Jürgen always helps our families out by reserving two boxes and organising tickets, so now we just needed to arrange travel for the staff. We just didn't want any distractions, so travel and ticketing should run smoothly – even for the staff who would normally stay behind. Jürgen and I decided to offer to the club to pay for the buses to get them to Wembley. Everyone should be thinking about how to help us to win this final and not how to get there.

Jürgen started the Wednesday session with: "Yesterday's training, the 'gates game', was so intense. Like this, the future is bright!" I later heard Kaide had said that the Tuesday session – the one which was "deliberate chaos" (not his words but the senior boys') – he loved more than any he'd ever done before. In fact, there was a moment he tackled Millie even though he was on his team! It's great to see how much he loves training; it's great to see he is maturing and to see that our game style has fewer secrets for him. Just little notes are enough now for him to understand and recognise patterns. For example, I took him to one side separately while Jürgen was speaking with the team. "You decide how small we make the pitch when the ball is on the other side, Kaide. It's like this: the players who are furthest away are always the most important. It doesn't feel like that, but it is, because counter-pressing in a big space is impossible. You and only you give chances for the closest two to win the ball, and when they find a way out of this 'tornado' you are ready to catch and surprise them from the blind side." With the first opportunity in the session, he then pressed an opponent intensely from the blind side when the team wanted to switch from right to left.

That evening we received news Vitor had tested positive for COVID. "Pete, you are the last one," he sent to our coaches' WhatsApp group. Pete replied, "Unkraut vergeht nicht," which basically means "Sick weeds don't pass" only for the next morning to test positive too. Our last man standing fell over as well. This virus doesn't have family. That meant on Thursday it was only Jürgen and myself with the outfield players on the training pitch. We split the group and on both pitches we drilled the last line with balls in behind, with unorganised attacks, always with the target for them to move as organised as possible, anticipating each other's defensive behaviours. The day before, we had battered our centre-halves already with Bobby and Jota playing one-v-ones over and over again against them. When I told Roberto before training he would play one-v-ones against Virgil he started dancing around him. Virgil just laughed it off and in the session he was like a rock: every wave collapsed on top of him. He was in control, ready to intercept at the right moment and forcing Jota and Roberto to the outside.

He was, by now, completely his normal self again; in 2022 the best defender in the world of football once again – and for a Dutch guy this is a truly special achievement. He did it before and will do it again, especially when he trains like this, finding new solutions for different problems in the sessions, but his biggest strength is he is smart in avoiding them. The best ones love difficulties, they overcome adversity and transcend themselves. He represents a singularity and an identity which differentiates him from the other Dutch defenders. We feel his identity every day in the training sessions. We are so happy we have the best players with us. This is the most important thing: sign the best ones, keep the best ones and develop talents into the best ones. Some might say there are better players out there, but there aren't better players for Liverpool Football Club and our team than the ones we have. We have a team. We have character. We are strong together. We have the ones who feel our club, who live off and on the pitch for our mission; who have this 'us against the world' mentality which took us to the top because there is always a way for the ones who want it. Evolution. We have a 'brand' now: the type of training, the type of coaching, the type of leadership. We represent our club's history but this team is making its own. I hope this book will showcase our brand well to everyone.

Friday morning and what a moment: Luis Diaz arrived at the AXA Training Centre. He was with us, finally. After taking some photos, we sat in Jürgen's office together. It felt incredible he was here. We spoke for half-an-hour, just the three of us. I translated each word Jürgen said to him and vice-versa. "We fought for you! From a sporting point of view we really fought," I told him. He said: "I'm so delighted I'm sitting here. I grew up in a small village, so making it into this team, this club, it means so much to me, it makes me so proud. I will fight, always with a smile. I only wanted to come here." We replied with: "This club is so big on the outside but very small on the inside, it's family inside. You will love that, you will feel that. The team was really happy when we told them we signed you." He smiled. "Mister is tall!" he then said out of nothing, about Jürgen. "Wait till he raises his voice, then he looks much taller!" I joked in reply. "He stands on his tip-toes as well in these moments but you will see and hear that really quickly!" Jürgen laughed without me having to translate because I was imitating him. The boss said to me, "Tell him that our style is organised chaos." So I told Diaz, "We call our football 'organised chaos'. It means you have to create chaos for us in the final third, let the rest organise." "We have staff football now," Jürgen told him, "it's not how we play football here – it's without the counter-pressing!" The staff game actually ended 7-6 that day, with Jürgen scoring the winning goal. We joked afterwards with Taffa, "What happened?" "Not my time this time," he responded, "Verrry bad," in his best English. We all laughed. Jürgen responded immediately, "January and February you mean?" Taffa laughed even harder. The best ones can deal with a joke.

I walked into the sports hall directly after the staff game, everything hurting. Let me say it like this: I'm not like a fine wine, getting better with age! Niklas and Patrick from neuro11 were sitting and discussing things – namely planning our penalty-takers should we need them in the upcoming games, with the League Cup final particularly in mind. The only thing I ask is, "Is Virgil in?" "Yes, I would put him number 3," Niklas replied. "So, no1 Milner, no2 Fabinho, no3 Virgil, no4 Trent and no5 Mo – you would go like this?" I asked. "I don't have any doubt," Niklas said. Done! Back to Virgil, he knows the secrets of the game, I explained to Niklas. Some play long balls really well but not at the right moment. Virgil will never do that, he understands where and when to go. Not many have this talent. You can see it in how he orientates his first touch, it faces the play, it faces the opposition goal, it gives time and is many times the start of a speed-up. This is probably the most common characteristic between the best players, the quality of their first touch. The first touch dictates the speed of the play, is how Cruyff once said it. There are no secrets in the game for Virgil. Now he needs to know the secrets of set-piece deliveries and he will excel in this decisive football aspect as well. Luckily, Virgil is like a fine wine and continues to get better with the years.

Turning attention to the game that was coming up, we felt our main strength against Cardiff would be to eliminate the set-play opportunities for them, first of all by keeping them far away from our goal and taking their chances away to reach free-kicks and corners. Against teams who play for set-pieces this is key: a high last line and a smart second-ball fight. For example, Brentford three weeks prior, they didn't have one corner or wide free-kick against us – that's quality and all down to our last line. We had won 90 offsides by this point in the season – the second-placed team were behind us on 49. Our defensive attitude should create the offensive rhythm, this would allow us to have the ball most of the time. It would be about doing good things with it and it would depend on us what open spaces we used. So, we'd use 95 per cent of our training time on the Friday to show how to create as many speed-ups as possible to be able to shoot from all over the pitch, inside and outside the box. Creating chaos only works with loads of bodies in and around the area. We would need a real finishing attitude to create set-pieces, but our new idea was paying off.

On Saturday, Jürgen opened his meeting with, "I can say a lot of nice words about the football player Luis Diaz, but he will not understand anything yet, so it doesn't make sense! Maybe the Spanish-speaking guys can explain to him. Milner, you as well – you can explain to him the rules and where the money from fines will go!" "Multa [penalty fee]," Millie responded! But if we needed a warning about complacency against Cardiff, we just had to look at what happened to Manchester United against Middlesbrough at Old Trafford and the scares West Ham and Chelsea had also had to survive. We all love these kinds of stories, when a lower-league team beats a Premier League team in the FA Cup... but only when you are not involved in them. This tournament is made for these stories, so the only way to go into a final is respecting the game in front of you. We didn't know how much Cardiff wanted it, but we could decide how much we wanted it. As we were preparing to head over to the hotel, I looked outside from the coaches' office and Trent was still out there practising free-kicks with Niklas. It rained, it was windy, it was cold... Jürgen even said sorry to Luis in Spanish when he came outside to train.

On the Sunday morning Jürgen's last message to the team started with, "Two words. It will only work if you do them both: fight and play. Has anyone won the FA Cup in here? Anyone reached the final? We know how big it is to reach a final when we played Arsenal away and felt it ourselves. Our defence is an offensive thing so it creates rhythm. Create chaos! Only with one reason, to get one step closer to the final." The game ended 3-1 and moved us into the fifth round. We had the ball 80 per cent of the time. I said to Thiago on the bench, "This is our total football." "Yes, but Bobby on 8 defensively," he said. I replied, "When you have the ball you don't need to defend because we play with one ball – you should be the one who understands this!" He and Adrian started laughing. In the game we eliminated their set-piece opportunities, restricting them to a minimum of one. Our game had this constant fluidity and I was so happy with that after two weeks without a game. We had a good impulse when we lost the ball, maybe not always making the last step well enough but our immediate reaction with all of us was just good. If you look at Manchester United, West Ham, Leicester or Chelsea in their games, then we had to be satisfied. We played with quality, but when we changed and brought Diaz, Harvey, Bobby, Taki and Jota together on the inside there was so much technique on the pitch, it made it a different game. "We became a different wine," Vitor remarked. The highlights were Diaz counter-pressing on the touchline, which ended up with a Taki goal. You could see he was hungry and assisted immediately. Carlos Carvalhal had compared his signing with a size shoe: our team has a size eight and he is a size eight so will fit perfectly. He has a profile. He has our profile. He has this clean, technical style like Laudrup or Stoichkov. If we are comparing Diaz with these kinds of players, then I have to say that Jota has so many similarities with Romario… he's just missing the toe finish! The best teams in the past had so much technique together on the pitch: Ajax, Real Madrid, Milan, Barcelona, United… And when we won trophies, our front three were just unstoppable. If we wanted to win again, we needed this extra magic in attack.

Back to this game and the first half had actually ended goalless. The problem against a 5-3-2 Cardiff is that you don't have this natural 'step-in' from the back when you play against a 5-4-1, so you need an extra midfielder to build up. Our forwards were coming too much to the ball, which meant our midfielders, Curtis and Naby, were moving to the outside with Trent/Taki and Kostas/Jota not creating the important width and depth. We were able to correct this at half-time with a clear image showing the opportunities we had to create speed-ups more often, but the opening goal was a studied wide free-kick which Jota headed in with so much timing, technique and power. Create set-pieces, use them – and we made them decisive once more. Harvey also marked his comeback with so much control during his first touch and volley, all inside their box with so many players around him, as he scored our third and final one. It meant so much to him, to our fans and to us. We had our little diamond back, finally. The draw gave us another home tie, this time against Norwich, and our dreams were still alive. Drawing at home in the cup competitions makes such a big difference as it means no extra travel in our busy schedule.

Later that night it was the final of AFCON. Egypt v Senegal, Mo v Sadio. How can you choose between brothers? The whole LFC family were proud of our two boys, but we knew they'd be experiencing different emotions come the end of the game: joy for one, disappointment for the other. No matter what happened, they were already both legends – to us, to everyone.

‘A GOOD
TEAM SOLVES
PROBLEMS,
A TOP TEAM
AVOIDS THEM’

WEEK 29

BUENAS DIAZ

THIS WEEK BEGAN WITH ANDREAS AND I SPEAKING through every single player in our squad on our day off. It obviously took some time, but it's important to relate and connect the gym programme with the training intensity. 'Think as one' is the only way to control this process because we are always on the limit with our players, so unbalancing this process is a forerunner to injury. The main thing we do in our job is to change the thinking of our players, the way they look at the game, the way they look at our team, the way they look at our club and the way they look at gym work. Andreas has this special gift to do the right things with them, so the football game becomes better and not worse. I have a feeling that, generally speaking in the football world, there are a lot of people working in the gym with players who make the game worse. That doesn't happen here, but one of the hardest things in the world of football is to understand the gym correctly.

The Tuesday was Luis' first real training session, a 'counter-pressing introduction day' we called it! After the warm-up and rondos, we did the counter-press rondo and then go into 'stopping counter-attacks' with 'create-to-score'. Press. Play. Finish. Again and again. Repeat until the opposition vomits in a game due to tiredness! Mo was also back at the AXA. We got him back as soon as we could. Credit to Mo, the first thing he said to Jürgen is that he was ready. Jürgen spoke so highly about his performance at AFCON in front of the team, saying what an achievement it was reaching the final, that he probably would not feel this now but he made us proud showing his talent and leadership. "This deserves a round of applause," Jürgen continued.

It was an intense training day for Luis, but it's clear what we want to achieve in the game. As I've said before, the main impression is the first impression and I had no doubt he would fit like a glove. Organised chaos, his dribbles and movements should make sure we got more direction in our game. "These are the best ones," I shouted just after Fabinho intercepted a pass and played Milner immediately free in front of Ali during the drill. "We want to steal the ball as high as possible. We steal the ball because they feel under pressure and make a worse pass because of this. Next time they are free but will still feel under pressure." A few seconds later, Joe took a ball off the goal-line with a well-executed slide tackle. "Passion makes the difference, Joe. It makes the difference between winning and losing," I yelled. Jürgen stood back and was observing, always ready to react. He took Mo to one side again for a short one-on-one talk following his return from AFCON, while I addressed the rest of the boys about Leicester. "Leicester will set up to counter-attack," I explained. "Daka will be lurking from here, Iheanacho will be hiding himself here, always ready to be the outlet. A good team solves problems, a top team avoids them. Stopping the pathways into them will be key, always making the last step to cut the passes to them." While the work was intense, there was a light-hearted moment during the warm-up when Harvey knocked a cone over twice. Immediately you could hear from all directions, "He's still thinking about his goal!" And that was it, job done: the boys make sure every day is a 'zero start day'. Similarly, when it was unclear who would go to which rondo, I sent Luis to the one with Milner, Robbo and Trent, just for him to feel how quick and lively we play our recovery five-v-two rondo. "So much technique on the pitch," I said to Jürgen when we walked back inside to the warmth of AXA.

I was reminded of the first time I felt that Jürgen really respected me. It was when he came with a letter to my desk, about six years ago – probably two months after he'd arrived. He asked me to read it because he didn't understand it, so I started reading and I told him it was from a coach who said he wanted to work with him, to help him on the pitch and assist. "So basically he wants your job?" the boss said. "Basically, yes." He took the letter, tore it apart, threw it in the bin in front of me and turned around and walked away without saying anything. Of course, he understood the letter. He didn't need to do that. But that was the moment I knew we would work together for a long time and I would help him with all I've got to become the most successful manager he could be at Liverpool Football Club. I think you can see online, I did an interview just after this, explaining Jürgen's philosophy through my own eyes at the club. I had this idea before this moment, but it was a feeling he created that hasn't gone away even to this day: trust. Do we disagree? Of course. Does he want me to leave his office sometimes? Of course. But I believe and feel I can count with – and on – him. He is so much more than a colleague to me. To explain our early relationship, this is a good example: wherever I'd worked before, I had my playing ideas on five big flip-charts printed out. The middle one was my game idea explained with core principles over eight steps; the other four were the principles for when we have the ball, when they have the ball, counter-pressing and individual principles in and out of possession. It covered a big part of the wall of the old coaching office. It was my life on there. When Jürgen first came into the club, after a week or so he asked who they belonged to. "They are my way of believing, gaffer," I told him, "you want me to take them off?" He replied: "No, I like them – keep them there." Wow! Every year I would add new ideas, or tweak the existing ones. Stability in coaching is what creates consistency… and aren't we coaches all searching for consistency?

We reinvented ourselves this year, not because we said this and that. No, we went back to our basics with some little tweaks and by accepting going back to basics we went beyond ourselves. We were clear, the tweaks were so clear. A cup is made of two per cent talent and 98 per cent hard work, that's how it is. Nowadays the levels on which the Premier League, the cups and the Champions League are operating are so close to each other, so it's all about which team is preparing itself better to reach these last percentages of dedication. One of life's oldest lessons is the most true one: your hard work does pay off. Of course, we were clear with what we wanted in pre-season, from the first session, but it wasn't rocket science. It gave a clear direction, it gave imagination and room to grow. If your team wants to go beyond limits, accept you have them. I'm pretty sure that is how Einstein would have said it if he'd been a coach. The numbers '24-12' were showing on all the televisions inside our building. No, not Christmas Eve. It was the score after the latest old v young game on the Wednesday. "A new signing and you still can't win," Milner shouted after the latest game; Joe approached me and said, "We need some help, Pep – this can't continue like this!"

"Tomorrow we will need to be organised but really brave as well," were the opening words as Jürgen spoke with proper conviction to the team about Leicester [at home]. "We go for everything, we have to show ourselves this, time and time again. It's only the fourth game in the Premier League in 2022, it's the main competition, it's a proper target for us. The plan? A full-throttle Liverpool FC performance." The last time we set up this bravely was against Chelsea; we'd chosen the calculated risk again, leaving Virgil for three or four seconds in a one-v-one while we would be attacking. Joel would need to push up and help Fabinho in protecting against James Maddison. This would give all the rest the freedom to attack and would give us so many bodies to stop counter-attacks at the start. We expected them to play in a diamond again, but the higher we come with the ball the less interesting systems become anyway. We needed a formation which directly faced them in the eyes when they had a goal-kick because you should never ruin a good counter-pressing situation by thinking about how bad your pass was. Four, five or six of these situations would make it a top game for us. Jürgen continued: "Pep spoke about it yesterday during the counter-press rondo: the last step, being in it, the challenge, making impact, is what makes all the difference, these last two percentages. Use 'the line' to close another option, so know where you are chasing him from. Our midfield-three will be against their midfield-four so we need to 'leave' our man to press."

We showed images from the game we lost 1-0 [away], we showed the good and bad habits of our midfield press that day. We correct and are clear: like this and not like that. We needed more options around the box, we should have pushed up quicker into better positions so the player on the ball had more and better options to choose from. Today's analysis was to show the extra option players have when we'd do that right. Why do we do all of this work, all of this hard work? To stay in the opposition half more often, to give more offensive freedom to all the others, to lock them in, to shut the door. 'Which door?'

you must be thinking. The imaginary door is the whole of the halfway line – the line we use so many times in training as the definition to defend. We decided to go again with Curtis. He wasn't at his best against Cardiff, but Jürgen asked, "When did we give Curtis a second chance?" I agreed. Let's go, Curt. I like the brave decisions. Watch the games of us back where Curtis started. The first chance, the first shot, the first real press, the first moment in the box… it's always him. He has this desire to be the one who wants to prove he is different. I told him exactly this on the morning of the game: "Be the one who creates our first shot, play from the first second with the goal in mind. Don't let the last game take up too much of today, Curtis. Put the goal again in your mind."

Matchday morning. We were standing outside at AXA. The sun shone but it was cold. Luis was shivering. The sunlight was deceptive. He had his snood over his ears. "It's fake sun," Virgil said to Thiago. "Not the real one. It's like when you expect Coca-Cola but get a fake cola." We practised our defensive set-pieces. It's always tricky with Brendan [Rodgers] because the first set-piece is always a new, creative, studied one. Our formation needed to be ready for everything. Robbo and Trent were repeating their deliveries, over and over again over their first zonal man. The work with neuro11 was really paying off. In the previous four games, our corners had been excellent; we'd targeted closer to the goal and went with more bodies in this space, so this in combination with the quality of the delivery made the chance of scoring with making first contact so much higher, and our second-phase remained a real second weapon.

That night, final no23 finished 2-0 against Leicester and featured Luis Diaz's full debut. I had never seen someone fit into our style that quickly. He was just a tailor-made signing. He has 'collective', like Jota and like Harvey. They pass the ball so naturally with an incredible overview and technique and they move constantly into different spaces. Harvey is exceptional in this as he moves in spaces where other midfielders don't move into. Jota and Diaz have a signature of us all over. I think Luis didn't miss one pass on this night. We were superior and the team was in a good moment. Let me say it like this: I felt if we'd played City in our next game we would beat them. We were now nine points behind – six if we won our game in hand. Let's see in what kind of form we'd be when we actually had to play them, and more importantly what the difference was in the table. But in this game Thiago and Curtis were so aggressive defensively, constantly on the front-foot to steal balls and it gave Fabinho time to read and intercept the passes. We scored with two corners. The first one, Virgil timed his run perfectly, lost his marker and made first contact at the near post. Schmeichel saved but Jota finished it off. Virgil, by the way. What a performance it was from him.

The second goal came from a second-phase corner where it ended up with Joel passing through to Jota and game over. I liked how decisive our second phase of corners was becoming, but I loved that we were scoring with first contact now as well. A new and extra weapon. "Clean sheet," I said as I high-fived Virgil in the tunnel afterwards. "Joel didn't want one!" he responded, laughing, referring to the two passes he missed that created danger. Directly after the game we sat in the manager's room and Billy Hogan was with us. It's great when he is around. "Buenas Diaz," Jürgen joked. "What a player!" Billy replied. "He looked like he could have played 100 games already!"

Burnley was our next task in just a couple of days' time. They were last in the table, but this is the Premier League and we knew a Sunday fight was waiting, so our thoughts were very much: let's get prepared. Early morning the day after Leicester and I was sitting in the chair next to Jürgen's desk: 'Were we too harsh with the team yesterday after the game?' is what we were discussing. No, we agreed – because it sets the right tone, so don't worry. We played a great, great second half. We then go through the line-up for Burnley, with Inter in our minds as well. As I walked out of the office I turned back to the boss and said: "If we played tomorrow against City, we would have a chance." Jürgen replied: "In life this is the only thing you always get: a chance. It's about us and what we do with it." Top.

Outside, Mo was still on the pitch speaking to Harvey. Penalties, life, professionalism… I don't know what they were discussing but I couldn't have felt prouder seeing Mo like this with Harvey. The mega-star being really busy with the mega-talent. Teaching to deliver. Teaching to prepare. As I've said repeatedly, talents need models and not criticism. I use it a lot because it is one of the best sayings to explain the last step of development. It's this principle that allowed our squad to evolve. Love for each other is what gets the most out of each other. Burnley do what they do with 100 per cent. Yes, at this stage they were bottom of the table but had only lost eight games. That doesn't happen a lot. Seventy per cent of their chances came after winning second-balls, so we were going to set up differently. We would be higher and in better positions to attack the second phase of the second-ball fight. We felt this idea would keep us higher on the pitch, further from our goal. It's a little tweak with great influence on where the game is played. For the public eye it's not that interesting, but for the coaching eye it is decisive. It would hopefully give us the possibility to play 14 times higher up the pitch more often. Every set-up should be to let our boys shine more often.

And wow, our boys filled it with so much conviction and life. The moment Jürgen and I explained it with the tactics board on the pitch they were immediately all in. These tweaks give our players success, and the players give these tweaks success. 'Win-win tweaks', I call them. You take their strength away without them even recognising it!

In the meeting we showed the goal against them earlier in the season: Trent between the lines and flicking it immediately to Sadio, who ran in behind. "One of the best goals we've scored this season," Jürgen tells the boys. They would try to close the decisive spaces and closed situations can only be countered with movement. Against teams who close spaces deep in their own half, you need offers and movements to open up these decisive situations. Against set-piece teams like Burnley, the worst thing you can do is give stupid fouls away. You make a foul on the halfway line and you know the ball will come flying in. The best way to combat a fighting team like this is with technique. The remedy against physicality is technique, it's the ball. It's the most powerful tool to avoid physical situations. Because this game is played with a ball, a round one, the better you are with it, the less physical a game can become. "Throw as many [players] in with pure technique," says Vitor. That's how we did it in the Academy, always; against the most physical teams we threw in the most available technical players possible. Together, taking care of the ball is making physicality less important. Last time we'd played them, it was with Naby and Harvey in the middle. Physicality is not the first thing you think about when mentioning these two players, I would say. On each occasion they put the ball on the floor and found quick attacking solutions.

Before the session started on Saturday, Jürgen spoke with Sadio: "Great tournament, incredible performances but not a lot of defending… welcome back!" "Even Naby didn't defend," Sadio laughed with Naby, "And when he did it was always with a yellow card!" We'd decided Sadio would start instead of Diogo, who picked up a dead-leg against Leicester. When Mike Gordon heard about it during a phone-call with Jürgen, he joked that Diogo would even score from the bench with the form he was in. We missed Mike, the pandemic made things really complicated for him to be with us. He is so close to all of us, close even to our families. When my dad got diagnosed with cancer in November 2015, he offered to get him to the USA for special treatment. Boston Hospital had the world's leading specialists, he explained. My dad had great care in Holland, but had things started to go wrong it was absolutely an option for us to take the hand he had so kindly extended to us. I'm grateful for loads of things, but I am really grateful for our relationship. I'm glad that we never had to take it, even when the cancer came back, but what Mike did in this phase of our lives was incredibly generous and compassionate. In life you meet many people and many pass by, but there are just one or two you meet who will influence your life forever. Mike is one of these people for me.

After our session on the Saturday, Jürgen and I watched the FIFA Club World Cup final, Chelsea v Palmeiras. He said, "That tournament was my biggest surprise in football." I explained to him how, when I was 12 years old, I listened on the smallest radio to Ajax winning it on penalties in Tokyo. Winning it ourselves was one of the proudest moments in my life. Beating Flamengo with Jorge Jesus as the coach, whom we confronted so many times with Porto against Benfica. Extra-time, Bobby, our Brazilian, scoring the winner.

Matchday. It felt just like they ordered 'wind and rain' every time we played them. I told Luis just before we headed out for our traditional game-day walk, "Today you will see the real Premier League." Milner, standing next to him, nods his head and laughs. I spoke with James and we decided let's go first half with the wind if we win the toss. Start with the advantage. As always with James, we went through all of the advantages and all of the disadvantages before deciding. There's no-one better to discuss them with. Final no24 ends 1-0 at Burnley. "We earned our money today," was the first thing the boys said walking back into the dressing room. Thiago created 'control' in the second half. Technique. Naby was outstanding on the ball. Technique. Our new set-up for the second-ball fight made it so that we could always stay in their half. Wonderful.

For the goal, again an in-swinging corner, Sadio makes first contact and Fabinho scores. Again Fab! Since we'd put Fabinho as the sixth player in the box, he'd scored three times. The new set-up was working wonders. In the previous five games we'd increased so much pressure with our set-pieces. We needed this to keep the chase going. We needed this if we wanted to win cups this year.

WEEK 30

CHASING LIKE WOLVES

CHAMPIONS LEAGUE IN FEBRUARY, AWAY IN ITALY. Tell me a better situation at this stage of a season? It's the most interesting competition, fighting with the best teams in Europe. You want to be a part of this. "A normal effort doesn't work against these teams," Jürgen starts the team meeting with.

"Inter Milan are too strong for this, they have the quality of a champion, the swagger of a champion. But they're not used to playing us, they're not used to our rhythm." This would be target number one for us: make the game quick; quick throw-ins, quick re-starts, quick free-kicks, spot and play. It was clear after analysing them that we would need to be at our highest level, both in our attacking and defending. Simone Inzaghi has clear, clear plans in possession. He is a typical old-school 'big' player; he knows what he wants and wasn't afraid of us, but I love it when teams want to show they can play against us. We knew we'd need to be chasing like wolves. Not 'attacking' them too early; preparing the press well, but when we go, we go with all of us. As a pack. We would need to find the right moments because we felt they would try to play with bravery – and too early means run and run a lot. Who starts the press for us? The one who sees and smells the trigger should start and follow to cut the pitch. "You see – you go!" we shouted over and over in the session. "Prepare! Compact! Go and follow!" We have this image of being the team no-one wants to play against again; that's us. Inzaghi said this, that we were the team they didn't want in the draw.

Offensively they insist a lot on returning the ball to the back-three, even when they outplay the opponent, always starting again with trying to keep the ball. If they broke our first line of pressure, they would go back to do it again until we became passive. Inzaghi-style. It was clear if they had more of the ball than us it would be really difficult to press them with the intensity necessary to cause them problems. The ball and pressing are like twins. That's exactly the reason why we chose to go with Thiago and Harvey in the centre – we needed the ball and we needed to treat it well. Individual class in combination with our system.

They went man-to-man over the whole pitch, so we needed one-v-one offensive quality to make sure we kept the ball, found openings and used these openings with the speed of Mo, Sadio and Jota, or with overlaps from Trent and Robbo. We felt this would keep Edin Dzeko, Ivan Perisic and Lautaro Martinez, their main guns, out of the game most of the time. I gave my view, with no illusions, that this was our year. It's exciting preparing for the knockout stages in the Champions League and hopefully you can read my excitement through these words.

"We need our full package of defensive tools tomorrow night," Jürgen finished in his meeting. "It's a challenge to play for us, aggressive against the ball but class on it, so tomorrow we have to be us. There are no secrets in football. You feel our secret only when we stand in front of you and the whistle goes: intensity. Everything in football is analysed except the feeling when you face us." I read a quote from Antonio Conte: "You can't buy a winning mentality." Spurs had just lost their second home game in a row at the weekend, this time against Wolves. He couldn't be more right in this – you don't need to teach an Italian about winning, they are born with it. It showed again, by the way, that stats are only there until they are broken. That he had won 20 of his previous 21 home games was big on Sky Sports – a combination of matches with Inter and Tottenham – but there is no bigger stats-breaker than the Premier League. The only stat that counts in football is the result of the next game; the only thing to keep the mood in a camp is to win the next game. Life as a modern coach, it's only about the next game. Names don't exist anymore, it's just about results. That dictates our life, knowing that 'the stats' can change every other game and with this our lives. But to come back to Conte's quote, it's so true – but I believe you can stimulate the little competitive voice inside these boys'

Marching on: (Top) all smiles in training. (Above) Bobby celebrates a goal at Arsenal; Luis bravely heads home at Brighton; Sadio's decider v West Ham and Diogo's winner at Nottingham Forest

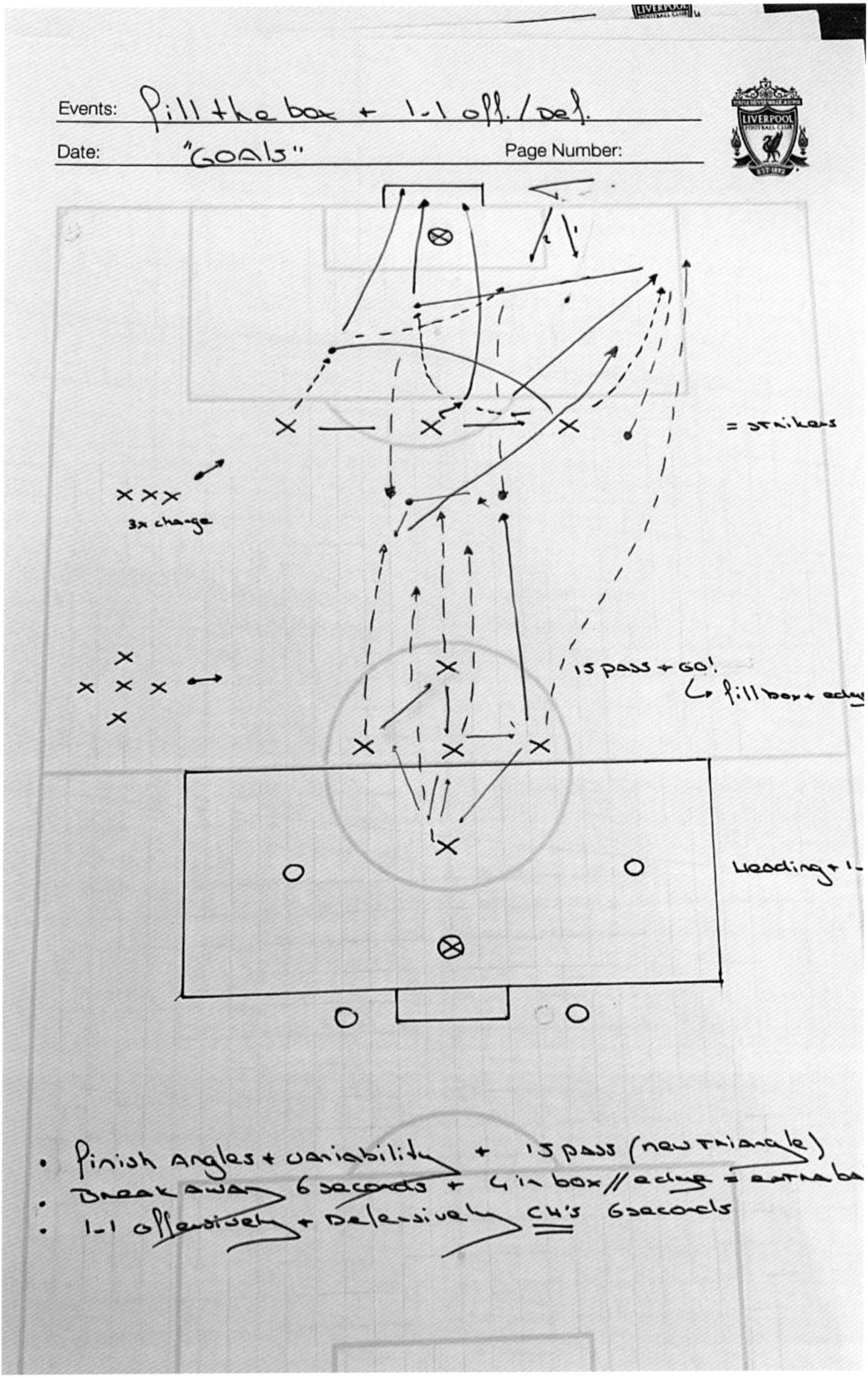

Fill the box: More tactical notes from training – if you don't drive forward, you don't score goals

Tale of two Cities: (Above) applauding our fans after a 2-2 Premier League draw at the Etihad. (Left) during our trips to Wembley last season, Jürgen inspected the pitch and sent this photo to our groundsman. (Below) Sadio pounces to put us two up in the FA Cup semi-final and Vitor's note to me after an amazing first half

Unstoppable: (Top) a hug for Alisson from Thiago before a Merseyside derby win over Everton at Anfield and (above) Mo scores the second goal in our 4-0 defeat of Manchester United

heads. Because you have to win in your own mind, that's the start. For me, Virgil is the best example of this. He wins with his mindset and you can learn this, I'm convinced of it.

Let me give an example, when walking off the pitch at Burnley at half-time. He said to me: "Pep, the wind is incredible, it's impossible to judge the long balls well, one moment I was already in the air and the ball ended up with Joel." I told him the only thing you can control is to make sure that you are prepared to push the line up, don't drop off; it feels uncomfortable but it's the best for the team to put pressure on the ball and with this there will be fewer high balls. He nodded his head. You see him thinking and I know he is playing the game in his head. Job done. He was massive in that second half, just massive. Every manager, every coach with time learns to ignore nonsense – you get surprised how much noise there is about you, which is so far from reality in the world of football. Win in your own mind is what makes you the next you. "Don't spit on your own mind," I say to the young players.

Our last session at the AXA Training Centre before we departed for Italy was rainy and cold. In fact, exactly the moment we walked outside, it started to rain like only it can in the North West of England, coming down vertically but horizontally. It looked like it was coming from all directions – just like how Bobby presses opponents. I walked over to Vitor, Pete, Jürgen and said: "I just love this weather, let's go!" "What's to like?" Jürgen joked, "What's the reason you say this?" I replied, "It's too cold for the players to stand still in training, so they will move!" Speaking of the staff, there was some activity in our coaches' WhatsApp group – 'Diamond Dogs'. Yes, Ted Lasso's name for his backroom staff is also the name of our group chat. Mona was organising another house dinner party. They're the best – they end up with everyone singing and dancing but in particular having some really good talks. Saturday after Norwich at home would finally be the next one. After the pandemic, everyone couldn't wait.

We left Liverpool for Milan that Tuesday afternoon. The plane was as perfectly-organised as always by our travel guys. Philip Holliday delivered once again – the fly-in-and-out principle, no waiting times, just doing business. I was listening to music and making notes when Jürgen asked me: "How many games in the Champions League as an assistant-manager will it be for you tomorrow?" He counted and it turned out Inter will be my 38th game in the dugout. Not bad. When we landed, we heard a quote from Pep Guardiola which said that Liverpool were a "pain in the ass" for City. Good! At least he feels our breath.

Matchday and I mention a question from The Times in a recent interview with Robbo: do we ask too much of Trent? Robbo replied: "That's why he gets paid so much – to do a lot!" I love our boys' down-to-earth attitudes. We decided on the day of the game that we'd change our plans and stay over afterwards rather than flying straight back to Liverpool. There was a storm back home and we didn't want to take the risk, better safe than sorry. The boys are happy, a better night's sleep and maybe a chance to have a beer after the game.

We arrived at San Siro later that night. The cathedral. "See the line-up? No surprises," Jürgen says of Inter's team-sheet. "The good, good teams never have," I say back to the boss. I walked over to Virgil and Ali who were on the massage beds and told them we needed a real playing attitude, don't make it a second-ball game, stay calm, we'd decide if it's a long pass instead of a long ball. Virgil responded, "Confidence in our boys." That's exactly how a leader should respond. Before we went out to warm up, Jürgen showed me the Bayern line-up for their game in Salzburg, with Kingsley Coman and Serge Gnabry as their wing-backs. I said it was like a Cruyff dream team – you see the line-up and just think: only attackers?

For us, it was a night to savour. A 2-0 away win against the Italian champions in the knockout stage of the Champions League. This night we saw how a bench can change a game around. We were efficient, which is always a good sign in these phases of the season. We were under huge fire at the start of the second half, they were bombing us over our right side. Perisic and Dzeko came into the game. We needed control again and Hendo, Naby and Luis coming on before the hour-mark gave us exactly this: the ball. Luis has the signature of street football – the best ones have this signature, by the way. For me this is art – art inside the game of football, unpredictability, imagination, and the feet are just executing. He can think and react a second quicker than others because of this. Bobby also came off the bench at half-time and got the first goal with a clinical header from a corner. And speaking of clinical, Mo got our second soon after with a good finish from a loose ball in the box. But we were only in the middle of this final. It was a good starting point, but a penalty and, for example, a sending-off would change the whole world, so we had to stay humble and take the result knowing that there was a big fight in front of us in three weeks' time. It was also the 50th win in the Champions League for Jürgen. Not many managers have achieved that number. And it was the 800th career game for Milner. Have a guess how many yellows in that time? No, I didn't put that joke into the WhatsApp group.

Back in Liverpool it was Friday morning and you know what is the best moment of the week? Sitting with Jürgen in his office after a game and speaking for five minutes about the good, the bad, the what we can do better, and then we move on. Move on, put a line through everything and move on. That day, I don't think the wind had ever been as influential in Kirkby as it was then. The expensive wind nets were even struggling. To be honest, I was scared when I walked out and saw the floodlights going from left to right. At Porto, one fell down on the pitch while I was training with twenty 15-year-olds one time, probably just 20 metres away from the bang it created. If you see something that big happening once, it will always stay in your mind. The storm is all over England and the north of Europe and it meant that Norwich would take the bus instead of the plane up to Liverpool.

If we wanted to play our way against them, we would need to change and bring energy into the team. We needed freshness but the team can't be like a fruit salad – it needs a collective. We needed to be spot on. It takes time to find the right balance and connections but when we found our solution, there was peace in our minds. The amount of games and travelling we were doing was just ridiculous. We would need this squad, all of it. I was feeling tired, so can you imagine the ones who played 95 minutes against an intense Inter at San Siro only 40 hours ago. It was like a bonus game for Norwich. "They will try everything without having anything to lose," Jürgen started the meeting with. We had four unbelievably quick and tactically good centre-halves and against Norwich we decided we would play with three of them. Joe hadn't played a lot so far this season but he would get in any other top-six English team, easy. For me, he is our best offensive centre-half. We decided he would play in place of Trent, who we gave two days off before the week of Leeds and the Wembley final. We'd need him fresh and fit to decide an important game once more. I took Joe out of the gym, told him he would start and explained why: I showed him four clips of Kyle Walker 'constructing' as a three for Man City against Norwich the weekend before and explained the advantages of this: "You can do this as well, Joe. Move inside to use your quality, touch and pass to switch quickly to Mo." Writing the notes for this book, I will tell you guys now: Joe will become one of the most important players for the final stages of the season, especially if the weekend goes well for us. He played 26 games in a row in our Premier League title season. We lost one game in that time.

Everybody was fighting for something at this moment: to get into the squad, to start, to get on as a sub, to stay in the team. The amount of quality we had available was incredible. That's the difference between a squad to play for the first four places or a squad to conquer prizes. It felt like it was helping us a lot to have this last push. I understood early at Porto that when a whole organisation or a whole team wants it a little bit more and tries to improve themselves, nothing is impossible. In 2010/11 under Andre Villas-Boas, we became champions, won both cups and won the Europa League in Dublin. "We are what we make of what we learn," Jürgen told me and Vitor that night back at The Titanic and he couldn't be more right.

Matchday morning, Jürgen started the meeting: "The challenge for a football player, the challenge for a player inside a massive club, the challenge for a player inside a massive club which fights for four prizes is to see each game as a special game. That's the key. Burnley was windy, rainy and we reacted with a super mature performance. Then we had the fancy game with Inter at the San Siro in the Champions League. Make the most special game out of each game we get. This isn't easy but we help you with this by making seven changes, using the full power of our squad. Yesterday we trained, that's our meeting-centre, much more important than this meeting now. I want us to be wild but organised. When we do this, the chance of a special game comes really close." While walking out of The Titanic, Mo whispered to Ox, "I will be in your ear constantly this afternoon, don't switch, keep it in our triangle."

Final no25 was a 3-1 win for us… with three goals in front of the Kop. "Life is about overcoming difficulty," Jürgen said straight after the game. Today we did. A little bit of help with changing structure, but we did. We had 29 attempts against a deep-defending Norwich; we were shooting from everywhere. A terrific sign for a good last half-hour is when your front three all score. Just before 60 minutes, we changed to an offensive 4-4-2, bringing Thiago and Divock on for Naby and Ox. Vitor told Thiago when he walked into the dining room afterwards, "You know what the headline of today's game is? 'How to win a game in 30 minutes.'" His smile could not have been bigger. What an impact he had, defining each attack – the ball always comes into the right spaces, or within the right players. We changed, we used the squad, we won, we rested the right ones. All with a good victory. And… Luis had his first beautiful goal in front of the Kop. Hendo outplayed nine players with his pass and put Luis in front of Angus Gunn. Ali put Mo in front of Gunn as well with his first assist this season. If your goalkeeper starts assisting, you know everyone is connected. By the way, the goal from Luis was made with 34 passes, the highest Liverpool FC sequence since Opta began in 2006 and the highest in the Premier League so far in the season. There isn't a better example for using the width, opening them up and attacking the centre.

After leaving Anfield, I was driving with Vitor to Mona's dinner party. We'd watched City versus Spurs in an empty Anfield until the 70th minute before we set off, at which point it was 2-1 to Tottenham. Inside the car, the radio was loud, the atmosphere intense. City had turned so many games around already, so the belief was there. In fact, sometimes it's good you listen instead of watch the game because you can't see how close they are to the goal. It goes to 2-2, it's injury time… and then 3-2 to Spurs. Incredible. And what a moment to have a dinner party. Like I say, at least they feel our breath.

'COUNTER-PRESSING ISN'T A PROPOSAL – IT'S A LAW'

WEEK 31

"WE DID IT!"

I READ A STAT TO BEGIN THIS WEEK. SO FAR, VIRGIL had only lost one league game at Anfield in his entire career… and that was when he played for Southampton. What a statement. The night before we played Leeds, I sent him a video of his header against them at Anfield on the opening day of the 2020/21 season. What a game-changer he has been since we brought him in. "Academy and game-changers, that's where we need to invest," I said, while sitting in Jürgen's office. "Not second-line players who take the space for our talents. Diaz and Kaide, or Thiago and Harvey." Room for talent, space for our Academy to give a chance to these young boys to evolve into game-changers. We have to buy premium and use the Academy. Liverpool deserves a process like this. A good system always gives freedom and the chance for interpretation. This is what our boys want: dominant football, freedom. This is what we as Liverpool dream of: play like Cruyff's dream team and defend like a red machine chasing like devils. That's why we want so many attacking personalities on the pitch. We shout many times in training, "Everyone has to touch the ball before scoring!" That's why it's extra-cool that this happened with our third goal against Norwich, I couldn't have been prouder. A little bit of Cruyff was there, 'Total Football'. I celebrated that goal for many reasons more intensely than others. We always said at Porto, 'There is no need for food after quality football like that'. Bring together a German who admires Sacchi and a Dutchman who admires Cruyff and you create a monster! Jürgen has said this so often.

We just had to make sure that in our build-up we sped up the positional game as many times as possible with these simple passes; it changes the situation, it's to move the opposition. Here was where we'd improved so much over this year with better positioning, a collective display of 'we want the ball and we want to move it quickly' attitude. We are more together in simple defined triangles and with this we can find and create the 'free player' much easier. We were showing Anfield good football, both tactically and as a collective. There was a constant tactical improvement by reminding the team to occupy key zones in width and in depth, to be flexible on the inside spaces while still being close to each other. We tried to create tactical confusion for the opposition with our flexibility. It gave us the chance to open up the pitch and move the ball in situations where we could outplay, where we could provoke, or where we could unbalance them. There were so many of these moments our boys were creating together and it's all on them that we were so dominant this season. The best teams are always a combination between system, talent and a positive energy. For example, we gave our front three much more offensive freedom this season and they were all thriving on it. Just look at the numbers they were providing. But the good thing was, it did not influence our high press defensive attitude at all. To be honest, I actually thought it improved it, if anything.

I asked Dan to get me the stats and he surprised me: at this point as a team we had so far 301 high press successful ball-recoveries in the Premier League, with number two, Man City, having 242. It was an obvious sign that all of our players were really committed to doing what's right. Our adjustments in pre-season were coming off; teams had found a way to outplay our first phase of press and we had to change. Offensively we wanted our front three to play 'the space' and not 'the position', which means constantly searching for the decisive spaces to break the opposition's last line. We wanted to take it to the next level with a complete false front-line. Freedom… surprise…chaos! They needed this freedom to find the spaces nobody can show on a tactics board. When they did this with timing in the training sessions, we felt we could score at any moment in the game. Jürgen called this 'organised chaos'. It is organised because the rest constantly adjust to them and make sure that when we lose the ball we are close enough to them. The only aspect that needs a permanent answer is respect for defending – "respect for the 30 per cent" when we don't have the ball. This is where we wanted to be different from any other team in the Premier League. Our best offensive games were defined by much better defending. That's the truth – it was with fluidity. Basically, we tried to improve the team every day to give stability in being more unpredictable by defending better. So far at this point, so good. At game no25 we had the highest number of goalscoring opportunities at home in the league in a statistic Manchester City had dominated for over seven years.

Preparing for Leeds and our next challenge, I have to say Trent was so strong in our Tuesday session, hitting one long pass after the other under pressure. It was no surprise, though – he will have hated not playing against Norwich on the Saturday, but Trent being Trent doesn't cause a scene or anything even close to it when he knows it's a done deal. He has the perfect balance: he always wants to play; if he can, he will make his case to play, but at the point the decision is made he trusts us and gets on with it. Don't lose any anger with something you can't change anyway. If we speak about Trent being out of the last game, we have to speak about Thiago being in the last game. He defined the moments to risk so well. He defined where to attack so well. The only thing we, as coaches, do is give direction towards this collective development. For example, the main thing I'd told Thiago before he came on against Norwich was: "Read where we can attack them well… just read it well. Through the outside? Through the inside? Define it well!" But just to make it absolutely clear one more time, it was the boys' talent and attitude that had put us into the chase we were in. With the seven changes we'd made against Norwich, we still had the ball and owned the pitch. Seven changes and still being that dominant. Our whole team – even the boys from the Academy – feel and act in our system. We can change knowing that our 'we want it more' mentality in the end will put us above the others.

Our philosophy has always been to create a special game out of the next one and with this mindset and with time, we would create a special team. Game by game, session by session. Normally we change only one player in each line, or one in each triangle. We are 'consistently consistent' with our changes, which makes it easier to control this process. But the intense playing periods we were going through asked for more substantial changes. And when these boys come on from the bench, they come on to strike. Our squad had proven that in the last games. They had to trust that their moment would come like it does in boxing; you prepare and prepare and when the time is there you hit. Now it was time for Robbo, Trent and Fabinho to do exactly this: to hit. We would drill them ahead of Leeds with high-intensity exercises because it was good for them to train and build some sharpness within their bodies and make an overload of quick decisions again. At Liverpool FC you need to reach a very high level every single day because the speed in training is much quicker than in most of the games. Just before the session started, Jürgen made a compliment about how the squad was dealing with the amount of players available to the boys.

We had Robbo practising his corners with Niklas from neuro11 this week. As I arrived to take a look, he said, "I feel after the last time I worked with them, I really put it right." He turned to Niklas and added: "But it's better to ask Pep if he thinks the same – he could still think they're shite!" I laughed before Robbo added, "Assists for Virgil and Bobby!" I told him we were definitely on the right path and just keep it simple and focus.

Matchday and the team meeting in The Titanic began with Jürgen saying to the lads: "I'm not making this story up, guys... Pep and me play a lot of padel tennis, our level is equal. Maybe Pep is a little bit better but we're pretty much equal. It happens often that one of us is 5-0 up, and we don't know what changes but it goes from 5-1 to 5-2 and suddenly you are thinking about the result. I learned myself but can't always change it, so I say to myself: don't think about the result, just play the point. Many times it ends up 5-5 and the one who was in front still wins 7-5. We ask ourselves the why, what changes in the head? It's quite obvious it's 5-4 to City still, so what I want to say is don't think about anything else other than playing our football, being ready to face problems, being ready to do things right. Be the team full of energy and desire. Nothing changed, guys, nothing. Be the most annoying team to play against. The real race starts now! Go and be yourself." When we arrived at Anfield that night, there were so many fans waiting for the bus. You could see in their eyes something had changed. These are the moments I love the most in football, when you see in people's eyes how much it means to them. We could close the gap on City to three points and everybody knew it.

And that's what we did. Final no26 was a statement for the outside world: we beat Leeds 6-0 at home. Just wow, what a game! We played 95 minutes with maximum concentration. Leeds, in the end, were not even watching the ball anymore – they just had eyes for the man and that's not a good sign when you are man-marking. We were 3-0 up at half-time, with one of the goals coming from one of Joel's classic runs forward from the back, which he finished superbly after a pass from Mo. Incredible. We'd played really well in the first half with 13 attempts against none from Leeds, but during the break Jürgen made sure the boys knew the game wasn't over. Leeds had proven this in a recent game with Aston Villa in which they came from 3-1 down to get a point. We were too experienced for this to happen and our mentality should never give them anything, so we would go for the fourth goal. We knew what to expect. Our man on the ball would have to make the difference. For example, the moment you can hold a ball with your back to the goal, or when you outplay your man, it will automatically create a one-v-one situation in a big space facing the goal – and that's what we wanted, one-v-one facing the goal. We told the boys to be really mobile and Sadio was the playmaker, he was always available. It was impossible for Leeds to control his movements and, with this, our possession. Again I found myself asking on this night: how can Mo dribble so quickly and break speed so fast at the same time? It's just not human. The ball is like a magnet to his inside and outside foot, while Luis Diaz treats the ball like a yo-yo, the ball always finds a way back to his feet. These are the type of players we want and need for Liverpool. As well as Joel's goal, there were two each for Mo and Sadio before Virg got one right at the end. As I said, just wow.

Then, of course, it was straight into our work for the Carabao

Cup final. On our way to Wembley, each second counted because we only had two days to prepare. We had surprised our boys after Leeds with a necessary day off. The League Cup was all about the journey and that it would end with a final was so special. It felt like my mind was buzzing 24/7 with this game. Because I had been asked to take care of the 'presser', because it was a final, because it was Wembley and above all because it was Chelsea and their way of using the free spaces. Our pressing had worked so well in the home game with them because we had surprised them. We understood our favourite coaching phrase: we chase them over the whole pitch. Unpredictability in our pressing; we needed to come from directions they were not used to. The new way. Because when it's predictable they were more than capable of finding the free spaces and putting their technical and quick front three in the game. They were just too good for predictability, especially because they overloaded our last line with five players. When those players received the ball facing our goal it became uncontrollable. I was sure we needed to come up with something that would surprise them again, this time at Wembley. I knew our intensity could do this but it'd only work if we had a great balance between possession and pressing. The trick would be that we only had to do it for 40 per cent of the time and do it right. Our pressing dynamics had to be spot on and we could not be too worried too often about what was happening behind us. Creating a wild game instead of a chess game… and anyway, chess isn't the right direction for the future of the football game, in my opinion. Disciplined and compact is what we would have to be, always, by applying our principles and ideas, then we could do what we want to do: create chaos. Leave the tactics board at home, I would say.

We talked with our analysts and we all agreed the key would

be a front-footed 9 and front-footed 8s. We knew Chelsea better now after playing them twice, the good and the bad. "The most important message is that we can still improve after watching both games back," Jürgen said after the meeting. We all felt the best Premier League team in terms of playing between the lines was Chelsea; they were the best playing with an overload from out the back, so we had to take 'the lines' and 'the overload' away with our striker and midfielders going one-v-one against Thiago Silva, N'Golo Kante and Mateo Kovacic. We would try to take these three out of the game and with this the pathways to their creative players. A lot of times, the brave but simple solutions are the best ones to get a grip of the game. "Apologies – I'm sorry!" Jürgen said out of nothing in the team meeting on the Saturday afternoon before we headed down to London. "With us, our offensive players have to do a lot – a lot. But tomorrow you have to work together on the next level. Anyway, I'm speaking to the best football team in the world, so I don't have to make clear that we have to outplay their pressure." With time as a coach you learn what to say, and you learn the hard way what not to say. Clarity to work hard and encouragement to freedom.

We received a boost in our preparation on the Saturday. It's really incredible what the mind can do. We had Diogo back and training without problems with the team. We knew it would be an absolute advantage to have Jota ready to play. I pulled him out of the gym for a conversation and we decided he would come as the impact substitute instead of starting, so I discussed this with him. Playing football is the best way to bring players back from injury, anyway. I don't have a doubt about that. I'm a nice guy… or, at least, I think I'm a nice guy. All of our staff get a lot of praise and freedom from me, but when I feel strongly about something I'm really strong in expressing my opinion about it. I'm Dutch, is how Jürgen explains this characteristic. That's not always easy, especially when it's about a player coming back on time, when it's about set-pieces, when it's about a line-up or even when it's about subs or tactical decisions. But it's important to me to speak what I feel – it's healthy. That's the culture we have at LFC. Jürgen and I discussed both games we'd had against Chelsea and it was clear, we'd need the brave approach again. I said not to watch our last game against them, watch the tactical résumé our analysts made of our home game earlier in the season. Jürgen put it on his iPad and we started watching… "Look, they try this… We have to be more front-footed with our striker here… Jota is too busy trying to cover Kovacic, that's why he isn't on time to press Silva… We can only do this with our 8s staying central and surprising both Kovacic and Kante…" We had to correct the two or three dynamics that would give us more unpredictability and that last one was the most important one, it would take the lines and the overload away. When I looked back at the away game a little bit later in the day, I just started laughing. The sheer intensity of this game, it felt as if the ball wasn't out of play for the entire first ten minutes. I remember taking my eyes off the game for literally a second and when I looked up again so much had happened. That's the game you want to have when the manager is out with COVID, away against the Champions League winners after a draw at Tottenham and a defeat at Leicester.

Matchday morning. The final was here. We took the boys for a walk around the pitch. Sky TV was there trying to ask some questions. The sun was shining, it felt good. I took a photo of Jürgen pointing at the pitch to send to Warren – we joked, "That's how a pitch should look!" I felt the hunger that morning, the conviction. I could feel we really wanted this, we were really ready. The last message from Jürgen: "It feels different today, fans are drinking beers early, our families are flying in. But there is no difference to winning this football game – we need to do the things we always do." It proved to be a special day. A final at Wembley and conquering our first domestic cup together. We were back in business. Liverpool FC was back in business.

We did have to make a late change to the line-up when Thiago got an injury in the warm-up. He told us he felt his hamstring when we went back to the dressing room, but he insisted he wanted to play. I grabbed Jürgen and we went into the corridor. We decided to go with Naby and not take any risk, but Thiago was in tears. He knew to play a final at Wembley for Liverpool was a huge deal, even with all the medals he had already won in his career. Naby needed 15 minutes to get into the game but once he did, he dictated play in a way only he can. How this game finished 0-0 is a miracle, really, after 120 intense minutes. It could have been 5-5. The flag was up many times and even the VAR intervened against us when we thought Joel had given us the lead. Games against them are just incredible. Football reaches another intensity and concentration-level in these moments. This is the reason why all the penalties were so well-taken, for sure. I couldn't have been prouder. So many decisions on this journey were spot on. It's cool that they all are described in this book because, as I've said, you don't prepare for finals in the week leading up to them – it's a long, long journey.

The 'small plan' with our high and midfield press took the pathways to their front three out of the game. In the first half we had 61 per cent possession and in the other 39 per cent we could create the chaos we wanted. Top. You could count the moments Kante and Kovacic could turn and progress on one hand. Hendo and Naby were all over them. The attacks they had came from us having technical breakdowns in spots or moments when we should have been clearer. Thomas Tuchel made it a chess game by putting a fresh Timo Werner and Romelu Lukaku on and pushing Alonso right up there as well. The speed, the overload and the freshness created problems on the side of Trent, but wow, what a game he had defensively. Everyone who doubts his defending should watch this game back. We had to react strongly and brought Ibou on for Joel to give some new power on that side and we spoke with Fab to drop into our last line when the spaces between Virgil and Ibou became too big.

Kelleher showed why he only started late in goal in his career, demonstrating he used to be a striker when he finished his penalty in the shoot-out. Scoring the winning penalty must be the ultimate feeling in a final. When he hugged me at the end, he thanked me for the opportunity to play but I told him: "I'm so proud – you deserve the world." I walked to the side of the pitch during the celebrations and embraced our owners before I saw Robbie Fowler and Jason McAteer. This is what makes our club so special; legends commentating on a final and being so proud of the current team winning it. Culture. When Naby came over to hand me the cup and the boys started waving with their arms, it was an incredible moment for me. I took it to the fans and for a few seconds this was my moment. I don't need any more than that. In those few seconds I looked into the eyes of our supporters with a trophy in my hand. Done. That meant so, so much. After that, I took the cup to Sir Kenny, to neuro11 who were in the stands, and then to Billy Hogan. Together strong. I found the co-author of this book, James, in the dressing room, someone who has become a real friend to me. "We did it!"

We celebrated in the dressing room and for once we were able to immediately have a few beers to toast the success. I asked Robbo to put Freed From Desire on. I didn't know the name of it, actually, so I said to him: "What's the song we always play?" On it came and my feet went quicker than the beats, creating some memorable scenes. Our club media team was there to capture it – to record some of the dance moves. Most readers won't know this, but we actually played that song during a couple of our staff get-togethers in Austria the previous summer, where our 2021/22 journey had begun. We didn't have a party that night because it was back to Liverpool, so I felt it was important to create that moment – staff and players together, as one – to celebrate our achievement. For me, the achievement was the journey, the road to the final.

When we were back on the bus, we got the call from Mike Gordon. "Who invented the offside rule?" Jürgen said to him, laughing. "Congratulations – we are so excited!" said Mike. "I can't feel any difference to the Champions League," Jürgen continued. Mike again: "Absolutely outstanding!" Jürgen explained to him how we had the penalty-taker list from the neuro11 boys ready for a long time, but only our first five were in the exact order. Then it was suggestions and explaining the characteristics of the other takers when we decided who'd go from six onwards; at that point, it wasn't in our hands as much anymore – the boys had to decide then. When Ibou walked up, Jürgen asked me: "He wasn't even on the list, was he?" Thankfully he sprinted and smashed it. He'd had a few sessions with neuro11 and the main thing they'd told him was to put more power behind it. Luckily he did because Kepa got a hand on it.

On the plane flying back that night, I got emotional. 'Life can't get better than this – we won this in Austria', went through my mind. It all started there back in July. Flying back from London, there were so many emotions. It was time to just enjoy the moment and be proud – proud of everyone who loves Liverpool FC.

WEEK 32

BATTERY CHARGERS

WHEN LIVERPOOL FC WINS A PRIZE, IT'S A MAXIMUM feeling because so many, many people give their maximum effort towards it. Because of this, we brought the whole staff together in the sports hall at the AXA Training Centre – and I mean the whole staff – for a group picture with the cup. Everyone was smiling. Jürgen spoke to everyone: "This will be the one picture I will keep. There were so many incredible moments but this picture I keep. Thank you. This one was about the journey and we did this one all together." A cup is as big as the effort you put into it, that's it. But the best picture I saw from the final was when the group stormed towards Kelleher. The expressions on their faces made me so happy, seeing the boys I love and respect so euphoric. These pictures become iconic and this will be the one I keep, knowing that we scored all eleven penalties and did not get distracted, even when Kepa stood in the 'go to' corner.

As an aside, my favourite picture ever from in and around a final was one of me with Trent, my captain, directly after the Champions League final in Madrid when he leapt onto my back after the final whistle. These moments define a cup as well. Virgil later explained to me that the penalty from Kepa was a proper 'head-fuck' because in this moment the group realised that if he scored everything would start all over again. In the brain it goes from, 'I did my job – what a relief' to 'I have to go again – what do I do and where do I go?' To illustrate this, you can see in the pictures that Milner was focusing and getting concentrated again – that's why he couldn't move with the others. Beautiful. You have two types of people in football, at each club: the ones who see the cup as half-full and the ones who see the cup as half-empty. Make sure you get those who see it half-full around you because they will search and bring ideas to fill the cup more. The others will only create and start problems. At the Academy, we called them the battery chargers or the battery drainers. Be the one who gives energy.

There wasn't much time to celebrate winning the final, though. We had Norwich – yes, again – in the FA Cup on the Wednesday night at Anfield. On matchday I was sitting with Ray and John in our dining room at The Titanic. Ray was due to leave the next day for Bangkok and Singapore to prepare our pre-season tour. In his expression, you could see he was looking forward to the long flight, honest. John was in the opposite mood because our Under-19s had beaten Genk in the last 16 of the UEFA Youth League on penalties, with Harvey Davies saving two of them. One week and on two occasions one of our goalkeepers had been the hero.

Jürgen started the team meeting by telling the boys: "Only our skipper stays on the pitch from Sunday. We changed the rest because of two reasons. The first one is simple: because we CAN do it. The second reason is because we respect Norwich. We've always found the right attitude after a high moment and that's what I expect today as well. We believe with fresh legs we can show who we are. Be yourself with a real counter-pressing attitude." I love this part of coaching. If you want a dominant team, tie it to counter-pressing, not to possession or to skill. That's why our main football idea is that counter-pressing isn't a proposal, it's a law. The boys didn't disappoint, either, as we reached the quarter-final with a 2-1 win. In these types of games I felt so much more comfortable with Hendo and Milner on the pitch. They made the others collective, they led and corrected every second of the game, nobody got a chance to do a little bit less defending. Not that Taki needed this kind of leadership – what a performance again from him in a cup game as he scored both our goals in the first half.

Speaking of leadership, just before we went out of the tunnel Ali spoke to the team: "They want to counter us, they have quick players, so we need to stop the counters." Everybody listened. We shocked them, we pressed from the first minute, really intense. We had a good mixture of a winning attitude and quality, the best combination in football. On these nights when we change a lot, our main guns make sure we don't drop concentration or intensity.

Wow, we had come from such an intense playing period with so many intense football games still in front of us. West Ham, Inter, Brighton, Arsenal and, now after the FA Cup draw, Nottingham Forest. All before the next international break. I'm used to a lot, but this is the new version of modern football: non-stop with no breaks against good opposition constantly, needing to win each game if we want to achieve. But Bill Shankly said it like this: playing football at the highest level isn't pressure – it's reward. I say we take that: pressure is the reward for working hard. For example, in one month Mo had played 120 minutes on five occasions.

It was the first time we, as a group, had reached the quarter-finals of the FA Cup and, of course, the first time we had won the League Cup. Our target was to reach the maximum number of games this season. The more we played the better, as it would mean we were en route to becoming successful. But it does make preparation harder because of the time limits.

In the next period, it would all be about recovery to create fresh legs and a fresh mind again: who needs rest, who can go again and for how long. The time off is as important as the training time. They go hand-in-hand. Training only works when the boys are hungry for information and hungry to play. For this reason, we had left the ones who played the whole 120 minutes at Wembley at home against Norwich. Except for Robbo, who during the warm-up asked me, "Am I the only survivor of the 120-minute boys?" I told him, "Yes, because you are the only left defender we have!" Owen Beck was unfortunately injured otherwise Robbo would have had a day off as well. I'd told Hendo at half-time that we were going to give him a maximum 60 minutes with West Ham and Inter coming in consecutive games. Giving all the others a day off against Norwich gave us time to really train them, they needed to get concentrated and connected again; keep focusing on what we wanted in our way, always with the idea that everyone was responsible for everything, because when you know what is going to happen it gives a split-second more time to be creative. It's about what we do, we do together and we do with a 100 per cent winning attitude. Every day, again and again; that we defend them to attack them and use counter-pressing as our playmaker because the best way to start a decisive attack is winning the ball back high up the pitch. The players have to feel during the sessions there is just 'no escape route'. From the moment they arrive till the moment they leave, each department has to give their all to guide them to reach the right levels.

Sitting with Mo, Robbo, Virgil, Fabinho and Trent in the canteen on the Thursday, Virg asked me in Dutch, "What are we going to do today?" I replied and walked away and immediately all the others knew as well what kind of session to expect! When I came back, I told Trent in front of the others that Niklas had sent me a message after Norwich saying we really missed Trent's deliveries. "I need to be on set-piece deliveries as well because I will create even more assists," Mo responded. "But then you don't score as many goals," Robbo replied. "And you should be more careful with these penalties because the new boys are in town!" he joked, referring to Trent and himself scoring in the shoot-out against Chelsea. In the session I called the group together just before we started our high last line work. While looking into the eyes of Mo, Virgil and Trent, I told the boys: "Attack wins you games but the defensive line wins you championships. We saw this really well in the final against Chelsea. We are good but there is always space for improvement, so really focus now on keeping the last line compact against these world-class attackers. The last line adapts to how the ball rolls." In my mind while I continued talking, I was thinking: maybe I pushed this one too much. Then some guys started laughing towards Mo, but Trent immediately chipped in with, "The truth hurts, guys." He had my back!

I would love to see the 'pre-assist' becoming more important in football. On the Friday night we watched Inter against Salernitana in the hotel and [Nicolo] Barella was superb. Jürgen asked me why I was laughing; we were in the middle of a discussion but I was watching the game with one eye and saw him play another incredible pass. "I'm just so happy that he doesn't feature against us," I said. "Every attack starts with him, it's scary." At Porto I introduced initiatives where I would count the amount of successful passes or dribbles to reach zones A, B and C of our main pool of talents. Zone A was the space between the lines, zone B the space on the outside of the last line, and C the space behind the last line. I would then compare the amount and the successful initiatives with the best players of Porto's first team and the players who were so influential in European football. As you can imagine, when I wasn't preparing or giving training sessions, I was just with a pen and paper all the time analysing games. It gave them an idea of where they wanted to go. With the Under-16 team at Liverpool I would show each of my players all of their 'successful and unsuccessful initiatives' on the Monday. I would print the numbers and hang it up on the dressing-room door. No escape route as well – 'initiatives' don't lie. Trent, Herbie Kane, Ben Woodburn, Rhian Brewster, Yan Dhanda and Adam Lewis breathed it. They were constantly encouraged to take more initiative in the game and, in training, always pushed to do more and do better. Even centre-halves started searching much more to bring the ball towards the three key spaces. It's just a great development and game-idea tool to support improvements.

When Brendan Rodgers brought me up to the first team as a coach, I held a presentation with our players to explain this process: "This is where we want to bring the ball, zone A, zone B, zone C. And this is what we are going to train. Attack and press. Attack and press!" I remember one day Adam Lallana came and said to me, "You can't be right about Coutinho's numbers?" In his good games, he was just unstoppable. I think he reached 48 initiatives with 40 being successful. Plus, an assist and a goal. Now I mention Adam, I need to share that I really miss him at our club, that he is and was the heart of our way of playing.

Matchday against West Ham and our matchday walks were getting busier. It was feeling like the pandemic was over in England now. "What a team we have," I said to John as the boys walked in front of us. "What an addition Luis is," he replied. He's right – he was proving a game-changer. Milner was in conversation with Mo when people shouted out of the window on the other side of the street, "Yes, Mo!" You can feel the season we are having in the way the people spoke with us. The sun was shining and I said to Ali, "When England is like this, it has everything." "You can't have everything in life," he tells me. I laugh, "You can have everything… just not at the same time." We laughed but I'm a believer in always focusing on what you have. The trick in life is to learn to see the cup as half-full. Back in my hotel room and the 12.30pm Premier League kick-off was about to start: Leicester v Leeds. "We will not be perfect, and that's okay, but we need to fight like the team always did before me." I loved that message from Jesse Marsch before his first game. So smart, it takes pressure off.

In our own team meeting, an hour-and-forty before kick-off, Jürgen delivered a strong message. "We come from an interesting week: an emotional game at Wembley, ten changes with a great attitude and approach in the FA Cup and now we go into the third competition this week. People speak to me about the quadruple, they want to create a nice story I guess. It's true that the only team who can do it is us because we won the League Cup. The problem with this can be that it softens our approach to see the next game as the next final. If everything goes well, we will have 21 more games and that means 21 more finals. How can we go through a period like this? Only one way: focus on this game. We are good at that, but we have to stay like that. A mindset to realise that there will be problems. Us with the highest intensity, we don't want it the easy way, we jump as high as we can. Guys, a lot of words but it's not complicated, let's go for them. Create an atmosphere inside and that will create the atmosphere outside."

The next final – Premier League final no27 – 1-0 at home to West Ham. To be honest, we paid back with the result but not with our performance. It was not that we were bad, but we just gave too many clear opportunities away. We knew it would be difficult because West Ham were just very good. Take, for example, their biggest chance where they ran from deep behind our last line. These second-line runs with such good timing only happen in the Premier League. But as always, Trent saving the ball off the line and Ali flying in with his body kept the clean sheet. Passion made – and will always make – the difference. There is only one way to play against them and that is to have more of the ball so you can control Michail Antonio and the three runners better, but when you counter quickly as we did, how we want, there was always a chance for them to use the space we left when losing the ball. The way you attack influences so much the way you suffer counter-attacks. We went 200mph so often. The amount of counter-attacks we had, the amount of times we were three-v-three over half-a-pitch, this happens of course much more often with a front-line of Sadio, Luis and Mo. All three want to go. Sometimes we could slow down and control the attack to give time to stay together. Anyway, Sadio scored and played the role of Bobby as the false nine outstandingly once again. Chapeau. Last time we'd played them in November, they caused us problems with their set-pieces, we'd suffered two goals against, but we improved with our defensive set-pieces, which was crucial otherwise you don't win these games. In the year we became champions we had many games like this – only difference was that we were ten points clear!

"What a signing Luis is," said Milner while walking out of the stadium. "He was like a rocket in the counter-attacks," said Jürgen.

Tough game, but we did the job. We'd move on to Inter and Brighton.

‘OUR TRAINING IS OUR COMPASS – IT JUST MOVES US IN THE RIGHT DIRECTION’

WEEK 33
DREAM BIG

IT WAS THE MORNING AFTER WEST HAM AND I WAS sitting in the office with the analysts and Vitor. The sun was shining through the windows. It looked like spring was coming – and spring in England is the nicest thing. But just seeing the sun again was nice. We were watching back the first leg against Inter and we had identified three massive improvement-points: in our high press, in our midfield press and in our goalkeeper build-up. It's cool that you discuss and analyse for over two hours to achieve a conclusion of two sentences to be able to explain to the players clearly. Until this moment, analysis means nothing.

I had the feeling there would be nothing easy in this next game with them. It looked like Inter had played at their best at San Siro because for 65 minutes they reached levels I hadn't seen them reach in Serie A. Let me say it like this: if we weren't good that day they would have won, for sure. We engaged our extra power sources after 65 minutes and with Hendo, Luis and Naby giving new tactical energy.

It was a tough opponent, in every position there was real quality. [Samir] Handanovic showed in our game that he is probably one of the best goalkeepers in the world with his feet, for example. We planned to adapt and give them the first pass and go with the 'second-pass press' principle. We would also need an out-of-the-box solution versus their man-on-man high press, I told the guys. We'd lost each goal-kick and suffered counters over and over again – and their midfielders grow if the game becomes a second-ball battle. I spoke with Jürgen and we went through so many different options until we agreed: Ali is the spare player so we should open the space around him, he is the extra man and has to show he is better than Handanovic, that will help. Jürgen gives the perfect example, saying each one-v-one you win against a man-marking side kills their structure.

I walked in the dressing room; Jürgen was already changing. "It's Sunday," he says. "If we win something more this year it's because of these sessions." Every day you have to conquer your team. Then they are happy – and a smile makes the biggest difference. I took Jota out of the canteen and told him he would start as the striker on Tuesday. We went to the analysis room where Dan had selected two clips of Sadio in the Wembley final where he put Silva under massive pressure from the centre. "Like this, as many times as possible towards [Stefan] De Vrij. If you try to defend [Marcelo] Brozovic in these moments we will lose timings and one per cent less in these moments will change the whole type of game," I tell him. With Diogo, it is nice to speak with him because he thinks and talks as a coach. It's incredible how he sees the game tactically. When we signed him, I'd said, "He is technically on the level of our front three." But knowing him now much better, I have to say that tactically he is among our top boys. Coaches and players, it's the same as how you see your kids, you are part of their life, not the other way around. That's how I try to see coaching nowadays: helping the team to be superior, helping the team to avoid mistakes, putting them into their strengths. We knew very well how it felt to have a comeback: it always started with the other team feeling that they are already there, maybe not on the game day but all the days in between. This didn't happen with us, though, in my opinion.

Matchday-1 and it was analysis meeting time. "Good news, guys – Champions League tomorrow. Not so good news, guys – the opposition still thinks they can go through and they are good," Jürgen warned the team. "We should expect an intense game again, nothing is decided. We need very good defending from the starters and the subs. Guys, it's the old story but we are one of the five teams who are able to win this competition. If you want something desperately, you give everything. It should be allowed in life to dream big. If you can imagine it, it's the start of making it possible. Look around here and see the quality we have – that's why it's allowed to dream big. End of May, Paris. There are players here who have won it and want this feeling and memory again. You have players who never won it and want this feeling. That's a good mixture, I would say. This is the reason to make the extra yard or when there are problems on the pitch to give this last per cent. It's a night game at Anfield, every special game started when we put the extra intensity in. Just be yourself and I will be happy."

Ultimately we did make it into the last eight but only after a 1-0 defeat on the night at Anfield, meaning a 2-1 win for us on aggregate. It was job done, but there were not many happy faces in the dressing room afterwards. I was glad we didn't have to play them again this season – wow, they were tricky to face. The Champions League is like this; if you are not good on the night, you are out. But we were ready to face the problems. It was so important we spoke about this before so it wasn't a surprise. They were so difficult to play against. Inter also had one more rest day, which gave them a physical, analysis and training advantage. It was so hard to see what they were trying to do, who was moving where, that I had to look many times at the screen to see again. They had so much variability in their build-up, which is mainly caused by Brozovic. What was clear was with Lautaro Martinez and Alexis Sanchez they had two players who wanted to use the spaces behind our last line and give our centre-halves constant pressure. That said, Joel hit the bar, twice we struck the post with Mo and a shot from Luis was cleared off the line by Arturo Vidal. Normally on these kinds of occasions we need a goal to free ourselves completely, but this didn't happen. The speed of the simple passes and the quality of the first touch defines the fluidity of the attacks; doing these two small things right makes the big things happen, and we were missing exactly this too often. When Alexis was sent off it was game-over as we were able to control it. For me, what was most important was that we respected them and we respected our situation, not only on the game day but from the second we came back in the changing room in Milan.

We had three finals to go before the international break. I was a proud man driving to the AXA the following morning for an interview while listening to Dutch music. Three more finals, three more big ones before the break. Our training is our compass – it just moves us in the right direction. Thursday's session this week was a good example. Jürgen explained before training that the game against Inter taught us that we had to be more lethal in our counter-press – so many opportunities to hurt them were missed; that we needed to reach momentum not only through good play but especially through our counter-press. Both go hand-in-hand, of course, but what he meant was the attitude in the last step. So we trained hard on our counter-press, firstly in a counter-press rondo with three teams of four competing to earn the right to keep the ball in possession. In a space of 15x15 metres they train the pressing impulse when losing the ball. Secondly, in a 10-v-goalkeeper where the starting position is a midfield press, a high press or a counter-press, they needed to apply the first-pass-forward principle while recovering ball possession. The one extra rule in this drill was there must be five players in the box before scoring. Thirdly, we played a 'create to score' game where two teams of four had the opportunity to combine with two extra players in depth, so basically six-v-four, where the one extra rule is that scoring after a counter-press counted double. Winner-stays-on principle and magic was a certainty. "We should never forget who we are," Jürgen said when finishing the session. It shows sometimes when we get used to winning, details get lost. The counter-press rondo was exceptional, we'd just have to activate it on Saturday at Brighton.

Actually, while I was preparing for the session with Vitor, we looked back to our last week and we had the feeling we did too much on the day before the game against Inter and too much on the day before West Ham. Too much information, too much physical activity, basically not respecting the recovery process enough. The moment we were not creative or quick in our simple decisions during the game meant something wasn't right in the days leading up. It's not easy to know what it was, but I was pretty sure we did too much. We would adjust again to the less-is-more principle. On the Friday the doping control showed up at the training ground. They can arrive at any moment in time and on this day they surprised us by standing in the sports hall. "I understand why they want to test you, Trent, if you keep playing like that," I said. "I don't understand why they want to test Robbo then, Pep" he replied. "Clown – you are a clown!" Robbo told him in response!

"Brighton had a whole week to prepare and, let's be honest, they are a good football team who always find ways to keep the ball," Jürgen told the boys. "We have to focus on us and have to use all our defensive tools. We have to close the decisive areas with our formation going back to our oldest principle: one can defend two, two can defend three and our front three can defend five of them." I saw that Graham Potter said in his 'presser' about us: "They are very good but it's cool to face them." They had a plan, for sure. We had to be ready to reach our intensity to make sure it wouldn't work against us. Driving in the rain towards the Amex Stadium from the hotel on matchday morning, Sky Sports was on the TV on the bus. I saw a picture of Mark Leyland at Newcastle where Eddie Howe won the Premier League manager of the month award. They did the impossible by winning again against Southampton, and in their last nine games they hadn't lost once. For us, Joel Matip won the Premier League player of the month. That's not easy as a defender. Naby acted as if he was standing with a bottle of champagne next to him when we all applauded Joel at AXA.

Walking into the away dressing room, it was red. Our analysis department fixed big posters of our players everywhere, with quotes and nameplates of the boys. We try to create a little Anfield everywhere we travel. I caught a glimpse of Mo carrying an iPad with the behaviour of [Brighton goalkeeper Robert] Sanchez during penalties. Jürgen's last message to the boys was: "When you are well-prepared you can decide to enjoy. And that's what we have to do today. We want to, or we have to? That's a massive difference. We want and nothing else. We want to give everything. I want us today to be super-positive. Is it possible to win 19 games? Yes it is, but only when you focus on one." Our boys deal a lot with criticism. It's a big part of football, especially nowadays. We can't underestimate this part of being a football player or coach; it happens to all of us. The problem comes when they are lies or when it's to hurt someone without any context. This happened to me this particular week after an interview I'd given to Dutch television. I'm proud of our group, our boys are so strong mentally. They are an example for me. I always use this John Wooden quote to explain: 'Be more concerned with your character than your reputation, because your character is what you really are, while your reputation is merely what others think you are.'

Final no28. A 2-0 win at Brighton. We were good, especially after our first goal. Diaz timed his run perfectly and came in front of Sanchez, he headed it in and Sanchez took him out. 'If that's not a sending-off, what is?' I was thinking. You can put Diaz on a gravel pitch and he will play good football. It's just insane. It's the joker card – and so is Thiago when we can bring him from the bench. Whatever is happening, this card overrules everything! The influence bringing players like him on is just massive. Naby played excellently again. Our midfield was compact throughout. What was more important was that we learned from our first game against them, we were always in control without the ball. It's so hard to go to Brighton and we just gave an outstanding performance. I was so proud. Walking in after the game, Vitor showed me the result of the Under-23s who had won 7-1 against Tottenham. The Spurs coach said they just couldn't deal with their intensity. I loved that. One small victory for the U23s and a big, big victory for the one-club mentality. Well done, Barry and the boys.

WEEK 34
PURE LEADERSHIP

IT WAS MONDAY MORNING AND I WAS SITTING IN the office with Jürgen. "Remember I wanted to speak to you last week but we never got around to it?" he said. "Well, I'm thinking about extending until 2026. The club wants to extend. What are your thoughts and plans?" "I'm with you until the end of this project," I responded, firmly and directly. "Whatever happens after isn't important now, only today and tomorrow counts." Our agent spoke with us later that night and I told him: "I'm positive about the situation we are in with the club, the team and staff. It's the right moment and time to commit longer with the club I feel as well. It gives stability and it gives trust. We can keep improving the process like this and fight for each prize. There is stability, leadership, control and with this constant evolution. We are pushing and it's an honour to represent this club and Jürgen. We are pushing!"

Away from the contract discussions I had a thought: it's about pressure now, who can deal with it best? Ten finals for them, ten finals for us. Could we win them all? That would mean we'd have won 18 in a row by the end of the season and I'd say we'd deserve the title if that happened. City were away at Palace that night and it ended in a 0-0 draw. I had watched the first half but then had to go to sleep. The amount of games was taking its toll. We would see Man City face-to-face very soon, but on the Tuesday morning it was a one-point gap in the table and we had Arsenal away the following night. Our building should know that every single department would play its part to support our team to continue the successful run. When the pressure rises, the exercises should be highly competitive because that's the moment the guys don't think about the season and the rivalry. They just think to compete, to win... one of the oldest characteristics of the human brain. And with this they adapt to attacking with and without the ball. Wanting to win. You see it with a three-year-old, you see it with a 30-year-old. We would be stimulating this in the coming period, so the boys would be training with their whole bodies – always having to earn time to play more football or earn the right to attack more, always with the goal in mind.

The boys who played at Brighton looked tired, I could see they weren't smiling, so we put on a foot-volley 'old v young' five-v-five game after the recovery rondos to stimulate this competitiveness in a controlled way. In the end this race would be about who wanted it more, but only with having control emotionally. Remember: it's just focusing on the next point. City were pushing us, we were pushing them, to limits that we'd seen in previous seasons. Game on, let's keep dreaming big. All good things start with that. There was a perfect example of James Milner's exemplary attitude this day, too. He had fined himself a few weeks back because he was late to a meeting – and, by the way, when he did arrive, I had never heard so many players make the 'ker-ching' sound! But he had to text Bob Windle, our first-team operations officer, to check why he hadn't had the fine taken out of his salary yet… he is even on top of himself.

In the analysis meeting the boys were listening carefully. Jürgen started the meeting: "We can all pretend we don't know what happened yesterday [City drawing]. It's important because results of other teams influence the league table, but it's not important because we are preparing for an away game at Arsenal. Now we spoke about it, so we can draw a line under it right now and focus on us. We should try to be a nightmare for them tomorrow, they should wake up a few times in this game hoping it's just a bad dream." Jürgen was leading this team with real power. Pure leadership. The analysis was clear, Pete had selected good clips to prepare the behaviour of our full-backs and our 8s. Always in between! Five metres doesn't matter a lot for many teams, but for us it's the difference-maker because we want to counter-press – so push up! "Anyway, like that you are closer for the goal celebrations," joked Jürgen, "so stay together!"

That night, we arrived in London. We were staying in an old prison that had been turned into a beautiful hotel. Watching the Champions League that evening, I was thinking there was nothing better than being through in the tournament and watching the other teams without any pressure, knowing that you are not playing a knockout game of your own the following night. We watched Manchester United v Atletico Madrid while keeping an eye on Ajax-Benfica.

Matchday. Ten weeks previously, when City looked gone, I spoke about the gap of 14 points and to remind ourselves that we wanted to go on a mission. Eighteen games were left at that time, Arsenal was now 'half-time' and there were nine more to go. A lot had happened since then. The real pre-match meeting, Milner did with his text message in the group: "Let's go boys, let's not let up now, keep the throttle at 100 per cent and be ruthless, horrible bastards to play against." Jürgen continued with: "Go at them tonight as a thunderstorm." And the boys did. Final no30, a 2-0 win away to Arsenal... but it was a game with two opposite halves, to be honest. First half, credit to Arsenal, they pressed us really well and with time and with the ball they put our lines too deep. Luckily, at half-time we could correct this. For me, in the second half, because of all the days off, all the moments we were able to rotate, a few players popped up and we were able to keep our tempo and pressing longer than them. That's why we won. Fitness is always in relation to recovery. Always. The highlight and decider of the game were the two counter-press moments before we scored our second, wonderful goal with Bobby. When we came back in the dressing room, Jürgen said: "Thank you for being a pain in the ass for the whole of the Premier

League!" "This one is BIG, guys," I added. "It's all about clean sheets," Virgil shouted while walking into the dressing room. These moments when the team is together are the most special moments in football, at least that's what I was thinking on that night. One more game before the international break. Jürgen said in the press conference after the game: "We have played six games more than Arsenal since we met last time. Thirteen to seven, if I am right, which is really mad. I don't think that will stop. You wake up in a different hotel and people tell you where the restaurant is and you remember the room number. That's our life." This is so true: the amount of times I'd woken up in the weeks before, needing a little bit of time to understand where I was, was incredible.

Back at the AXA Training Centre on Friday and we learned that it was Benfica. It was Portugal. It was Lisbon. The Champions League quarter-final draw had paired us with Benfica… Jürgen's favourite city, my worst city, only because of Porto being in my blood! But I respect Benfica. They helped us massively before the Champions League final in 2019 when their B team came out to our training camp in Marbella for a practice game. They simulated the system and style of Mauricio Pochettino's Tottenham in the best way possible. It gave us specificity before the biggest game in our lives, so I will be forever grateful for how they helped us in preparing for this moment. But first, the FA Cup. And Sunday would be the first time we'd played Nottingham Forest in the tournament since Hillsborough. We cannot – and never should – miss one opportunity to pay tribute to those who lost their lives. Some Forest fans came to Anfield to lay some flowers at the memorial. I really believe we can draw inspiration from the 97 children, women and men who died at Hillsborough. How is it possible for us to lose hope as a football team playing sport when you look at what those supporters and their family and friends have been through – and continue to go through? When our fans sing You'll Never Walk Alone they don't just sing it, they live it. This city is different. Before every home game I see the flag in the corner of the Kop by the Sir Kenny Dalglish Stand. It's the one of Owen McVeigh in silhouette holding the hand of his dad. It makes me emotional, it really does – especially as our fans are singing You'll Never Walk Alone in the background. We are different.

"If we take this draw the wrong way, we are halfway out," Jürgen told the team just before our prep started for Forest. It was the last game before the international break and this was the exact reason we made it compulsory for the players to travel back with us after the game. Nobody could travel directly to their holiday destination or to their national teams. It was to ensure the game received the full focus it deserved. We wanted to make Wembley red again. It's how Jürgen says: you show respect for the opposition by the way you defend. They are a massive club and they were in a good moment. It would not be easy – any people who have worked in England will understand this. To help the recovery process, we did a one-v-one 'move up, move down' 1-2-3 tournament. The winner goes up and the loser goes down in short one-minute games. Competitiveness. Firmino vs Virgil was the final. We all made a big circle around them while they were competing, Virgil forced Bobby to make errors, which we all know isn't easy, but Bobby was doing Bobby things. The subs played four short five-v-five games with the one rule that on the third corner they would receive a penalty. We took this 'rule' from Cruyff; he did it to practise penalties in the context of the game, I guess. At Liverpool we play the game to create finishes and this rule stimulates this target even more.

Normally the quicker you attack, the quicker it comes back. This was what we had to avoid against Forest: avoid the amount of opportunities to counter with [Keinan] Davis and [Brennan] Johnson. We would put Virgil and Ibou one-v-one against them if they did not change their system. Counter-pressing without pushing up into the right spaces is like sailing without a map – it's not only very dangerous, it just doesn't work.

In terms of our team selection, Kostas was still positive with COVID. Milner was still positive, too. I don't like Millie, I love him, because he is the one who makes us consistent. He makes sure we don't drop half-a-per-cent. Back to our line-up and Robbo was our one and only option for the left side. When we made the line-up for Forest we decided to go strong with our defensive triangle: Virgil, Ibou and Fabinho. We had to create stability with our spine. We needed to be ready to stop and defend counters, so this combination of speed and positioning at the back would be crucial. "It will be important to have the spine with experience and power," I said to Jürgen. "The spine with power and the rest of players who have to prove something."

Forest had defeated Leicester and Arsenal in earlier rounds of the FA Cup. We could not take this lightly, especially not in their home. It's one of the stadiums in England that can reach our Anfield atmosphere. "The FA Cup journey of Nottingham Forest is impressive, but they should feel after five minutes it was a really bad draw for them," Jürgen told the team. I continued: "They man-mark our midfielders, they will follow each movement which opens up gaps – this is what we need to use to progress; in and around the box we have to show how good we are, we need technique there." On Saturday, Robbo arrived at AXA having only slept four hours and when we asked if there was anyone who needed an extra recovery day, he asked to stay inside. That night we found out he had tested positive, meaning we now only had Owen Beck as cover for Kostas, who was back in contention. Trent was also out with a hamstring problem and we'd allow him to recover in Dubai – a win/win situation, recover and regain freshness. We also decided to leave out Mo and Sadio because of their World Cup qualifier play-off.

I'd met an old friend the night before in the city for dinner and I'd received the biggest compliment an Evertonian could give me on Castle Street. This moment will be with me forever, seriously. He told me: "Love your passion, lad, but I still hate you!" With some swear words in there, too. After I bought him a drink, he apologised three times! You fight bad with good in life! I had also bumped into Mike Kearney, one of the club's biggest supporters, and Lizzi Doyle from The Anfield Wrap. Mike, being a proper Scouser, invited himself – politely I must say – to visit our new training ground. I could not and did not want to refuse. These people make football a little bit more about life.

But I felt we were fully focused on the job at hand on Sunday and we duly got a 1-0 win. Forest were definitely the FA Cup surprise of the season and full credit to them. They put their hearts on the pitch. They were aggressive, front-footed and played a 4-2-3-1 instead of playing with a line of five. They were dangerous on the counter and were brilliant in some of the moments from goal-kick situations. The pitch was not great, the ball was not great, there was an incredible atmosphere… all that is a good combination for the 'underdog' team in the FA Cup and we saw it. At least we knew now how it felt for other teams to come to Anfield, so respect and credit to their fans, but only a team with our mentality was able to go there and win this game.

We were sloppy but didn't get frustrated; we never blamed, whined or made any excuses and I think this was the difference-maker. We were more ready to suffer. You need to expect problems, especially if you make changes, especially in this cup. At half-time we changed to 4-4-2, which helped our pressing but didn't help our playing. Against a high and jumping line of four, it is much more about the moment when you start than the real speed. It's about creating and using the gaps. We pressed them in the positions where we felt they were weakest technically. We got the win with Diogo doing Diogo things, tapping in from Kostas' cross late on. Jota has the quality of a real, real striker: not playing particularly well, the team not playing well, but making, again, the decisive goal. Not many have this. When he walked onto the plane, he said to me: "Being in the right spot is what counts." He'd done it against Arsenal and now again. Wembley, nothing more to say. Liverpool were coming again. But now it was time for our break. Our run in January, February and March had been incredible and we should be proud of our effort during that time.

‘IT’S A PRIVILEGE TO WORK WITH THESE PLAYERS, THEY ARE MACHINES, REAL TEAM PLAYERS’

WEEK 35

THE LAST PIT-STOP

IT WAS GOOD THAT THE TEAM DIDN'T HEAR OUR voices this week. This break couldn't come at a better moment – new surroundings and different voices explaining different things to the boys. I really believe that always having the same food will change the amount of appetite, so Van Gaal coaching Virgil for us is a good thing. Tite telling Ali and Fabinho, Southgate telling Hendo… and Ronaldo telling Jota! I was sure they would come back hungry again, to these guys who constantly shout "Press!" And this hunger, this burning, this real appetite to compete is something we needed.

I had gone to Portugal with Danielle immediately after Forest and was then due to go back home, but before I went there I opened the convention for all the coaches at Liverpool FC soccer schools all over the world. "You are the guys who represent our club, so welcome to Anfield," I said. It was special to speak with them all, so I took my time. I flew back from Portugal especially for this event. When it is for our coaches, I always try to make time. It is always a privilege to speak to coaches. We were sitting in the Legends Lounge at Anfield and we had 40 of the head coaches here for four days. I felt free and safe to speak so I gave complete insight into how we work, my pathway, our future and our last game. USA, Japan, Egypt and Cyprus were all present. It was special they were all here again after the pandemic. In these moments you realise how big our club is and how many good people are giving their all to support it.

What I like about the March international break is that it gives time to reflect, it's the last stop before this season will get decided. After the convention, I headed back to my home in Holland for four days. I used the time to watch back our last games, using them to prepare training for the following week and try to find an answer to the most important question: how would we attack the month of April with a Champions League quarter-final, an FA Cup semi-final and five Premier League finals? It's the last pit-stop. Anyway, the question made the answer: we needed to attack, with all the tools we had, show hunger and realise why we came into this situation, just game-by-game. Neglect all the noise and create finals. It's a privilege to work with these players; they are machines, real team players. We will push for them and try to create the right conditions to shine and deliver. But the problem during this international break was that my anxiety was not going away, it felt like there was just too much at stake. The rhythm stopped but the feeling continued; it was not that easy to deal with. I tried to release it by spending time with my family, drinking coffee with my sister-in-law, eating Dad's homemade pizza, working together at the house, and playing padel with my Dutch friends, which didn't help actually because they are just much better than me and they are 'bad winners'.

It was just an incredible chase. We went from 14 points behind in January to one point behind in April. We were in it – they certainly felt our breath. But getting in a good position is one thing, overtaking number one is something completely different. As Jürgen would say, we came back to 5-4. I had this gut feeling it would be a Verstappen v Hamilton kind of finish this season. If it happened, I knew it'd be fun for the rest of the world… but would not help my anxiety!

Jürgen called me while I was driving through the woods to my home village. We laughed a lot and spoke about how we saw the future, the future long from now, then we discussed our players and their performances during the first round of internationals. Jota, what a day; a curler and an assist from Luis Diaz. "I can wait to see you again," Jürgen joked.

I'd forgotten how beautiful spring in Holland is; it just felt right. It was nice to be close to my family, with all its good and bad points!

One of the questions from the coaches during the convention was asking how I relax. And when he asked, I couldn't really answer it. In fact, I made an answer up, hoping it wouldn't show that our lives are possessed by pressure and that in the season it's just really tricky. The best way to control the pressure is to control the plan, I told them; to focus on the process. The recent months had been just insane. There is a big 'shadow side' of being a manager or a coach and it's not the critical media – it's trying to control the uncontrollable, finding a way to be prepared for 95 minutes in the Premier League jungle. Only the Premier League coaches will understand this feeling. It's exciting and hard at the same time. One thing is sure: I want to win and I liked this slipstream situation… with Luis Diaz we'd got some new, quick tyres!

WEEK 36

THE PERFECT SITUATION

WE HAVE A WHATSAPP GROUP FOR THE PLAYERS called 'Avoid Payment'. We made this agreement that the boys have to let us know that they are alright after their international games. They are far away from us when they are with their countries physically, but like this they are still very close to us.

I opened the group on Monday morning and there were ten messages all saying pretty much the same thing: '90 minutes, I'm OK'. Jürgen would be a happy man; no issues and we'd be ready and complete for this final chapter of the season. They were open pages, so we needed to fill them with pride and passion.

At the AXA, Jürgen was standing in the canteen and greeted me with a high-five. I gave him my hand but I wasn't sure because, I have to be honest, I didn't fully understand. He then put up his hand to show five… five subs [allowed per match by the Premier League]. Ah, the rule came through! Top – finally and fortunately! Job done. It's a victory for the players, a victory for the squad and a victory for the playing calendar. With it, I'm convinced we can play every three days. The future of top football was saved, in my opinion, because the way it was going wasn't right for the quality of the game.

That afternoon I had a long talk with my agent. The contract extension looked good, I was hopeful we could announce it before the end of the season. But firstly we spoke about the long-term future and there was something I wanted to make clear: I will only ever assist Jürgen. After this project, I will manage myself. It was during this week, I had an interview with the Coaches' Voice [online resource] in the commercial lounge at the AXA. It was set up perfectly with the tactics board and the lighting. They had me booked for an hour, but in the end it took two-and-a-half and I was happy to do it given we were speaking about one of the most impressive games in our modern history: Barcelona. Why not, I thought, let's go back in time and show one more time what makes us 'US'. You get defined as a club, a team or a person in moments like these. Winning prizes is the start, not the end – and like that, hunger follows.

Jürgen addressed the team just before our final training session of the week. “If anyone would have told us at the beginning of the season that after the last international break in front of me was sitting a full and healthy squad, a trophy in the cabinet, one point behind City and still in the race for the FA Cup and Champions League, we would take that. People who speak about the ‘Quadruple’ try to create a feeling that we have something to lose. What we did is that we created a base for the end of the season. We have a chance because we created this situation, that’s what you want. But what I always say is that giving your absolute everything doesn’t mean you will get anything, but it’s the only way to get something. There will be tough moments but when we do the things we are used to, the things that made us incredibly consistent over the last four years, we will have a chance. This is the perfect situation, having this room full of world-class players.

“We will play another 16 games maximum, that’s a lot of football so we have to use this room, we have to use five subs when we can. If something is proven this season it is that we will need the whole squad. We will achieve everything together, we can’t use any trouble-makers. We need to be the most annoying opponent for everyone, then we will see what we will get. You guys are a team that is ready for something special. We can only do this focusing on our way of playing; everyone is responsible for our offensive stuff, everyone is responsible for our defensive stuff. If we do this we will create a positive situation.”

Later, walking off the pitch, I said to the boss: “I will never take it for granted.” “What?” he replied. “That the boys are so concentrated.” We created some different problems for them to solve during the session: high press, midfield press, goal-kick build-up and open-play. Four different 11v11 games, each lasting four minutes. Milner was captaining the yellow team, the 'non-starters'. I've given a lot of praise to the players but would just like to say that it's never, ever enough. We are only as good as the non-starters are and how they look to these sessions as well. We don't expect them to be happy at not playing, but we expect them to deliver and that's what they did and do. Like this we all grow. The training was important for all of them to reconnect again with our principles and ideas. They all came back from different national teams, different ideas, different roles and different competitive contexts; some were playing for their World Cup chances, some just friendlies. So what we wanted during those days was that they reconnected again together. In the end you don't need a lot, but you need something where they can find the collective again.

Walking in after that session, the World Cup draw was on the television. These types of games are incredible, I thought to myself, but it is only special because it is once every four years and people have to understand this. There is a flip-side when you play more and more of the same – it will lose all the uniqueness. The shock between cultures, the shock between styles, the shock of how countries live the same game but express themselves so differently. We will see all of that this autumn; we will be in Dubai for our training camp watching them all. That night we would watch Braga against Benfica and then in four days we'd play the latter in Lisbon, so perfect timing to see them live and what they were all about. We also laughed about the staff game earlier that day, so much happened in it. I won't mention any names, but one player got the nickname 'The Bermuda Triangle' because every ball disappeared when it went in his direction!

And so, final no30 in the Premier League and a 2-0 home win over Watford. We saw a typical Roy Hodgson side, organised and with belief. Respect. Formation 4-5-1, deep defending but with quality. It was a good game from our side, especially in the moments we lost the ball. It was the final phase of the season, it was about mentality and winning, nothing more. All our boys showed mentality towards the team. I love that. Respect again. Watford had some real good footballers, but we felt they wouldn't be able to stand us if we counter-pressed at our best level. That was the best tool because Watford would fight for 95 minutes defensively to have these two or three counter-attacks. We told the boys before the game we needed to be ready for these by protecting our attacks with full conviction and concentration. Fabinho coming on from the bench and his well-taken penalty was the game-killer. Joe Gomez's cross from the Trent position was impressive, but how Jota scored again with his head to open the scoring in the first half was Falcao-worthy. I looked behind me to Trent and joked if we could add these quality crosses to our game it would be great! "Being top of the league at the start of April is something that makes me happy," I said walking into the dining room afterwards. It lasted for five minutes as City went ahead at Burnley. Anyway, we were still in the race. Champions League next, and after that, the game against the champions.

‘FOOTBALL IS A TEAM SPORT AND WHEN ONE LOSES THE BALL EVERYONE REACTS AND GOES IN – NO DISCUSSION, WE GO’

WEEK 37

BRAVE, BRAVER, BRAVEST

HEADING INTO THIS WEEK, WE'D BEEN WORKING ON our set-pieces and on the blind-side movements from the second line in behind. We needed to improve both again; both were always important but also very specific if we were to get a result at Benfica. On the plane to Portugal I was reading back over the notes I'd been making for this book. Time goes so quickly, I was thinking to myself, it goes at the same speed we play! It was on the flight that I picked out two sample pages and sent them over to Jürgen. 'Have a look if you like', I wrote to him in the message. Coming in to land, we could see Benfica's stadium: Estadio da Luz, the Stadium of Light. When Porto became champions in 2011 it was in their stadium, the celebrations were on the pitch...so the hosts decided to shut off the lights and turn on the sprinklers. The photos taken that night with flashlights are iconic – the Stadium of Light without light, possessed by FC Porto. For me, you need to deserve to become a real champion with consistency and with direct confrontations. We won that night 2-1 away at Benfica. This is what we'd have to do next week: earn the right by winning away at the Etihad, something we hadn't done in the league since 2015. We'd won one in the last ten encounters away against City, so it would be a statement of a champion. I liked that we'd need to deserve it directly against them.

But it was Benfica next up and our focus was firmly on them. To explain one more time the rivalry between Porto and Benfica, I remember the moment when I signed my first long-term deal with Porto. It was three months into my one-year contract; they called me into this typical southern European directors' office and started speaking. "Pep, this contract means three things. First, you are part of our family now; second, you are going to make much more money; and third, the most important thing is that this contract means you can never, ever work for Benfica!" I laughed but they were deadly serious. No red allowed. You learn quickly when people are honest.

During the meeting between Pete, Jürgen and myself, we found the right words: let's try to surprise them with our attitude and timing of press. We decided to go brave, braver, bravest against them with our organisation. We were preparing a wild game. We would give them the first passes, so they had time to find their building structure with [defensive midfielder Julian] Weigl between the centre-halves and both full-backs high on the pitch. This would mean three players with big space in the centre, so we'd go with Luis, Sadio and Mo against them. This had to become an advantage for us when we won balls in our midfield press. On the game day we trained at the Sporting Lisbon stadium, the boys were smiling; there was no extra information for their brains, it was just to get a good feeling to play quick passes. We did some passing exercises and rondos, but we'd brought the weather with us from England, cold and windy. Unlucky. What we knew was Benfica would play with their entire soul. Their key offensive players are Rafa Silva and Darwin Nunez. Rafa is so quick with the ball, stopping him would be of great importance if we wanted to control and dominate. He is this 'all-or-nothing' player; give him space and it's all, that's for sure. In the high press Virgil would be responsible, in the midfield press we had to be so compact that Robbo, Virgil, Fabinho and Thiago could always get close to him. From a set-piece perspective, it was [left-back] Grimaldo who was key – he had Kostas's type of deliveries, so we should try to avoid set-pieces against them. On the morning of the game I had a call with my good friend Joao Tralhao, an old Benfica Under-19 coach, to get some extra information… Well, to be honest, we spoke just five minutes about them and the rest of the time we spent catching up.

That night we took a big step forward in the Champions League quarter-final, albeit it was only half-time in the tie. A 3-1 win at Estadio da Luz… the boys deserved a nice glass of wine that night. Our fifth away victory in the competition in a row and our eighth consecutive victory on the road in all competitions. History. And with Luis Diaz, Diogo, Vitor and myself having a history at Porto, for us it was a little bit sweeter as for many years winning against Benfica would define a season for us. The game itself was wild, but the opening goal from Ibou was exactly what we needed. The second came from a full-pitch press, Trent playing the first-pass-forward – and how, so similar to the one he played against Arsenal. Luis came from the blind side and headed it across for Sadio to tap in. Trent plays the passes our forwards like to receive, always on time. And that was the speed we'd spoken about, that was the 3v3 we'd spoken about. The other three, by the way – Fabinho, Naby and Thiago – gave us so much control with the ball. Then the three subs – Hendo, Bobby and Diogo – changed the game into control again after Benfica came out for the second half with the knife between their teeth. They recovered what we had lost: the ball.

As we'd anticipated, Benfica played with their soul, that's for sure. The goal from Nunez made the stadium believe again, but we pulled the trigger with Diaz's speed coming from the blind side of Nicolas Otamendi in behind. On this occasion he outplayed the goalkeeper, Odysseas Vlachodimos, who was in my opinion their best player on the night. That's always a good sign in terms of attacks but sometimes not a good sign in terms of finishes. But anyway, our players showed their class on this night.

After the game I was speaking with Joao and when I walked back onto the bus, Jürgen asked who I'd been talking to. When I explained that he was a good friend who worked for many years at Benfica and had a huge influence on Bernardo Silva's development, he immediately said: "So, he is responsible for him being that good?" "He helped a lot," I said. "I will kick his ass for that!" He went out of the bus to give him a hug and gave two pretend punches. I laughed so hard. The morning after, as we stayed over, I tried to improve my mood, get some sun and clear my mind by walking into Lisbon city centre. I went in search of A Bola, the daily football newspaper, to re-live the night before. I headed into the first coffee shop I found; the smell of croissants and coffee hit me and memories of the past came flooding back. Reading over the game, I thought to myself we had watched one of Europe's purest and most powerful strikers fighting against our centre-halves in Darwin Nunez. Not many make life hard for them, but he certainly did. He is, for sure, one to keep an eye on; he has a lot of potential... and how can you not like someone who has 'win' in their name? We returned to Liverpool later that day and the following morning I was back at the AXA. Mine and Jürgen's agent, Marc, sent me a text: "All is sorted, contract is done." "And happy?" Jürgen texted me. I replied: "I'm proud! Let's make new memories together. We are going to add new chapters to our collaboration – how cool is that? It will be good fun!"

The day before City, I was sitting with Jürgen and we went through our line-up, creating the small plans. We had to be ourselves: a pressing machine that wants to play. Over the years Pep improved his team so much against us in the direct confrontations. Patience with the ball, finding solutions against our press, trying to go to the left to attack over the right and vice-versa using our free spaces. Most of the goals they scored were with our team open, attracted to press, moved to one side, leaving our full-backs in a one-v-one and loads of space. We had to learn, we had to adapt as well without losing ourselves. This was the tricky part. Our defensive plan should be spot on. First and foremost, we had to overplay their high press, something we didn't do well and consistently enough in the last five confrontations against them.

So, in training and in the analysis, we focused on exactly this; we showed how we could create options to outplay the six players who pressed. Trent and Robbo would stretch their midfield line by opening up the pitch to its maximum, opening up the inside spaces for Thiago, Fabinho and Hendo; with this they are ready to receive line-breakers on the outside. Robbo and Trent would be crucial. "Be quick but don't rush!" and "Use the gaps!" I shouted during the tactical overview. "I love video analysis," Jürgen said, "because we can show our boys their weaknesses." We showed the eight-v-six several times and that when our orientation, our overview, is good we were able to bring the ball to their half and into our creative players. The boys needed to know and feel it was right, what we were doing. That's why 11-v-11 training is so important; we do it always the day before the game focusing on what we think is decisive. We create focus with a six-v-two rondo but with teams of two – when you lose the ball not just you but also your partner has to go inside. Jürgen called the team together and said, "There is a hidden message in this exercise: football is a team sport and when one loses the ball everyone reacts and goes in – no discussion, we go." Our boys got sharper with each minute that went on.

Game day, finally. The preparation was over. Manchester City away was here. Jürgen started the meeting: "We are back in Manchester, same hotel and the same room as before the United game. Don't think about the result, I want you to think about how good we are. Imagine us sitting in the bus after and we'd won this game. We have 550 million supporters, we just Googled that, but this was in 2015 so there are probably a few more now because of you guys, they will all be watching. Everyone who watches thinks: one day I want to be part of this game. And we are." Jürgen told the boys he was in an excellent mood: "Why? The reason is you guys. You raised the bar, it's impossible but because of you guys it's possible. I'm asking nothing special, just us. For the right reasons, because we are incredibly difficult to play against. But we have to show how much we have improved with the ball. Brave. It's not risky, it's football. The way we have to play against them is that we defend all with all we have, we attack all with all we have. Give us this extra bit of aggression. I feel so good because nobody else can do this better than you guys. Make our counter-press wild. City are a passing team who try to make us passive – don't let this happen, be active and unpredictable to create an impact stealing balls. De Bruyne, Bernardo and Foden, don't give them the one-v-one they want."

Final no31 ended 2-2. It was a 'football anthem', this game. Two brilliant teams trying to create problems for each other. These games are always about how consistent you are on your good things during the 90 minutes. In our case, how good is our pressing, how together we are in terms of distances with and without the ball, how long we can stay in the opposition half attacking and defending, how we can always bring the game to our creative players? That's what we tried and that's how we felt after the game. A fair result and with the feeling that it is possible. We'd be seeing them again soon at Wembley and, hopefully, as much of that as possible would be spent in their half of the pitch. Vitor said it like this: "The brain beats the muscle, but the heart beats the brain." This is a good way to describe what happened here: 2-2 against City, twice coming back into the game, that's an incredible sign of 'heart' being away from home. When I walked back into the dressing room I said, "If we win the next seven games we are champions."

What started with overplaying their 6, ended with one full-back finding the other. Robbo's cross and Trent assisting Jota, who again scored our first goal. A copy of the 'total football' goal we scored years ago. But this was a game where each imperfection resulted in so many aggressive attacks. Anyway, if we should just remember one thing, it should be the pass from Mo to Sadio for our second goal. Both teams were good but weren't perfect – how could they be? So, I couldn't wait for Wembley, but first we needed to try the following Wednesday to get into the semis of the Champions League.

WEEK 38

THAT'S INTENSITY, THAT'S OUR IDENTITY

HOW DID WE FEEL WAKING UP THE MORNING AFTER the away game at the Etihad? Not bad, really not bad at all, because we were still in it and anyone who would have said that months ago would have been considered a lunatic, so all good. Next time we would be braver with our subs, earlier and more, how we had done all season. We have to – our way costs a lot of energy. If we use the five-sub rule right next season it will be an incredible addition to our playing style. But there was no time to think too long about it while sitting in Jürgen's office; we went through the good and the bad for just ten minutes and then we moved on because we had Benfica in front of us and we would need to be in a killer mood for it. This was the not-so-good news for Benfica. It was half-time, but it was Anfield now. Our fans. No coasting, no complacency. "We go and make changes," Jürgen told the team, which influenced the intensity of the training session. During training I focused on aggressive pressing, aggressive counter-pressing and aggressive finishing, all this in combination with the first-pass-forward principle. Especially after an emotional game like we'd had at Man City, it was good to go back to basics. We were not in the part of the season to play well – we were in the part to win games and this was the mentality we would need against Benfica. It would be defined by how good we defended together. Again. This should be represented in our line-up: changes to play with 100 per cent intensity and concentration.

Jürgen and I tried to clear our heads with a game of padel tennis later that day. I won the tie-break after being 4-1 up in the set, but the German mentality and his new state-of-the-art racket brought the boss back in the game. On one of the decisive points, he threw himself into the fence catching a ball and ended up with blood everywhere. He had to go inside with some wounds. My heart stopped for a second seeing him flying into that fence, but like a real leader he came back after seeing the doc and won the game he was losing. Even the staff use adversity as a trampoline. It's the most powerful teaching tool: your own example, your own character.

The day before Benfica, it was early morning and I walked into our analysts' room. "This Pep [Guardiola] will make me burn out one day," I said, laughing. Watching the City game back, we noticed he had pushed Cancelo and Walker to Hendo and Jota, our 10s. We'd never seen that before. In the second half he put Bernardo next to Ederson bringing the ball out from the back; he overloaded our last line exactly like Chelsea did, trying to attack each gap. We have nothing less than huge respect for Pep and his staff. For sure, he would come up with new plans in four days when we would see him again at Wembley for a season-defining game, not just because of the opportunity of reaching another domestic final, but also for the confidence it would give for the rest of the season, knowing you will go back to that famous stadium to compete for the prize with most history and tradition in England. As we were in the room, Margaret Aspinall walked in. We each gave her a big hug before she spoke with Dan Spearritt, our analyst whose family have been directly affected by the Hillsborough tragedy. She had just finished a talk with our Under-23 and Under-18 teams before she popped in. These moments are so much more important than months of coaching. They teach Liverpool and they teach life. Never forgotten.

In the meeting with the boys we focused on following our press. "It's not written down in one tactical book," Jürgen explained to the team. "Press and follow to show the way – Robbo became famous with it when he did it four or five times against City [in 2017/18]!" Late in the afternoon, we took our starting line-up and went through our defensive and offensive ideas. Jürgen delivered clear messages. While they passed the ball quickly and with ideas through the thirds I shouted at any moment "Counter-press!" and the boys needed to press me intensely. At one moment, our 'Greek Scouser' slid into a tackle right in front of me, winning the ball back. "He is ready for tomorrow!" I shouted. Again, Jürgen demonstrated why his meetings are just the best on matchday at the hotel. They are probably one of the biggest reasons why we always leave everything behind on the pitch. "A big part of my job is to think. To think about what might happen. Think to find answers. Influence them. Villarreal went through [in the Champions League] yesterday. People assume things will go our way but that's dangerous to think. When they see that we change seven times they probably think we rest. Yesterday showed that Chelsea entered with the right mindset, with heart. Real Madrid learned only during the game. It's mid-April… mid-April… and we can go to the semi-finals of the Champions League. We need to be top from the first until the last second, so that's why we chose this line-up. Everything can happen, we learned that in our away game. Tell me one team in world football that can change seven times and have this team. From now on, the incredible bench, the starters, we all need this mentality to win. Commit to defending, everyone, then we will feel good and start using our triangles. That's the plan. Unbelievable chance, semi-final, how many people do you know who reached that? Start to get excited for this game and we have a good chance."

Quarter-final, second leg. Into the semis. The fourth European semi-final in the last seven years. We achieved it with a 3-3 at home against a Benfica team that refused to give up. Life only helps the brave ones – and we had changed seven times in a quarter-final of the Champions League. In the end we not only won qualification but divided and managed game-time as well. Win/win, I would say. Let's hope life will help us at Wembley with this decision… We showed trust in the squad, you saw that when the players coming on were still a little tired and we lost control over the game and they could exploit the imperfections. For example, we lost pressure on the ball, and with a high-line against quick strikers like Darwin Nunez this is a recipe for danger. Tempo and energy are always the biggest tactical problem-solvers. On the positive side, Luis, Jota and Roberto were incredible on this night. They gave attacking solutions to each other constantly. They were super-aggressive in the pressing, following their own press on each occasion. They didn't play the piano, they played the drums. Tempo and energy, no shortcuts, always giving time for the team to push up by keeping the ball in difficult situations. After the game it was deadly silent in the dressing room. We walked in and the players didn't know what to expect because of having given away the 3-1 lead. Jürgen was clear, however: "If there is a moment we don't celebrate reaching the semi-final of the Champions League we become our own worst enemy. We are in the SEMIS! The semis of the Champions League!" After this, the entire dressing room applauded. Musica!

Thursday morning at the AXA, the middle of April and we were having an English heatwave. Well, it wasn't that hot, but it was time for shorts. Time flies when you're having fun, I thought to myself. I was excited that we were going into the really interesting phase of the season; it's like seeing the top of the mountain but it's the steepest and roughest part we still have to climb. In front of us was this semi-final in a competition we – as in this current group – had never won. Which, by the way, was the only competition we had never won. The game was at Wembley again and this made me so happy. We felt City hadn't seen the best Liverpool yet, so it was time to really show this. This wasn't meant arrogantly, it meant that it was time to reach our full potential for this last phase. Put some real wind in the sails. This game was about who has to adjust to who: Pep to us or us to Pep? That's the trick, trying to be one step in front of them so they need time to adjust to us. When you analyse the opposition, it's always what they did in the past; when you analyse your own team it's what

Walk on: I'm so happy to be extending my stay at Liverpool with Jürgen. The future is exciting

Paris here we come: (Above) Sadio scores against Villarreal as we head for another European final. (Above left) team spirit before 'Final no37' against Southampton and (right) hard work in training

Cup double: Our second major trophy of the season. With the team at Wembley (top) and (above) all smiles with Andreas on our flight home. There was no time to rest – our next game was in three days

Best fans in the world: A sea of colour and noise on the final Premier League day against Wolves

All together: (Above) a team talk during training in the Stade de France ahead of the Champions League final against Real Madrid. (Left) man of the match Thibaut Courtois denies Mo late on with a brilliant save – it wasn't to be our night

Turning the city red: It was a proud day showing our two trophies to the fans in Liverpool. It was a season we'll never forget

you want to happen in the future. So we focused on us; we should be confident, trying to be a step in front. Just before we'd gone out against Benfica I'd told the team: "We've got this, guys, put a smile on and go and do this." The real confidence, the confidence earned by training hard and having no doubt what to do. This confidence, a feeling that's only built over a long time, is what makes you in life. That's Liverpool FC, that's our team. That's Milner, that's Hendo, that's Virgil. That's all of us. That's intensity. That's our identity. Nothing good happens in the comfort zone.

Before our final session on Friday we gathered as a group at the Hillsborough Memorial at the training ground to observe a moment of silence in memory of the 97 children, women and men who had lost their lives as it was the 33rd anniversary of the tragedy. As I mentioned earlier, this is something that brings everything into perspective. You do not – and should not – only have a connection to Liverpool FC to understand what happened that fateful day and why it's important to pay respects to not only those 97 fans but also the families and survivors. They are never forgotten.

In preparation for the game we did the finishing rondo. If you score, you get another try. If you miss, you wait for your turn. Basically, good = stay, bad = out. Love that. It's my favourite training methodological principle: earn the right to attack more. Balls are drilled in by Jack, and the boys can't come out of the 'D' of the box. It's perfect to train the first touch, but the best is that the boys train in dealing with pressures. Dealing with Robbo's live commentary, Virgil's laugh and the 'trash-talk' of the goal-keepers. You get tested. "You want a coffee?" is shouted when somebody takes too long between first touch and shot. "Should throw those boots in the bin!" when there is another miss from the same player. A hard laugh when there is a bad touch.

"Thank you!" Jürgen said to the team. "Thank you that we are in the situation we are in. We go to a neutral venue, there is no advantage like last Sunday. Put conviction in our press, put conviction in being ready for the balls in behind, and put conviction with the ball to outplay their no6 players. I wouldn't ask if we couldn't do this. What always helps in life is that you know what's coming. So orientate yourself."

We needed to 'turn the screws' before we went to the Etihad, but now we needed to be wild and free again using our physical advantage; our boys needed the feeling we can GO with freedom and press from each position. Vitor said: "If we put clips of our good things together from Sunday's game we will say it's incredible; unfortunately if they put their good clips together they end up thinking the same!" It showed it's a game of give-and-take. I really believe Liverpool v City is the best game in the world of football at the moment, the new 'classico'. But we couldn't overthink it, there was so much at stake and these are the moments the boys start to think almost too much. Don't think too much – in the end it's either inside or outside the post that will make the difference, anyway. The best example was that in 2019 it was outside the post for us and inside the post for them in the direct confrontation in the game at the Etihad. In the end this is what gave them the title. What I try to say is that we should leave everything behind on the pitch and then we will see what the score gives us. "James, we don't want to put pressure on you, but you know you are the difference between reaching finals or not, it relies on you!" I joked during the analysis meeting. I have a lot of time for James [French], I really like him – he and Pete make sure we always have new variations on our basic ideas. Our analysis department made some great steps this year; whereas in the past they just delivered the analysis, they are now fully in the 'small plan' process and with this they know much better what we want and how we want it. Greg, Dan, Robbo and James are the brains of our building.

Jürgen opened the matchday-morning meeting by saying: "It's my seventh season and I said so often the same things, BUT this I never said before: welcome to the semi-final of the FA Cup. It's really cool to be here. Make it special by being normal. We are historically very lively against them." When we arrived at this beautiful stadium once again, I took a moment to soak it all in. Andreas and Conall making the boys physically ready; John with the penalty-takers watching images; Pete getting the tactics board ready; our analysts finding the right changed City line-up; Mona making sure the boys were getting enough fluids in; Lee and Brendan running to get everything the boys need in terms of kit; Smalley, Lee, Lena, Michelle and Chris massaging and stretching the boys on the beds. You realise you are in a fluid machine, you realise we should be so grateful with all these incredible people. It's the passionate LFC team behind the best team in the world of football. And so… Wembley… FA Cup… semi-final… Manchester City… and a 3-2 win for us. Wow!

It was a masterpiece in the first half, with and without the ball. They had to adjust to us. One step in front. The early goal in the second half gave them the boost they needed and they tried to control the game more by opening the wingers outside and we got deeper with time. City were really clinical until the second goal, but even so… WHAT A GAME! At half-time and 3-0 up, Vitor surprised me with a piece of paper, which he handed to me without saying a word. I thought there were some improvement points written down but it just said: "UNBELIEVABLE!" After each game it's about this one thing: 'the mirror'. Can you look at it and say, 'I left everything behind on the pitch'?

That's what Luis could do. That's what Naby could do. That's what Sadio could do. Our team respects 'the mirror' and that makes us intense. Sadio scored two goals and they couldn't have been any more different. One where he follows and chases Zack Steffen and tackles him on the goal-line. The second was a volley after some outstanding combinations inside when attacking the centre. Ibou scored his third goal in three games to get us on our way. Jürgen joked after the game that he had probably scored more goals in these three games than he would in the rest of his career. After the game our fans sang, so loudly, One Kiss by Dua Lipa. It was becoming our anthem. I looked at them bouncing and thought: this is why we are different – it's you guys. When we came back into the dressing room Jürgen said: "This is the first time I say this, guys, welcome to the FA Cup final!" Wembley, we are not done with you this season, I thought, and I hoped this game was a mental statement to them as well. We are here, we are really here.

The following day I was at home, sitting on the couch with my chamomile tea watching Chelsea against Crystal Palace to see who we would face in the final. Life couldn't get any better and more boring at the same time. Yesterday Sadio had played the false 9 with so much conviction; this is a Sadio who can win finals for us. We needed him in this physical mood, where lethalness is written all over him. Could someone reach Bobby levels as the false 9? Well, Sadio wasn't far from it. Later, I used Easter Sunday to watch the new documentary about Cruyff. If we speak about false 9s why not watch the one who invented it? I fell in love once more. It was Chelsea who would face us again at Wembley in the final after they defeated Palace. It would be tough, no doubt, but there was no time to think about it just yet. Another huge week in our season was coming.

‘THE HARDEST THING IN FOOTBALL IS MAKING A GOOD TEAM LOOK WEAKER THAN THEY ACTUALLY ARE’

WEEK 39

A CULTURE OF WINNING

I BEGAN THE WEEK BY REFLECTING ON A FEW THINGS from our day at Wembley. Firstly, from a coaching perspective, it was absolutely brilliant because it demonstrated we had learned and improved over the two games with Man City. Secondly, I was in no doubt that it is a football game and not an opera show, but when respect should be shown then it should be, no matter who you support or who your opponents are. The minute's silence for Hillsborough before the game was interrupted by some City fans. Unacceptable. Thirdly, and probably the best news of the day, Bobby's ankle problem he picked up at Wembley isn't a bad injury. He had his scan at 10.30am and it looked as though he would just be missing the Manchester United game. Fourthly, you know when you have a good team when you ask the boys for aspects of the game to improve and they do not only do exactly that but even make it better.

1. A more active and braver Ali in the build-up ended up with another level of orientation and playing mood from all the others.

2. A front three with more intense pressing and being more unpredictable ended up with Sadio literally scoring a goal from pressing.

3. A last line who read the passes in behind them better, focused for 90 minutes, and finding the right balance between being high and dropping ended up with Trent taking Foden, then Sterling and then Grealish, out of the game.

4. Our midfielders and wingers closing the gap better between them and the closest being really aggressive on Bernardo ending

up with Naby taking that job very literally. What a performance from him.

What I liked the most over those last two games against Manchester City was that if you stopped either game at any particular moment, you would see completely different build-up structures and completely different pressing dynamics, time and time again. This, for me, is pure quality: understanding, freedom, clarity and adaptability all at the same time. Is it easy to reach these levels of flexibility? No, absolutely not. But life is not supposed to be easy. I can't stress it enough – our players make difficult look easy. One thing is for sure, we have become so much better at dominating games over these last years. That's why we were so 'big' on the ball. This idea is always present in everything we do. For example, for training on this day, we played four-v-four with Harvey and Curtis as the extra players in the centre-circle. Ten passes was one point to connect the attackers. With this exercise, we created this mentality and concentration to compete for the ball. Vitor was on top of them. The boys had to make new triangles constantly, they had to 'come out' of the difficult situations and outplay the press. The circle creates – unconsciously – good body positioning and orientation. After that we did our 'go and go again' exercise, where stopping counter-attacks and creating aggressive attacks alternate constantly. It's how Cruyff said it: 'Development is about do, do, do – it's simple and logical'. "We will repeat until we vomit!" I shouted in the session. There was no let-up for our boys. The schedule simply did not allow for taking the foot off the pedal even slightly. Manchester United were coming to Anfield next and they would want to make a statement.

We knew what we would get with Ralf Rangnick's United, we knew his blueprint very well. Quick wingers ready to counter-attack and a defensive 4-4-2 really orientated to how the ball moves. Jürgen described it well before we went out to train: "We have to use this good mood we are in but make sure we are still the team nobody wants to play against." I spoke with Pete and we made sure we went for some clips of our game against City to prepare for United; the boys had to see and understand why we did what we did. Focus on us to focus on the future. The day before United, Jürgen opened the analysis meeting with the boys: "Nowadays we are constantly aware about what the whole world thinks about us. Social media has a big influence. In the past it was only 20 people who thought something about you and it was not that difficult to ignore 20 people, to be honest. The whole world thinks United isn't doing good enough. But the only thing that is important is what we think. Four weeks ago Arsenal were finishing fourth; two weeks ago it was Tottenham; now the number four spot is up for grabs. The 5-0 at Old Trafford was ages ago. We have to try to understand them – they smell there is something possible. They will be ready to show up tomorrow. And with this we have to make a decision before the game, we have to make a decision now, not in the game. Sorry to say, knowing we did all of this only two days ago, but that's what I'm asking. That's how it is if you want to be successful. Chase and make the last step, how Naby does here against Bernardo [pointing to a video clip], exactly that should be the subject for these last eleven games."

Game day. This game is a lot of things, but for most people it's a proper derby. For them it's an all-or-nothing game because the weight of the shirt of a big club is really heavy when things are not going well. This is why we could not allow them to grow in the game. We'd decided in pre-season that 'defending first' was our agreement. And what an agreement this is going to be.

Our 32nd Premier League final ended in a 4-0 win over United at Anfield. A statement. We had the ball – mostly via Thiago! – and we went and went again. Almost 900 passes… there's nothing more to say. Our front three were clicking at the right moment of this season; they were playing the piano but playing it with soul. Luis, Sadio and Mo all assisted and scored. The goals weren't to defend, whatever system Man United would have played. I walked into the dressing room afterwards and hugged Milner. He said: "Pep, you know what the best counter-press situation of the evening was?" I was thinking really deeply to answer him and he continued: "It was you, Jürgen and Pete closing in on the fourth official!" "When even the staff are hunting in packs we are the team nobody wants to play against!" I replied. A great night for everyone who loves football, a unique night for everyone who loves Liverpool FC.

The following day was a special day, too. It was Vitor's bachelor party. Our plan was to surprise him in the afternoon by taking our big red team bus to his house to pick him up. We were then going to go bowling at PINS in the city centre before another surprise for him at Bacaro where all of his family and friends would be waiting for him with a glass of champagne. John even prepared a Benfica shirt for him to wear with his name on the back… you can't provoke a Porto boy more than by doing exactly this. It would hurt and go directly to his heart! The bowling was really good fun; four teams of four, with Carl Spellman [one of our transport providers] and Billy Hogan the standout players. Ray made sure Vitor got his own cup full of beer with some special rules: every time he left the bus he needed to drink, every time he spoke Portuguese he needed to drink (which led to so many funny discussions between him and Taffarel) and every time one of us threw a strike he needed to drink. Everyone would sing Allez Allez Allez. The mood was just insane. Ray's history as a travel leader came back and in these moments he is like the devil and made sure the cup was always full to the brim. "We don't win the Champions League with that attitude, Vitor," he said when our Benfica guy struggled to down his tenth beer. Vitor said back: "The beer tastes like vodka now!" But that wasn't the worst part for him… we drove through the city centre and at any moment in time, upon our command, he needed to sing a Liverpool song outside the bus. For example, a rendition of Allez, Allez, Allez in the middle of the docks, You'll Never Walk Alone in front of the Hilton. The bus was bouncing, people were staring. What the…? they must have been thinking, a guy in a Benfica shirt outside of Liverpool's team bus singing Liverpool songs?! At one point, which people later saw on social media, Jürgen left the bus to enter Jürgen's Bar when we stopped next to it in front of a red traffic light. All of the people inside thought he was a doppelganger, which made the moment of realisation that this was actually Jürgen Klopp so funny. The dinner party at Bacaro made for such a lovely time. His whole family was there and it became a real wedding party. We danced, sang and celebrated. Mission accomplished.

Waking up the next day, we spotted that one of the newspapers had run a story about Jürgen's appearance in the bar. It said he took some photos with fans and even a Benfica supporter. I couldn't stop laughing at it. But with Everton coming, it was back to work on the Friday. In recent days I'd received the same questions a lot: how can we be so intense, how can we be so consistent, how can we be so fit? I believe it has to do with the winning culture installed inside our club. It's a culture only acknowledged with time. It's a culture in which a draw can feel like a loss. A culture where everything is about the process and the training pitch. A culture where you see the next game as a final. A culture of winning by focusing solely on the process; no distractions, one direction, the direction to compete. A long time living inside this culture of winning makes you fit, intense and consistent. To create this we tell our boys: "You have to remind yourself each day is a character test." Because the biggest part of sport is honour, that's the reason Liverpool FC plays. And honour has nothing to do with results, it has to do with giving your all towards a team of fighters. Again, the 'mirror principle', I call it. There is only one guy responsible for where you get in the future, it's the one you're looking at in the mirror. If all eleven of our players do this day-in, day-out, the football world conspires in favour of LFC. Whatever we would get at the end of this season, it all started with hard work and we could not become soft. Let's keep this spirit up against Everton so we can win the ball back and go again and again. This time, the game against Everton was massive for both of us – more so than normal, not just because of the fact it was a derby but because of the league table. So, one job to do for us: we should turn into animals when losing the ball against them.

I was sitting in my office at home preparing the finishing exercises for Saturday's session. They looked like dot-to-dot drawings. Even I get lost sometimes. How can you draw freedom or unpredictability? It's impossible, but I try. I draw all the different options breaking the last line. I love my desk at home; it's full of the past with exercises, notes, game-meetings, pre-season plans and set-piece routines. For that next session we would focus on aspects we were still improving on during the recent period. Aggressive finishing and second-line runners, putting the goal in the players' minds immediately. What I liked the most over the past four games wasn't just the results, it was the fact we had different players on the pitch constantly and in all constructions we played very well against City, United and Benfica twice. This season, rotation had been excellent and it kept so many quality players with the right fire for the upcoming period. It gave options to change. I had no doubt that how we dealt with the whole squad during October, November and December was paying off now. We'd given the boys two days off after United, so we kept our two-day lead-in to Everton and kept them fresh for the last big, big run of games.

"I never saw a finishing session influence the next training game more than today," Jürgen said directly after training. The finishing gave freedom and with this it gave chaos. I loved it: open for interpretation, open for determination, the one who wants it more will give more; they look to each other and they know each other better after it. That, for me, gives colour to everything; the improvement of timings on the inside and the outside to attack. It's the opposite of mechanical. Harvey, Jota, Rhys and Naby won the identity game. They scored four goals in a row, which had never happened before. Jota was like Romario that day. I said to Virgil after the session: "You must have been a striker growing up?" "Of course," was his reply. All these things made me very happy, the time thinking about it paid off. And I even used the phrase "Is this all we've got?" at the start of the session. After that one little sentence, the balls were flying into the net left, right and centre. So many people were giving me a good feeling at this moment, I felt all of our fans had really started believing. You feel it and what's more important, our players feel it, too. It brought back memories of when we fought for the prizes years ago, the time before the pandemic. This feeling is incredible but brings pressure as well. One member of staff said when he saw me wandering through the hotel the night before the derby: "If you can't enjoy these periods, which ones will you?" "Football can be so unfair sometimes," I said. "Yes, but then we go again next year, we will be there again. If you want something desperately there will always be more pressure, that's a consequence of the human brain," he told me. It was probably what I was feeling in this period, but he took some pressure away, that's for sure. 'Game-by-game' should stay as our mantra.

Back in The Titanic, in the same meeting room as we were in for our last pre-season games. Couldn't be better, I was thinking: start the last run of games in the spot where this season had begun. Jürgen spoke with full belief to the team: "Football games are decided by attitude, and the level of attitude we decide ourselves. I will try to explain what is the perfect attitude. It's a mix of two things: first is to play with a fluidity and the confidence of a team who won a few games in a row; the second is to play with the greed and fight of one who didn't win a game for ages. We know we are good when we have rhythm. Rhythm means being constantly front-footed and proactive, both defensively and offensively. This is where we need to reach; the same level as against United. Greedy to press and counter-press. Over the years we became much better in the derbies. You know why? Because we don't have to give extra – we do this every game. Guys, the finishing session we did had real purpose, we want chaos and movement from the second-line. Show up, not to complicate things; no, to repeat the things we did thousands of times before."

Divock Origi, took the 'do the things we did thousands of times before' line very literally. We won the 33rd final of the season 2-0 at home against Everton. After a goalless first half, the change of system with bringing Luis and Divock on, paid off immediately. We felt it was important to fix their centre-halves more and create new problems in the outside spaces. Jürgen, Vitor and I discussed at half-time, when Everton got more tired we would bring on two at the same time to change our set-up. Robbo scored a header to set us on the way after Mo and Divock combined brilliantly in the box. I just love it when full-backs are in the area. "The manager and Pep at half-time, both said that we needed more bodies in the box, so I thought: why not me?" Robbo said afterwards. Divock then scored a header from the second-phase corner after Luis attempted a bicycle-kick trying to score. We saw him scoring a few with Porto so it didn't really surprise me. Back in the dressing room it was so funny when Thiago threw a bottle and Ali caught it and fell to the floor, replicating his ironic moment at the end of the game. So that was April so far. Seven played, five wins and two draws. One point behind in the league. We were right in there.

WEEK 40

KEEP THE GREED

THE DAY AFTER THE DERBY AND WE WERE STANDING in the sports hall at the AXA Training Centre. "Who cares about analysis after a derby win?" Jürgen said to the team with a smile. "Well done to all of you. How many times have our subs made the difference this season? Again! That's us, the strength of the squad." And he couldn't be more right, the amount of times we made an impact – or even changed the whole situation around

– by bringing players from the bench. For me, here was where we were different to the other three teams in the Champions League semis: we can and will change. At NEC [Nijmegen] my exact last words to [wingers] Arnaut Danjuma and Ferdi Kadioglu were: "See you guys in the Champions League." They looked shocked, like: what is he saying? It was the day after we missed out on promotion with a 5-4 aggregate scoreline [in 2018]. I knew I would go back to Liverpool and I was so convinced these two boys would have everything to achieve big dreams. Could I have imagined it would be the semi-final of the Champions League with one of them – Danjuma? Nope, but it made me a proud man.

During the Monday session Hendo trained with the subs and was pressing Curtis all over the pitch. I shouted: "That's how it feels for the opposition when you play directly against Hendo, Curt!" James, our analyst, handed over a piece of paper directly after training. It was Brentford at home when we decided to have more players in the box, a more central and closer-to-goal target area and with the same takers over and over creating real consistency in our set-piece delivery. He showed me that our goals scored with first contact had gone up from one in the first 31 games this season to seven in the last 22 matches. This meant two per cent to 22 per cent goals scored from first contact. Our xG [expected goals] on target went up from 0.98 per cent to 4.59 per cent. I would say we were making them decisive again by clear and obvious improvements. And for that, huge compliments need to go to Pete and James who worked constantly on the details. What I liked was that our second goal against Everton was from second-phase. This means it's not hurting the new idea, even with the subs we made. You try to have the best of two worlds: first contact and second phase. From now, we had to keep making sure our big targets kept getting close to the goal with better blocks. But in the first place we needed to keep creating corners because the trick in scoring from corners is…? Exactly. Just create many. Against Everton we had created 13, that's not bad. With the right ideas and the willpower of our boys it will be just a matter of time. We had towers in Virgil, Ibou and Joel. We had guys with great timing and technique like Fabinho, Luis, Jota and Sadio. We had players who wanted to shoot on the edge like Mo, Naby, Thiago and Hendo, and most importantly we had great deliveries from Trent and Robbo. For us as coaches, nothing compares to scoring from a corner. It's like the uppercut in boxing. It's effective, powerful and knockout material. "That's how we need to play against Parejo," I said on the day before Villarreal. He was as good as Bernardo Silva but with his right foot; they all like to dribble versus our press. In the tactical training I showed our high press and told Hendo to be all over their key player. We offer you up to press the hell out of him. In pressing, playing versus the ball and finding challenges must be in harmony.

It was then time for the analysis meeting. All our coaching staff were in. It was dark and silent in the room. Let's see what Greg and James had to say about Villarreal. We were favourites, yes, but the same counted for Juve and Bayern and they would be watching the game from their homes. We thought this said everything. Straight after the meeting we played a padel game: Jürgen and Marc, our agent, against me and Billy Hogan. We played for a bottle of red wine to spice things up. It's the 'quiet before the storm' moment because the following day Mike Gordon would fly in to close the deal on our new contracts. "It's insane it didn't come out," I said when we sat together in Jürgen's office. "We will shock the football world with this new deal." What was a dream for a lot of fans was becoming reality, but for us too. I couldn't wait to commit for the next four years to this wonderful family. I later sent the song Red, Red Wine to Billy to celebrate our victory in the padel match.

Our preparations showed that Villarreal just don't come out. We watched them many times; they closed the centre and defended the outside with the winger and full-back only. From there, they were so dangerous in their counter-attacks with Danjuma and Gerard Moreno. But we would try to catch the free spaces on the outside by finding our wingers early. Every reaction provoked a counter-reaction which meant they would open more spaces inside. Unai Emery said in his press interviews that they must produce the "perfect" performance to defeat a Liverpool team he described as "updated and improved." That night I sent a text to Jürgen consisting of just three words: "What a game." I was watching the first leg of the other semi, Manchester City v Real Madrid. 4-3. If this is the level of the last four, we have to be on top form against Villarreal. If you want to go to a Champions League final, you need to invest a lot of attitude in combination with pure quality. Both City and Real did in that game; football won and I was happy for that because this is what you want to see as a fan. The 'get the ball to Benzema' tactics of Ancelotti were working well. A talent is scary, but a talent with experience becomes an assassin. You have to accept the fact that this game is one from and for the players. You see immediately the ones who have this extra edge, that extra football smartness. Why do they have that? I've said it before, because of the best educational academy in the world: the street. It takes a village to raise a child, they say. I say, it takes a street to create a real player. Benzema, Modric, Diaz and Thiago are world-class examples.

The following day it was our turn. Champions League semi-final day. I had a buzz driving in to training. I will never take this feeling for granted. It's taken so much hard work to achieve it. Let's make it electric... but first we had to practise our set-pieces. Mike Gordon was watching while our starters and subs were heading in one ball after the other. Jürgen's meeting was short and clear: "I don't want to make it bigger than it is, but this one is big. Everything we did so far this season is made for games like these. We have a bench I dreamed of. They have to say after this game that LFC's identity is intensity. We need to be in this aggressive football mood. They are good, when they play, they really play, that's good news for us. It's good news for us that they have never played us so far. It's LFC 2022 vs Villarreal 2022, not 2016. I know it's over two legs, 180 or 190 minutes, but that's not important for now. Be prepared for surprises on set-pieces; they had eight days to prepare. Let's put them under pressure every time they try to control the game. Search and find challenges, and when you're there, win them. First pass forward! I'm not only in a good mood, I'm excited too, that's why I speak a lot. I will stop that now. Let's go and be ourselves." The boys listened. The first leg of the Champions League semi-final became the best game we'd played in the season so far. Not the highest score, or the biggest impact in progressing, but we were always calm and protected. It showed we understood the task. The fluidity and intensity was madness. There was a spell of three or four minutes at 13 minutes in, that shows this so well. The hardest thing in football is making a good team look weaker than they actually are. We avoided set-pieces and found the outside player early time after time. We stopped counter-attacks and had bodies in the box with real consistency. I would say that is controlling a game by being dominant. Hendo's deflected cross opened the scoring in the second half after he made the run on the outside. Then Mo slid in Sadio for 2-0 two minutes later. Anfield went nuts. I couldn't think for a second after the crowd roared Allez, Allez, Allez after Mane's goal. It was a sound of power, real power. So, 2-0, half-time and in six days we would have the possibility to reach the final in Paris. The following day we would sign and announce our new 2026 deals. So this was only the start…

The following morning at AXA, Jonathan, Julian, Jürgen, Pete, Marc and Vitor were all standing inside the manager's office. Mike Gordon spoke to us all: "This project has been the most incredible experience of my life. Thank you for contributing and having this important role." "Thank you, Mike, for the trust," I replied. Mike continued: "In 2015 I was standing in front of Stevie's restaurant and said we were going to conquer the world together. I'm not saying that happened but we are not far off." Mike added: "In life, the most precious currency we spend is our time; who we choose to spend that currency with says everything about us as people. I feel so privileged to be able to spend my currency of time with you and our group." Everyone clapped, signed and we moved on. Marc and Mike [Jäggle] represent me so well. I'm so happy they are at my side having the same values and same ambition. I walked straight out to the training pitch to put everything in place. Work goes on, we need to keep building the future. It wasn't the right moment to celebrate this new deal, I felt; there was too much at stake. I just couldn't feel it. It's sad but true. Move forward, we should just never settle. I hate that feeling. Especially when the next kick-off was only 48 hours away. We would practise stopping counter-attacks with an intense and concentrated counter-press. Defend to create chances.

Later that day we had a squad planning meeting with Mike and Julian. Margaret Aspinall came in to say hello and Jürgen surprised her with the news that we'd signed new deals. She hugged him so tightly and said she couldn't believe it. These are the moments I really feel the mantra 'we are a family' comes alive. The conclusion of the meeting was: we give space and trust to our squad and we will only sign if it is the right one, giving trust to the Academy pathway as well. When walking out of the meeting, Mike said that in America when you get elected they sing: 'Four more years! Four more years!' Jürgen and I had big smiles on our faces. Mike is class, very intelligent and funny. In life you meet many people, just a few change your life. Two of them were sitting together with me in the room that afternoon. And that wasn't all. Training was really good that day, which was important as many of the subs would be starting at St. James' Park so it was a good step towards control against Newcastle. "We don't accept the 12.30pm kick-off, but we shouldn't think about it. We are the 'men on a special mission' and this is never more true than now. You know why? Because of you guys." The Newcastle prep had started. Jürgen spoke to the team with determination. Vitor said: "The main thing they improved is their mentality." I said: "We will need a few energisers in the team." "It's the new Newcastle," Jürgen said. Strong in the air with [Chris] Wood, strong on crosses and a real aggression for second-balls. Bruno Guimaraes and Jonjo Shelvey were the key players and they had won seven of their last ten and would come into this one with real confidence. Jürgen continued to the team: "Pep spoke with Hendo after watching the Barça game back, 'Hendo, in the 85th minute of the Barça game you made a sprint of 50 metres'; 'Even if it was in the 120th minute I would have done the same, the crowd gave us so much energy.'"

Jürgen continued: "When we really want, the human brain and the human body can do incredible things. They will assume we cannot reach this Villarreal intensity again. Sure we can. This is how we are going to calm the crowd down tomorrow. Keep this greed, this is the greed which will show why we are men on a mission."

Matchday morning and an early walk in Newcastle to begin the day. Everyone was waiting for the one last man to arrive. "Ali, I told you to take a shower!" Jürgen joked when Alisson came out, saying he looked like it was the middle of the night. We always do this early-walk routine before the Saturday morning kick-off to make sure everyone really wakes up. Thiago ordered his breakfast before the walk so it would be ready before all the others had to wait in line to order. Jürgen saw it and said, "German efficiency!" "Or just really hungry!" Thiago responded. Our two captains were starting today, Milner and Hendo. It's in these moments you need your captains, away at a very difficult ground. I was convinced they would deliver. "It's a warm, sunny morning in Newcastle. Who can find the error in this sentence?" Jürgen asked the team just before we travelled to the stadium. "I hope it will get hot," he continued, "because then it becomes really about who wants it more. These are only words, of course – we have to show this to the outside world, show the outside world we are men on a mission. We changed only five times for the sake of rhythm. We improved again over the last games increasing the intensity in our press. Let's go and show exactly this."

Final no34 ended 1-0 away at the new Newcastle. I have to say, I love St. James' Park – it's hostile and it breathes football. These are my favourite games: difficult, no time, and we have to do it. It's down to mentality, and that's the one characteristic where we had to match them because they had won their last six home games. Ten wins out of the last 12 overall. We started without Mo, Fabinho, Trent and Thiago. We had to keep our main guns fresh with this insane schedule. We got the breakthrough early. I love second-line runners and Naby surprised everyone with his composed strike. Jota assisted brilliantly, these give-and-goes are so underrated, especially against a flat line. Just before the goal Milner stopped the counter-attack in a way only he can, a proper tackle on the ball, with a knife between his teeth. Hendo played the first pass forward immediately and from there we were living in the world of Naby Keita. Overall it was a hard game where Newcastle made a first and second-ball game with a good fighting spirit. Also, they had a really good pressing impulse and a good organisation on our goal-kicks, which killed a part of the fluidity of our game. In the end the bravery of our centre-halves and midfielders trying to play, to call the press and breaking lines, to mix it up with balls behind their line, was really good. It was a game for big teams, big mentality and as well for fresh legs. Three important points and a big win for the squad. After the game Jürgen complimented the team by telling them that we were improving every game, setting new benchmarks. We went back to the top for a few hours until City beat Leeds at Elland Road. But we were still there and were not planning on going anywhere.

The following day, walking up the stairs at the AXA, I showed Milner a clip where he pressed Guimaraes three times at Newcastle and then continued it onto Dan Burn. He was a pressing machine at St. James' Park. He replied: "The only thing I had in my head was: 'follow'." I love that, it proves that the same message over and over again, the same training over and over again, becomes the inner voice of our players. And when eleven players have a similar inner voice it erases doubt. That was us in April. That's how you become a dangerous football team. The way we – and especially Jürgen – erased doubt is what created this determined football during the month. This is what I like so much about football: a well-drilled team always has a chance. But this is why we would need to be really careful against Villarreal. We knew in a couple of days we'd have the chance to achieve the maximum number of games in the season. As I'd said to our fans in the summer: "This season we want to make you proud, with our type of football and our energy. We believe that the better we play, the more games we will play this season. That will be the target: play as many games as we can. Let's keep creating memories together! That's how Jürgen explains so well the essence of working for a club like Liverpool Football Club. Creating memories."

Together with Vitor, I went and watched the Under-23 team against Manchester United at the Academy on the Sunday afternoon. Conor, Owen and Tyler… my God, what quality. These are our boys. You see there is no hesitation with them. Compliments to Barry, they play with the same intensity and structure as our first-team players. Culture. Inspire one coach and indirectly you inspire 20 players. That's why coaches' education is the main ingredient in bringing players up.

‘COACHING CAPTURES THE BRAINS OF THE PLAYERS BUT FREEDOM AND TRUST CAPTURES THEIR HEARTS’

WEEK 41

CHASE

MONDAY. TODAY WE WOULD TRAVEL TO THE EAST of Spain. We were in early at the AXA for our meeting with the boys. "There they will want to win. The crowd will be there, the stadium will be on fire, we need to be ready for this. There are different ways to look at our situation being 2-0 up. We could look at it and say let's go there and defend the result. Whichever important result we got in the past we agreed before each game… OUR WAY! This means we have to be intense immediately. This is the third time in the last five years that we are in the semi-final of the Champions League, but we don't know if this will happen more often in our lives." We showed a clip on the screen. "What Luis is doing here [chasing 50 metres back] is a sign of the intensity we have to put in if you want to reach a final. We say it now, we say it tomorrow, we say it when none of you want to hear it: chase them over the whole pitch from all directions. They are a really good football team but they aren't magicians. Just imagine we win the ball here [pointing to the screen when Luis chased intensely]. These are clear signs of a good game. We have to be emotional and passionate but not with them. They started this second leg already at Anfield fighting directly after the last whistle. Let's speak about these problems beforehand, solve them now, then from now we only have to think about football problems. Villarreal are fired up, they changed eight times on Saturday, but we are experienced."

When there is a lot to win there is a lot to lose as well, this ugly voice can't take over in our heads. We were heading into the last four weeks and we needed the right inner voice: chase. To kill that ugly voice I went for a run through the city of Castellon after we arrived. My head was clear. "You should do that more often," Jürgen told me, with a smile.

On the morning of the game we trained at CD Castellon, a third division club close to our hotel. Time was standing still while we stood in the middle of this beautiful stadium, discussing everything except tactics. We work with human beings, so seeing them smile and focused at the same time made me feel very positive about what was to come that night. Coaching captures the brains of the players but freedom and trust captures their hearts. This is what I like most about us: we don't overthink or over-do.

That afternoon the boys were sitting in their spots at the hotel for the team meeting. Here we go! The weather outside was nothing special even though it was Spain in May, but the occasion was. Jürgen started the meeting: "Guys a new start, let's ignore the first game, let's make it a one-leg game. If this is clear, I would say, 'Welcome to the semi-final of the Champions League, 2021/22'. We improved throughout the whole season. Why? Because of our effort. We don't underestimate them for one second. Whatever happens tonight, we will write the headlines left or right tomorrow. My preferred headline would be: 'LFC are mentality monsters again.'"

And so it would prove as we came from behind to win 3-2. It's never boring with us, I would say. "For sure they will come and press more," we said to the team before kick-off. "We have to be ready." But we couldn't find the right solution. They deserved merit because of the first half, they wanted it a lot, put a lot of pressure on, especially Parejo. It's as Cruyff said: "If you dominate midfield, you will dominate the game." This couldn't have been truer than in this game. Half-time was crucial, bringing on Luis was crucial. We were 2-0 down and the tie was level on aggregate. Jürgen said: "The whole world now thinks it goes in one direction – we are the only team who can change this. Don't stay frustrated, it's time to show that we will earn the right to be playing the final. We will go and show this." The key of the game was to bring Luis on at the right moment. He entered at half-time and opened up free spaces for Naby and Trent on the opposite side. He kept the ball, and with him the others around him as well. Fabinho got us back into it before Luis and then Sadio got us the win. Job done. Paris, we were coming. I saw Luis' agent after the game and stepped off the bus to give him a big hug and say thank you. There was a game with and a game without Luis at this moment. We'd reached maximum games – the target of the pre-season accomplished. Now it was about reaching the maximum-of-creating-memories part. "I don't know what the papers will write," Jürgen said in the dressing room directly after the game, "but my headline will be, 'Monstruos de Mentalidad!'"

On Wednesday I took some time to reflect on the night before as we headed back to Liverpool. It was an incredible Villarreal we saw. They didn't only come out to dance – for 45 minutes they owned the dance floor. I said from the start, they were a good, good team and we felt for 45 minutes how strong they were. Juve and Bayern will not deny this. My anxiety was right up in that first half. There were two reasons for our performance before half-time. Firstly, it was Villarreal and secondly it was us. It was something we wanted to improve; overplay pressure, to give more time for our 'movers' to find the open spaces. Jürgen sent an iconic photo of Nat Phillips and Rhys Williams to the WhatsApp group. "Thanks guys, we would never have made the final without you." When we'd come back into the hotel the night before, we'd asked Dan to put the highlights of the 2019 final in Madrid on again after we'd watched the last ten minutes of Nat's Bournemouth getting promoted. Then we watched the last 20 minutes of the Barça game at Anfield and even watched the Roma away game from 2018. Watching those back, I realised that opportunity only arrives for the teams who work their socks off.

Back at home that night, watching Real Madrid's stunning comeback against Manchester City in the other semi-final, Jürgen texted me: "First time in history a team won all away games in CL." Liverpool v Real Madrid. The final. The final of the Champions League. Two giants, two clubs with real history in the tournament. Karim Benzema had scored 47 goals at this point in the season; he is a striker who needs one chance to score two. But we felt it was payback time. We were a different animal. Our team had five batteries now – and with this, we would try to suffocate Real.

Back at the AXA, thoughts were turning to Tottenham. "We know they are a great counter-attacking team, both Kane and Son are on fire," the boss said to the boys. "You guys know without having to show anything what they are. A compact defensive unit with counter-attacking threats. But these are all football problems – and for football problems we have all the solutions. What's most important is that we press the passer and not the receiver. Not because I say so. No, because it makes the difference. Cut pathways." In our training we repeated our high-press organisation and our goal-kick build-up. The tactical plan had to be right. However, we drew 1-1 with Spurs at Anfield in final no35. The crowd, incredible throughout, supported us until the last second. After this night, our Premier League aim became harder, but not impossible. If we lost or drew games, it needed to be like this: trying, pressing, attacking, fighting for every inch of pitch, with and without the ball. That's what happened in this one. It was not easy to break this Tottenham wall, especially with Kane and Son always with an eye on the counter-attack. Because of that, there was never a space or a second to lose any focus and that was really hard, especially after playing the amount of games we had. Still, we felt we could have won the game and, to be honest, that should have happened if we consider the amount of times we were able to arrive inside the box. But credit to Tottenham because they had their opportunities as well.

Three matchdays before the end of the season and we were first in the table on goal difference, but it felt more like two important points lost with City having the extra game to play. A draw that felt like a loss. People had given up on us several times earlier this season, but we weren't about to.

However it might look, it was not done yet. We'd keep playing for our dreams. That said, our focus – full focus – was immediately on our next game: Aston Villa, and not City. A must-win. Jürgen was absolutely incredible directly after the game, saying to the boys how proud he was of the team. We were all proud of them and rightly so. In Sunday's training we focused on 'the suffocated attack'... at least that's what I call it. Giving real importance to the moment directly after the attack. The quick organisation to the goal-kick press, the first contact and second phase of corners, the spot-and-play, the counter-press. I like to focus on the moments that should make this line of attack happen more often. I would try to link all these moments because it needed fluidity, and that's why we would practise it, over and over again, with so much still to reach heading into the last weeks.

WEEK 42

CHERISH IT, LIVE IT

WE HAD TO REMAIN A TEAM THAT KEEPS LEARNING. We showed the boys a clip of the Tottenham game where we displayed the options we had, or better the following action to take a player with them or to break the last line. But to put our performance and result into context, Son Heung-min said it was the most difficult game he played in his life… and we weren't at our best. However, when Anfield wants something, I always get the feeling that success comes so much closer. Jürgen gave our message like this: "Crossing is a solution but when it becomes the only one because we don't offer different ways to attack, we are on the wrong path. It's always about quality not quantity. Forty-seven crosses but how many were really dangerous? Exactly." Jürgen continues, "I'm just giving a few hints here, boys. Exactly these actions were missing, we are better than this." Jürgen continued the following day: "It's allowed for us to decide how we see things. The same situation can have completely different views. We played two days ago, imagine we would have won and City would have lost? We would be completely on our toes for this game against Villa tomorrow. It's just a question of perspective how we look at this game. It's exactly the same – we need to win the next football game. We need to do the things we do but at a really high level. If we speak in 20 years, what will we say looking back to this game? I believe it's an open race, but I'm not playing. There are no guarantees but just a massive opportunity in front of us."

While reading the newspapers I was thinking we should be deaf to the outside world. Erase this negativity and hopelessness:

we were in it. It was still an open race. We just had to believe it. I just hoped our fans still believed because with them, one plus one is three. We could reach 86 points against Villa, which is an insane number.

We cancelled the training session on matchday morning and went for a walk instead. We wanted to give the boys more time to rest. "Every team has weaknesses, Tottenham showed this against Liverpool," Stevie said in his pre-match media. It's true that we are not perfect. 'It's football, how can you be?' I was thinking while walking through Birmingham.

We had played every three days for months now, never with time to prepare for a game with consecutive training sessions. Don't get me wrong, I loved it, every second of it. About not having time, well in life you should never search to be perfect. You should search to give your all. The walk was a real energiser, loads of school kids got surprised passing us by, the sun was out and with every step I knew we'd made the right decision. Hopefully we could keep everyone fit and we were balancing on thin ice at that moment.

It was a busy day in the football world as Man City announced a deal for Erling Haaland. It's a proper culture shock between Holland and England, where people believe the more you spend the better. But this game is so much bigger than that. Fans will always be at the heart of the club's success, they should identify themselves with the values, the character and the leadership of a club. It was also the day stories came out about our front three and rumours Bayern were looking to sign Sadio. During breakfast Jota confronted him while seeing the breaking news on Sky. Trent was sitting next to Jota and we both started laughing when I said Jota could be a Scouser. He confronts without any hesitation which takes people by surprise. Jota replied, "They think I have Scottish blood!" 'McJots'.

Final no36 and a 2-1 win at Villa Park, but my god it was tense. They made it feel like a derby and losing Fab to injury in the first half didn't help. The stadium didn't help. What did help was our will to win in combination with the five changes we'd made to the line-up. What I loved the most was that when they had the ball we did everything to win it back. And when we had the ball we tried everything to score, from the start until the end. The people saw the essence of the Premier League. Two teams who applied the modern 'kick and rush'. It's attractive to watch for everyone.

I felt Villa couldn't cope with our intensity over the whole 90 minutes, but for the first 45 they could keep up, a little bit similar to Villarreal. Again, the base of all this was how our last line controlled the movements of Ollie Watkins, Danny Ings and Philippe Coutinho. They represented an incredible front three, I would say. They can play the piano. When we felt we couldn't win the game by suffocating them in their half we tried to win it back with a quick, efficient breakaway – like our second goal – after defending the throw-in brilliantly. Organisation and attitude, a combination of these two often stand on the base of something good. Thiago followed his press and won the ball, playing the first pass forward, Luis doing Luis things, setting up the goal for an incredible Sadio header. Winning balls in football always makes the difference and on this night it was proved, but this is only possible with a 100 per cent defensive attitude. When we can create opportunities through this, football gets its best mixture. Winning balls and loads of technique on the pitch, I love that. We were heading into the final straight for the big ones, going into the last decisive games. Four more finals, two Premier League games and two cup finals.

After the game I immediately sent a text to Thomas Gronnemark: "YES!! Defensive throw-in wins us the game tonight." He replied: "You guys are doing so well, it's a pleasure to watch, it means we scored seven in the last 10 games from throw-in situations." Wow. That surprised me, to be honest. I walked out of the changing room directly to their manager's room. With a beer, we just brought up memories. First with Michael Beale and Gary McAllister, and then later Jürgen and Stevie joined. What an incredible group together. On our long trip back on the coach I remembered again that ego only makes bad decisions in life and so that's why I respect the moments with good people so much.

Wednesday morning at AXA and FA Cup final preparations were beginning. "Trent, we still don't have this one!" I said to him. "Let's get it – it's the one which is missing," he replies. He and I grew together into this first team, so it was incredible we were fighting together for the last prize which was not in our cabinet. They say that tough times produce strong men, and strong men produce good times; good times produce weak men, and weak men produce tough times. We needed to keep signing the greatest players, the ones who make the team excel. Character. And this is exactly what can't happen inside our Academy – they need to earn the right to be with us. No easy pathways.

Outside, some of the pitches at AXA were already freshly-seeded, the others look like billiard tables. "Nothing compares to a five-v-two rondo to recover your players," Vitor told me while we were watching the warm-up. All the things you can do in the gym, you can do in the warm-up, there is nothing specific for the recovery-process of a football player, the only way is to be with the whole body in the training. Earn the right to attack more, even within the recovery process. A smile, a laugh and constant interaction between the players, not thinking about the stiffness or tiredness. When we have a big amount of games it's really important that we take care of the players who don't play as much. We do the 'half pitch – our way' exercise. It's the same as last week where one team has to try to suffocate the other with organisation, attitude and their talent. With training, the first thing is always about giving everyone some new energy.

We finally finished our pre-season planning together with Ray, Vitor, Jürgen and Andreas. I get asked questions about pre-season fitness by the media so many times. We are using the pre-season, first and foremost, to change the eyes and the mind of the players. What do we want and how do we want it? This changes the physique of the player and their bodies adapt step-by-step to our intensity. With this we charge their batteries. If you play intense football, the battery empties quicker so we start with short spells of maximum game-idea with long spells of active recovery. Nobody can tell me differently – when a coach starts losing interest in pre-season he should change to become a sporting director.

Later that night, Niklas from neuro11 sent me the replacement for Fabinho in terms of our second penalty taker, should he be needed on Saturday. It was important we kept thinking and preparing for all eventualities. In terms of stopping penalties, we were still thinking and learning there too, but John is a master in preparing our goalkeepers. I believe that intuition and reaction go really well together when trying to stop penalties. "Trust Ali," is my advice. Read the body of the taker while he's running up and go with instinctive power. I always believe that the more independent you make your players, the better they will deal with high-pressure environments. In life, independence is the main ingredient for a constant adventure.

I began to read up ahead of our trip to Wembley, everything I could find about the game. I came across an unbelievable statistic: Jordan Henderson could become the first Liverpool captain in history to lift six different trophies – and he would be the first player to play in two FA Cup finals ten years apart. Reading these, I felt we were on the brink of making history. I always receive two pages of information from the media department about the next game, no matter who we're playing. The stats come from Ged Rea and they go right back to the start of our history as a club. I told Hendo when we'd discussed a possible testimonial for him, "You're going to lift another seven trophies before that happens." Before we set off for London, Jürgen told the team: "Whatever number is on the back of your shirt, you are responsible for stopping counter-attacks," while showing a clip of Mo tracking back and defending like a full-back. "We should defend for our dreams. The pitch is as big as how many players we outplay when they are pressing. The pitch is massive if we overplay their press." We showed our second goal away at Chelsea from January. You could hear me shouting in the background, "PLAY, calm!" We used three or four passes to attract Rudiger and Alonso, and with this created space behind them. Mo moved behind them and the rest is history. I hoped we'd see a final where we and Chelsea were at our best to make a real FA Cup final.

Matchday morning. The same hotel we'd used for the Carabao Cup and FA Cup semi-final. Five hours before kick-off and I was in the gym. I just couldn't stay in my room any longer; on the treadmill, trying to ease my tension and lose any negative thoughts that sometimes pop up. I was looking directly at Wembley. It was a real fight against this machine; the problem with treadmills is you can never beat them, but I tried anyway… This little voice in my head kept saying to me, 'Tonight you will be screaming to the players in the 80th minute to sprint back and you can't even do an extra 15 minutes on a treadmill!' When the exterior of the stadium caught my eye again, I relived the moment of Kepa missing his penalty in the Carabao Cup final and me running towards our fans, feeling free as a bird, though I was hoping there'd be no need for penalties. Leaving the gym, I bumped into some fans and told them: "Don't forget how special this is today – cherish and live it."

It's not easy to always find the right words if you play many finals, but Jürgen hit the nail on the head in our final meeting. "We had to learn to arrive in finals and to win them. In our first season together we squeezed everything out of it and arrived tired in the finals. We had to learn, the club had to learn. It's about how clear we are when we think about what we are going to do. When you guys get asked when joining Liverpool you say, 'I want to win silverware with this club'. So today is that chance. There are two facts at this moment: the first fact is the sun will be shining, the second is the atmosphere will be incredible. All the rest is still up to us to decide. Just think what will Tuchel say now about us? What will he say when he speaks the truth? Just think about that. Today it's Easter, Christmas and a birthday all on one day. Every time we win the ball, we play first pass forward. Nobody else arrived in four finals this season, but you have deserved to. Just put everything on the pitch and we will be fine."

A few hours later I was the polar opposite to Jürgen in the meeting: I was lost for words. The FA Cup was finally coming back to Liverpool. It was the prize I'd grown up with, watching football as a little boy back in the Netherlands. It was the prize with the most history in world football. And, above all else, it was the one that had been missing from our collection. So much happened in this game, so much I can speak about. For example, our insane positional game around Kovacic and Jorginho in the first 25 minutes. The concentration levels of Ali. Our high-press domination. The two tackles from Trent saving us late in the second half. The way Milner entered and gave us control again on the right side. The chances created by Luis. The passes from Trent. The cross from Milner to Robbo at the second post. The injuries to Virgil, Robbo and Mo. How even with a penalty in a shoot-out Thiago showed sheer class. The 'Greek Scouser' who scored the decisive penalty. The missed text messages during the game from Niklas… So, so much.

When I ran to Ali I waved my arms like a bird, I have absolutely no idea why. As you guys can see, there are so many things I could speak about, but what will really stay with me happened towards the end of the celebrations when I saw Milner. It was the best hug I ever had. I respect him so much, he is so special. Thank you for leading the team with commitment and example; I will be forever grateful that I met you as a player. You gave my understanding of professionalism a new dimension. Just before that, I was searching for my best and oldest friend in the crowd to give him a wave. We grew up together from a young age and he came to the game at the last minute, flying into London that morning after I'd told him I felt we needed him there to win. While trying to pick him out, someone grabbed my neck. It was Jürgen. We went to our fans together and celebrated with three massive fist-pumps. This was our moment. It meant the world to me. In front of my friend, in front of all the fans together with Jürgen sharing the moment. On the plane home I became emotional. The flashlights of our photographer kept going as he shot everyone with the trophy, but I realised my two sons will forever remember this day. They were in Madrid but were so young; now they were here for the League Cup and the FA Cup finals. They must think that all finals are so incredibly joyful to watch with a Liverpool win at the end! In the background, I hear our boys singing, 'I'm so glad, Smalley is a Red!' I'm sure, as a staunch Blue, he'd have loved that! Our idea of creating another special game was achieved. Our idea of creating new memories together with the fans was still going on. There were three more finals to go for: Southampton, Wolves and Real Madrid. I had to stop writing my notes at this point, though… the club photographer, Andrew Powell, arrived with the trophy for me and Andreas to have a photo together with it. Memories.

The morning after – and after a terrible night's sleep – we were back to work, analysing Southampton at 9am at the AXA Training Centre.

Jürgen spoke to the team: "I'm proud of you guys, more than ever before. In this season, where 90 per cent of humankind would have done a little bit less, we didn't. It's a lesson for life that when you are in the zone so much is possible. Normally we would be on top of a bus today and pissed at 11am but we have a game in two days. Whatever happens with City this afternoon, we will need a team full of desire and fresh legs at Southampton." What happened with City was a 2-2 draw at West Ham, meaning if we could win at St Mary's we'd take the title race to the final day. That had to be our target.

'THE ONLY WAY FOR A CLUB TO BE SUCCESSFUL IS WITH PURE LEADERSHIP, FROM TOP TO BOTTOM'

WEEK 43
THESE ARE THE DAYS

AFTER CITY'S DRAW AT WEST HAM, THE SITUATION for us heading into the final Premier League week of the season was clear: they were four points ahead of us, but we had the Southampton game in hand. Life is always about perspective. The Premier League should thank God we were here in the way we were – can you imagine City just running away with it and winning it by February every season? It's how Jürgen had said it last week: "The world is not full of winners, the world is full of triers." That's us – and we will keep going. I really believe that everything happens for a reason and we would try with all we had until the end. It was good because it also kept the team focused until the end.

Southampton was, therefore, a must-win to take the title race to the last game of the season. We'd had a lot of these 'must-wins', with so many changes, without time to train, but never with so much pressure to stay in a title race. But these are the challenges we like the most; the toughest ones are the ones we like the most. Could we pull this one off? We had just one day to make the 11 a collective, one day to refine the ideas. The line-up we went for was good. Can you imagine Southampton playing against us with this exact line-up? Jürgen said it like this to the players: "Tell me one team in world football who can change nine times and line up like this." We would set up the right-outside triangle with Joe, Harvey and Taki, combining their natural characteristics. Harvey would catch the space on the outside, Taki would play in between the lines and Joe would build up right next to Joel.

All that said, there were big decisions to make about our line-up at St Mary's. It was the schedule that was haunting us at this particular moment – three days after 120 minutes at Wembley in an intense final against a top-class Chelsea. Jürgen and I sought out some of our 'keys' to ask how they were feeling and, in the end, we opted for only Ali and Ibou to remain in the XI and refresh all the other positions. People ask me a lot if we use data in our decisions, but you can't measure tiredness in football by only using data. Vitor gave the right example: a player could have run 11/12k but in all the moments when he received the ball he always delayed the first touch, he never anticipated an offensive or defensive action, the timings of his decisions were different, he was never coordinated with the other players. That's the real measurement. So it's through a coach's eye, it's through intuition, it's through knowing our players, it's through an anticipated collectiveness that we make and deal with all of these decisions about who will start again. Andreas thinks and works as a coach and it's brilliant working with him so closely. So much pure knowledge. If anyone deserved credit for this season's training process, it was him and Vitor. Mona fuels the players to the highest level and this gave us the chance to train and play the way we do. Remember, a Bentley without fuel is nothing.

On Monday at the AXA, Jürgen started the team meeting: "Whatever eleven will be together on the pitch tomorrow, we could meet tomorrow morning on the parking lot here and I'd expect you guys to defend well." I think that a coach feels proud, whatever the score, when he sees his reflection in the team. It's like this: we are tolerant with the offensive but we are so strict with the moment we lose the ball that our boys know this is where we want to be different. We have this one idea: to grab the opposition by its throat when they have the ball. "I couldn't be more excited," Jürgen told the boys just before we went to the stadium. "The outside world will ask questions, people forget how good you are. Thank God we coaches make the decisions. In the unlikely case it doesn't work out, it's my fault. Forget that you don't have rhythm – it's about getting rhythm in the game. First – and this is most important – don't expect everything to go well! They are a pressing team, but what's a much more important question is: who are we? We should be the team nobody wants to play against. They will expect a tired opponent, and you know what they will get: a fighting unit instead. It's all there boys, now it's time to show the outside world."

At the stadium, Milner yelled just before we went out on the pitch: "This is why we train each day with everything we have, we are ready for this, but we need to show it now!" And we did. Final no37, a 2-1 win at St Mary's. It was a top performance that showed how important the training process is and how everyone taking care of the players with less game time was. It's not easy to put a team out who had never played together and still be able to perform like we did here. We suffocated them. We were proud of ourselves and proud of our players. Jürgen after the game said it well: "We will keep going, this season, next season, we will not stop. It's so much fun to see you play. It feels like a crime not using some of you more often. I'm very proud of you."

This was the week where it was confirmed Erik ten Hag was coming to the Premier League with Manchester United and Alfred Schreuder was going to Ajax. What a season for him, leaving Barça, becoming champions with Club Brugge and now making the step back to Ajax as the manager. It was also the week where this Premier League season would get decided by a crazy amount of points. Ten Hag would enter the world of the Premier League when he arrived: welcome to the most intense league in the world of football. He is a fighter and a dreamer so he will do well, but also he will need 90-plus points to become champions of England. To put the evolution of the game in England into perspective, Sir Alex Ferguson once said if you want to become champions of England you can lose a maximum of eight games a season.

Friday morning at the AXA I was called into the manager's office. "Pep, congratulations! We are manager of the year!" Typical of Jürgen to use 'we' instead of 'I'. "LMA and Premier League!" he continued. "Wow! Congratulations, so deserved," I replied. "There is only one problem," Jürgen added. "The awards are in London and I will only go if the whole staff go with me next Tuesday." "Yes, let's do it – these are the moments you should cherish and really live." Later, Jürgen spoke with the team: "We have the most exciting ten days in front of us." Milner nods in agreement. In my mind it always goes like this: if he nods then Jürgen has said the right thing, but if I see his eyebrows frown, maybe not exactly right! The boss continued: "The whole outside world didn't ask about us playing against Wolves in any interviews. It's all only about Aston Villa, Stevie and City. We need 100 per cent focus on Wolves. I was never proud in a way I was proud after the last game: nine changes and a game like this, with an extra hurdle of being 1-0 down. We are a new version of my ideas; I dreamed about a team who was incredible against the ball, but we have a team that is even better with the ball now." Milner nodded again.

I'd used Thursday afternoon to prepare Friday's session: rondos, finishing and finals. During the rondos Thiago told me from a distance: "The pitch is dry, Pep!" I replied: "It will be dry in Paris! We need to play well on whatever pitch, so start getting used to it." After that, I never saw a better rondo before! They used the conditions; sometimes in life you just need a different view about the same situation. In the finishing, six players had to pass the ball quickly between them and on my signal counter-press me, play the first pass forward and end with five players in the box. Simple but very effective to train the connection between our lines. I have this passion to keep our ideas simple. After that, we focused on second-line runs, second-line shots and entering the box after quick, low crosses. Finals (three teams who play winner-stays-on format) were won by the team of Sadio, Naby, Trent and Luis. Some of their combinations and finishes you will only see on YouTube. When you bring good players close to each other on a big pitch, unpredictability is a guarantee.

"There are a couple of things we have to say before we start our second-last game of the season." Jürgen stood in front of the team the day before the game. The analysis and coaching staff were sitting at the back of the press room. "A few days ago, we played an exceptional game. It was a proper statement. You guys fulfilled my dreams, that whoever wears the shirt knows exactly what to do. Pep reminded me today that it's about HOW we play, not WHO will play. It's not like, 'Thiago is next to me so everything will work out'. Who knows what Aston Villa will do tomorrow? The only thing we care about is what we are going to do, and that's why we have this meeting."

Sunday morning, I'm the first one in for breakfast. It was early but everything was set up already. The last Premier League matchday. Straight after breakfast, I had a long walk next to a nearby canal. I was thinking: whatever happens today it feels already completely different than in 2019. It felt so unfair at that time. Why? Because it felt that this amazing group of people, that amazing team would come away with nothing. It was probably my lowest day in football. This time we won the League Cup, we won the FA Cup and in one week we were going to play for the biggest trophy in the world. It brought a freedom to enjoy today. We didn't give up, not at all, we were still here. At least they felt our breath. These are the days. We go toe to toe with a rival on the last matchday.

Jürgen's last message to the team: "Three months ago we started our 'men on a mission'. Obviously we had an incredible series of games and here we are, this last piece of our mission. We will adapt a little bit to them, but from there we go. It never happened before in the Premier League that the team in front didn't become champions on the last matchday, but there is a German saying: 'I once saw a horse vomiting in front of a pharmacy'. Basically, it means for everything there has to be a first time. We need to know that stranger things have happened before. We can't play two games at the same time, which means we have to be here. No yard is too far today. The good news is that we have to do what we already did 500 times. To play football you need to be in a good mood. We would deserve to celebrate after this game. It's a final on the final day, this is what we wanted and that's what we got."

Arriving at the stadium was so, so special. Thanks to everyone for all the colour, thanks for all the noise… basically, just thanks for being yourselves. If anyone needed confirmation we have one of the most authentic and passionate supporter groups in the world, just visit Liverpool for a few days and end up with a game at Anfield. The real ones tell me it's their job to support us – not just a passion, their job. That's the exact reason the Kop can suck the ball into the goal, especially when Origi is on the pitch! 'FOOTBALL IS NOTHING WITHOUT ORIGI' was a lovely banner on the Kop on this day, by the way.

At Anfield the team sheet came through and we spotted that Wolves had gone 5-3-2 instead of 5-4-1. It was not the first time and will, for sure, not be the last time teams change their set-up to a more defensive/destroy structure. This time with Pedro Neto and Raul Jimenez purely to counter. Final no38 ended in an emotional, nerve-wracking 3-1 victory at home against Wolverhampton Wanderers. It was painful that we couldn't capture the title today; until minute 76, City were 2-0 down and looking at a home defeat against Stevie's Villa, which made us believe for a long time we needed the winning goal. When the Wolves end celebrated three times in quick succession, however, we all felt something big had changed. Seconds later when our stadium exploded and celebrated, everything went through my head but what I can remember was that I was thinking Villa scoring three goals away at City, wow, that's just surely not happened? The blood rushed through my body thinking it was going to happen, but ultimately those cheers were misplaced and it was 3-2 to City. For us, this game was a real final – and one we won, again coming from behind and losing again a key player in Thiago. We did what was inside our power. John Wooden says it like this: 'Success is peace of mind, which is a direct result of self-satisfaction in knowing you did your best to become the best you are capable of becoming'. That's so true, and only the people who give everything will admit.

In terms of our game, protection is at the base of the suffocated attack and this wasn't right in the first half. Too often we were only able to steal balls in our own half. Neto and Jimenez just had too much space. This was also the case when we defended with our midfield press. Without our most effective rule: 'the speed the ball travels, our formation travels'. It was very hard to dominate Joao Moutinho and Ruben Neves. And you know when these two can face the play regularly you can't avoid the dangerous passes anymore as they start using the open spaces. It's the same with Toni Kroos and Luka Modric by the way. That's why we are so happy with Ali because he has this ability to surprise us time and time again with an incredible save. The difference between a good game and a super-good game is when we make 'compactness', 'follow' and 'chase' our golden rules. 'Follow' and 'chase' without compactness is like chasing rabbits and this is what happened today much too often in the first half. This was, for sure, something we needed to improve before going into the European Cup final the following Saturday, otherwise Benzema and Vinicius would be very dangerous rabbits. We need to control the game with the ball by being dominant without the ball.

All the families joined us on the pitch directly after the game for the lap of appreciation. It showed that the best remedy for adversity is family – all the faces changed immediately when we saw our loved ones. My heart stopped for a second when I saw a new banner on the Kop: 'WE WIN CUPS'. I could have painted that one myself, I was thinking. A new culture of winning installed in this beautiful club, a new era. As I said, I get the feeling that our fans see the support not just as a passion but as their job.

The best thing that happened on this day is that we won our game. I think we would never have forgiven ourselves if we hadn't. The other good thing was the words of Jürgen directly after the game: "What I learned about life is if you stay on track, when you keep going, you get the reward. Not today, the maximum reward. We would have deserved it as well. But we will get it. It's up to us to keep going and that's what we will do. Next week, next season. What I said so often, the five minutes after the game are more important than the five days leading up to the game." This couldn't have been truer for us to prepare for the Champions League final.

Jürgen couldn't have done better when speaking to the boys, in my opinion. The only way for a club to be successful is with pure leadership, from top to bottom. Because it's like this: the only path to continuous improvement is to compete against yourself. I can't praise the players enough; everything we achieve is because of their dedication. Hendo is key in this. Why? Because he unlocked the belief in the other players even more. Hendo is the reason for the standards and the humility. If you ever have a doubt in life, just ask yourself: what would Hendo do? And you get your answer. Yes, we can look back now, where we missed points, but if you want to absorb and live completely the game of football you should never search for perfection. 'Don't let yesterday take up too much of today', is probably the best saying. Doers have errors, doers move on. We prefer the doers, it's much more about the ones who have courage than the perfectionists.

The morning after, I woke up to a text from Jürgen: "What a season ♥" I respond: "We took everything out of it ♥. What a journey… so much happened but always improving, keeping them fit, focused and hungry for the whole decisive period. We played each game, how bizarre is that. Men on a mission we were! Important we won yesterday. I think we wouldn't have forgiven ourselves… Honestly, just really proud here! Tomorrow will be great, staff together getting your prize. ♥ Enjoy the day off!!!"

I'm sure by this point you can guess what he wrote back… "OUR prize ♥."

WEEK 44

SCOUSE SOUL

MONDAY AND TUESDAY WERE DAYS OFF FOR THE boys as we counted down to the Champions League final. I wrote some notes while flying back from London to Liverpool on a seven-seat plane, with Jürgen and his full coaching staff, as we came back from the LMA awards ceremony at the Grosvenor House Hotel. We had to hurry out of the ceremony because the airport was due to close and we couldn't afford to stay longer because of the next day's training, anyway. Two more prizes in the pocket as Jürgen won Premier League Manager of the Season and LMA Manager of the Year. We went there and back via private jet; the only advantage in a plane like this is that each seat is close to the bar because it's so small. By the way, we all had to buy new suits that morning. It's funny and sad at the same time that nobody fits in the old ones. We are all getting older, let me say it like this. When, on the big screens, the previous managers of the year passed by I realised again how big it is to be here. Sometimes you forget that you are part of something much bigger. English football is just so special. Mike Gordon sat next to Jürgen at the event, our owner sitting next to the manager. Mike told me, "Remember when we first met at the Academy? We were so far away from this, we came from far, Pep." Which manager would not want his owner at his side collecting such a precious individual prize? It was good we had the chance to go; it was good because we could now put a definite line behind the Premier League season.

The moment the doors opened after we landed, we asked the pilots if they were sure this was Liverpool because it was dry and there was no wind! Honestly, the only thing that was in my mind the whole way back was, we could not go into 'survive mentality' to Paris. We had to go toe-to-toe. We would need our players to be their 2.0 version – and that's only possible when they have attack in the front and in the back of their minds. Driving back to Formby, it was clear something big was coming up with the amount of flags outside houses and even the little flags on top of car windows. When Holland goes to finals, the country turns orange – and Liverpool was literally turning red at this moment in time. This city deserved a parade whatever would happen.

"Thank you for making the world believe we are good coaches!" Jürgen began his address to the team the morning after collecting the two individual prizes. "We appreciate so much what you guys did during the year. Just exceptional! Thank you for that. As you see, there are five million journalists here today for the media day, this means there is a big event coming up. When you are healthy, life will always give you a new opportunity. It's good that this one comes quickly for us. We have the chance to put it right, in the moment when we are ourselves the world is open for us. Never forget they can only create football problems, these are guys who drink confidence in the morning – but we have football solutions for all their football problems. I can't wait to compete with them, we have been playing finals since January." The starting question before everything this week was: how can we be ourselves against Real Madrid? How can we be in this football game and be the ones who dictate what is going to happen more than our opponents? We needed a game full of everything, with all our strengths blended together, but placing more importance on, firstly, having the ball, and secondly, attacking more. So, for the goal-kick pressing, there had to be a clear idea of putting pressure and following the press, controlling the centre of the pitch and the back from each one of us. Hopefully with good execution, Benzema and Vinicius would not be comfortable. In our midfield pressing, we focused on just two rules: firstly, the one who is closest sets the trigger, and second, we always will recover the position from the centre.

Just before our main meeting with the boys, Jürgen, Pete, Vitor and myself were clear in what environment we want. When I walked out of the meeting afterwards, Vitor told me, "This meeting deserves a chapter in this book!" So I will try to recapture it. Jürgen started with: "When you are preparing for a game of this magnitude, it's important first to put everything into perspective. Three times in the last five years we made this final. We have a much better squad since the first time we played it. I can tell you, don't be afraid in the forest, but you guys have to feel it, be confident. They are this team who will be surprised if they don't win it. Some of them have confidence for three but we have the tools for that. We are the fairest team in Europe; the last five years we won this [fair play award] trophy four times – and twice we won it out of all the teams in Europe. What we need is this legal aggression, but it's allowed to be on the edge. Back to Real, if you don't watch them every week you think Benzema scores with every attack. They should have lost in all the last three rounds, but they are there and they will be better in the final. Guys, you know I think every single one in this room is good, super players, except for the persons on the last two rows [referring to the coaching staff]. Let's go back in time, who would have taken an offer from Real two years ago? Who grew up with this dream to play for Real? I can tell you now, if you are five or 12 years old you dream about being part of Liverpool FC. If you leave this room, look in the mirror and you see a world-class player. No doubt, it's the truth, we are ready. Whatever I could say if I was the Madrid manager, about this team in front of me, would be a lie. The question for the final is: do we get impressed with them? They will not stop fighting, but they also never played us before."

We discovered an interesting stat later that day. Opta analysed that our opponents had averaged just 6.8 seconds per sequence of play in the Champions League, the shortest amount of time allowed by any team in 2021/22. Surrounded. Fight that! Our target in the Champions League is reached: the suffocated attack. Now we needed to do it once more. Once more showing us being us. Jürgen explained during the video-analysis meeting – and before we started the tactical training – 11v11. I explained our ideas once more with pen and paper: where, when, what and how. Different voices Jürgen believes in but 'the power of the image' should always be present when you ask for consistency. Because without clarity there is no consistency. That's why I like so much this tactical training document we use. Carlo Ancelotti said it well: this game will be won by the team who manages to fit the game to their strengths.

After the tactical training I took Mo, Luis, Bobby, Jota and Taki for some finishing with striker movements. When you are in doubt about what to do as a coach, do finishing. Put the goal in their heads. Intelligence is what you use when you don't know what to do, Jürgen told me once on the plane after listening to an interesting audiobook. "Try to get in front of Courtois!" I shout over and over again.

During the UEFA open session we focused on second-line runs with finishes. It's insane how much Kelleher pushed these world-class finishers, everything that was not five centimetres next to the post was for him to catch. He was probably our hidden secret of the AXA and I'm so happy the big clubs just don't know how good this Irish cat is.

On Friday, we made the journey to France and had a last short session in the stadium. There, the old v young competition would finally be decided. It's strange how it always goes to the last matchday. "If you just could measure my level of excitement," Jürgen tells the boys while we were standing in the middle of Stade de France. We'd gone straight from the airport to the stadium for the session. Back in the hotel afterwards, we spent the night watching all our goals in 2021/22, a route-to-Paris video and a compilation of crazy Virgil van Dijk things. When we were watching Virgil, I told the others he reminded me of this red button you see in sports-car movies. Maximum speed, the other car passes, and you have this button which gives you an enormous boost. Anyway, we also watched Liverpool v Real from the 1981 European Cup final in Paris. The next morning, we took our squad to a pitch not far from the hotel to do some passing and penalties and throughout the day, pictures of our fans came in. Insane. The story that struck us was the one where a group of supporters hired a speedboat to get to France after their flight was cancelled. Respect. We have culture, we have tradition when it comes to supporting in finals. The Reds were taking over Paris.

And then here we were: the last game of the season, the last team meeting of the season, one last push for the season. "Anybody know what I said before the Tottenham final?" Jürgen looked at our boys and nobody reacted. "It shows that it's not that important. The only job I have in this moment is to transmit my conviction to you guys. The real talk is in the sessions, they are in the video analysis. I don't have to tell you to be motivated. You will be motivated. We are all motivated by different things:

money, your family, the history of this cup, for the supporters, making history, revenge. It will probably be a mixture of these things. What drives each person, you need to know where each person comes from. Where did it all start? Where did you become different to the others? Many of us were not loved from the first day. We had to convince. But we belong here now. But where we really come from is this: matchday 28 last season being eighth in the league. What we did until now is a miracle. We did it the hardest way. Ali scoring, midfielders at centre-back etcetera and so on. Reaching the Champions League and having this campaign. That's what we need to know. If you feel any pressure just go back to the feeling when we beat Villarreal. Tonight there will be struggles: it will be the 'mentality monsters' against the 'comeback kings'. It's not normal what they did. In the world of football they say we are favourites, this means we are good. For us, being good means two things; a red machine without the ball and with the ball really brave. The football pitch is big. This means two things as well: we need to run to find challenges, but secondly, there will be space to play the first-pass-forward."

But sadly the last final of the season ends in a Liverpool defeat. You try and try really hard but the odds were against us tonight in a game where Courtois was the standout player. We knew a goalkeeper can win finals; Ali proved this many times over the last few seasons. Real are a good team, they had a back line who were all individually very fast – that was a killer for us – and a midfield who knew how to win finals. If Kroos is a good player, what's Modric then? That's a different grape, Vitor would say. We played well, we could bring Benzema and Vinicius back many times, but it just wasn't enough to take the cup back to Liverpool. Afterwards the changing room was deadly quiet.

Some were in tears, some were just with complete frustration and most of us with disillusion. Jürgen spoke: "This one felt different than last time. Honestly, maybe not for you guys now but for me it does. It's not a cliche, and I know I used this one more often: we will be back again. I promise you that. I know you're not feeling proud of yourself now, but with time you have to. Thanks to all the staff, to you guys and thanks to our families because it wasn't easy reaching this. We need to be there for them tonight and we need to be there for them tomorrow. They deserve us. It wasn't easy for them coming into the stadium as well with the problems outside. Losing last week, being close for ten minutes, losing this final by the smallest margins. Don't forget that winning two cups is a good season, it can't be that because of our own success we see this as a failure."

The tone was set for next season. We were proud. Hopefully the fans were as well: we crossed through the whole of Europe leaving our Liverpool mark in all the cities we played in: Milan, Lisbon, Porto, Madrid, Villarreal and Paris. In years to come, people will remember our identity, that's for sure. That's the most important thing: a legacy, not just with prizes, and for a Dutch guy that means a lot.

Back on the bus I sent a message to our backroom staff: "It was an insane adventure this season, a journey that will never be forgotten. This team makes so many people smile, so many incredible games played. It's a joy of attack. The only thing I want to say is thank you for being the best GROUP in the world. It was a season with everything. How Jürgen just said: we will be back and the adventure continues." We decided to go ahead with our post-match party in a venue on the Champs-Elysees. All our families were there and, yes, what a party it was. A proper Liverpool party. All of us together. Drinks on ice all over, a brilliant DJ. It was special, though a few times I did wonder how it would have looked if we had won. The one thing you learn when you lose is that you appreciate much more when you win, though it's better not to think about that too much. It made me realise that life is about humility, that our club is ONE at this moment in time. And... our club knows how to throw a party. Basically we celebrated our two trophies in Paris on the Champs-Elysees. I left just after 4am. It was difficult to get my missus to come with me as she was enjoying it too much.

Strangely, I woke up on the Sunday morning with pride instead of disappointment. That was unexpected, I would say, as that didn't happen before. Only when I woke up did I remember the whole situation before the game. Thiago didn't do the warm-up as he couldn't feel his toes after his latest injection. He told me just before going out and he said make sure Naby is ready. I will tell you one thing: these are the things a coach doesn't want to hear just before a final. The problem was that if he would not start he couldn't be on the bench. We were in doubt and only after the fast-feet work we decided to trust him that he felt he could play; he was experienced enough to make this call. Naby was insane dealing with this whole situation, I have to say – credit to him. Back in the dressing room I saw Danny Stanway rushing in and he told me there was a 15-minute delay because of issues outside the stadium. At this stage neither he, me or anyone of us were aware of the magnitude of the situation. I told him we would wait until tomorrow if that meant our fans are all in, and Milner used the time to give a proper speech, calling everyone in: "If you need a little bit more motivation, just look around to all the staff who give everything every day for you guys to perform."

UEFA, by the way, didn't warn us about the delays. It was only after we'd finished our warm-up we found out. Can you imagine that, before a Champions League final? But more important than this was the terrible treatment of our supporters outside, trying to get in to watch the game. A complete failure by the authorities, UEFA and the police. Treating football fans like it was a riot. We couldn't believe what we saw and heard when we later received the images, videos and stories from those caught up in it. That included family members of my own who told me they cried – firstly in fear when outside and later in sheer relief once they made it in. They told me the only ones who were calm were the Liverpool supporters. Sorry to say, UEFA has to do better. You can't be surprised about the amount of people in a city when Liverpool play finals. When we arrived back in Liverpool, we set off around the city on our end-of-season parade. Wow. What can I say?

I got interviewed on the bus after having a few beers: "We see the Scouse soul today. The people are proud. There's something bigger than winning. If the people are proud when you lose, that's the next level. Seeing your family and the fans is the best remedy after losing a game like that. We have to cherish these moments. Being an LFC supporter in this moment, in this era, with this team, so much passion... we have to shout as loud as we can." The 15 minutes going down The Strand was in the top three moments of my life. I said to Luis: "Can you imagine when we win?" And Calvin Harris with us as a pure Liverpool supporter made the bus trip worth every second. A sincere thank you from the bottom of my heart to each and every single person who came out to greet us. I cannot express what it meant to us and what you did for us.

A few weeks before, I'd given my opinion about celebrating cups. Don't let one moment get unnoticed, even when there is a game coming quickly around the corner. Even if we have to celebrate later, we have to do it. My dream, for example, is to lift a cup at the Town Hall at the top of Castle Street, the day after a final. Can you imagine the scenes? Maybe something for the future. On the bus back to Anfield, everyone sings the Virgil song… and then the Bobby song. Ox was making extra lyrics. Then the Origi song came on the playlist and everyone lost it. The roof came off. I'd definitely drunk too much. And that was it. Season 2021/22 was over and the holidays would begin. Like all the seasons before it, it was a marathon. Actually, for teams like us who do well in Europe, more like an Ironman. Now, for the first time, it will be sprinting in 2022/23 and totally different. Two sprints: one before and one after the World Cup.

I'd like to say thank you for reading. I'm becoming emotional as we document this final piece, but it was an honour to take you on our journey with us and even though it was intense, it was a privilege to write about this team, this club and our unbelievable fans. Big thanks to Jürgen for being who you are. Above being the best manager in the world of football, you're not a bad person as well! You're the one who gave me everything. Vitor, thank you for your contribution. You are the most special and loyal coach I've met in my life. Thanks to Pete for explaining football in a simple manner. Thanks to John, Jack and Taffa for making the best goalkeeper in the world consistent – and thanks for all the banter. Thanks to Korny for making our players as robust as a rock. Finally, if you take one thing away with you from this book, let it be this one. Make sure you ask yourself more often when in doubt: what would Hendo do?

Never forget, guys, only the best teams play finals.

WITHOUT WHOM...

PUTTING TOGETHER A PROJECT SUCH AS THIS would not have been possible without the help, support, guidance, know-how and input of a countless number of individuals outside of myself and Pep, all of whom we're incredibly grateful to.

Firstly, thank you from the bottom of my heart to Jürgen for believing in the idea and providing backing and support. The culture you have created inside Liverpool FC is what makes something like this achievable in the first place. I don't take for granted for one second what you've done for me since you came to the club.

To the amazing players and staff at the AXA Training Centre, who make the honour of working for the club such an enjoyable, inclusive experience, both on and off the pitch. The club is blessed to have such incredible, warm people within its ranks.

To Billy Hogan for providing us with the green light to do this and for your constant support on this and everything else.

My colleagues-turned-friends in the club media department, sharing the highs, lows and everything in between with you across the globe is a privilege. It's never boring. Thanks for putting up with me and making me laugh. The same applies to far too many to mention individually across the club, who make it such an incredible place to call work.

Paul Hepworth, Steve Hanrahan, Paul Dove, Dave Cottrell and Mike Jäggle, thank you for your invaluable guidance, expertise and help throughout this project. It's been a pleasure to work with you.

To Matt McCann, Chris Shaw, Joe Questier and Tony Barrett, the only reason you're able to hold this in your hands right now is because of you. I'm massively indebted to you all – and not just because of this project, but everything else too. I don't know how I can pay you back but I will try. Thank you for everything.

Paul and Lorna, thanks for everything you've done for me and keeping me going when I needed it most.

To my mum and dad, whose unconditional love, care, support and encouragement made my career possible in the first place. I'm nothing without you and I appreciate all you've done for me.

And finally, to Pep himself. Your dedication and enthusiasm for this project – and, indeed, everything else – is infectious. You're the definition of someone who lives and breathes football and I've learned so much about so many things from you.

Thank you for trusting me to help you tell this story. It's been an honour for me to do so.

James Carroll